Redeeming Time

 T. S. ELIOT'S *FOUR QUARTETS*

Kenneth Paul Kramer

Cowley Publications

Lanham, Chicago, New York, Toronto, and Plymouth, UK

Published by Cowley Publications
An imprint of Rowman & Littlefield Publishers, Inc.
A wholly owned subsidary of The Rowman & Littlefield Publishing Group, Inc.
4501 Forbes Boulevard, Suite 200
Lanham, MD 20706

Estover Road
Plymouth PL6 7PY
United Kingdom

Distributed by National Book Network

Excerpts from "Burnt Norton" FOUR QUARTETS by T.S. Eliot, copyright 1936 by Harcourt, Inc. and renewed 1964 by T.S. Eliot, reprinted by permission of the publisher.

Excerpts from "East Coker" in FOUR QUARTETS, copyright 1940 by T.S. Eliot and renewed 1968 by Esme Valerie Eliot, reprinted by permission of Harcourt, Inc.

Excerpts from "The Dry Salvages" in FOUR QUARTETS, copyright 1941 by T.S. Eliot and renewed 1969 by Esme Valerie Eliot, reprinted by permission of Harcourt, Inc.

Excerpts from "Little Gidding" in FOUR QUARTETS, copyright 1942 by T.S. Eliot and renewed 1970 by Esme Valerie Eliot, reprinted by permission of Harcourt, Inc.

Library of Congress Cataloging-in-Publication Data:

Kramer, Kenneth
    Redeeming time : T. S. Eliot's Four quartets / Kenneth Paul Kramer.
      p.   cm.
    Includes bibliographical references and index.
    ISBN-13: 978-1-56101-285-5   ISBN-10: 1-56101-285-8 (pbk. : alk. paper)
    1. Eliot, T. S. (Thomas Stearns), 1888–1965. Four quartets. I. Title.
    PS3509.L43F647   2007
    821'.912—dc22

                                                            2006019340

Scripture quotations are taken from the New Revised Standard Version of the Bible, © 1989, by the Division of Christian Education of the National Council of the Churches of Christ in the United States of America. Used by permission.

Cover design: Zan Ceeley, Trio Bookworks
Cover photo: Houghton Library, catalog no. *AC9.El464.Zzx Box 2.
    Used by permission of the Houghton Library, Harvard University.
Interior photos: Kenneth Paul Kramer
Interior design: Wendy Holdman

Printed in the United States of America.

////

REDEEMING TIME

COWLEY PUBLICATIONS is a ministry of the brothers of the Society of Saint John the Evangelist, a monastic order in the Episcopal Church. Our mission is to provide books and resources for those seeking spiritual and theological formation. COWLEY PUBLICATIONS is committed to developing a new generation of writers and teachers who will encourage people to think and pray in new ways about spirituality, reconciliation, and the future.

In Loving Memory of
Rose Meredith Tracey Kramer

"The single Rose
Is now the Garden"

Contents

Abbreviations

BN   *Burnt Norton*

CPP   *Complete Poems and Plays*

DS   *The Dry Salvages*

EC   *East Coker*

LG   *Little Gidding*

Preface

Although Thomas Stearns Eliot (born 1888, St. Louis; died 1965, London) was born in the nineteenth century and wrote and published poetry in the years spanning the two world wars of the twentieth century, his work continues to attract readers in the new century, perhaps because of the unsettling power of his flashing phrases and the memorable music of his thought as it reaches beyond words. Who can forget a first encounter with J. Alfred Prufrock in "The Love Song of J. Alfred Prufrock"?

> Let us go then, you and I,
> When the evening is spread out against the sky
> Like a patient etherized upon a table. (CPP 3)

I was immediately grasped and amazed by the man who "measured out [his] life with coffee spoons" and by the undiminished freshness and audacity of his overwhelming question "Do I dare / Disturb the universe?" I still recall an undergraduate professor's highlighting the lines "I should have been a pair of ragged claws / Scuttling across the floors of silent seas." As I imagine it must be for many of Eliot's readers, I was captured by the unmistakable eloquence of these images and felt myself drawn to engage the poetry.

Sometime later, as a graduate student, I had the opportunity to spend several weeks studying *Four Quartets* under the guidance of Cleanth Brooks at Yale University. Once again, I was completely drawn into Eliot's "intenser feelings," but this time Prufrock's "overwhelming question" was replaced by a more confident, meditative speaker whose immediate interest was not "the usual subjects of poetry" but the redemption of time and the exploration of "intenser human feelings in terms of the divine goal."[1] As if in response to Prufrock's question, the poet of *Four Quartets* wrote:

> We shall not cease from exploration
> And the end of all our exploring
> Will be to arrive where we started
> And know the place for the first time. (LG V)

Then, when I submitted my dissertation at Temple University on Eliot's *Four Quartets*, I thought that I understood the poem in a way that would serve me for many years. This thought, as I continue to study the poem, has proven remarkably naïve.

From my early encounters with Eliot, this book has evolved intermittently over thirty-five years. The road that led to its publication has been marked by a full range of experiences, including the anxiety of almost losing a version of the manuscript in a fire; the excitement of student responses to *Four Quartets* in seminars at San Jose State University; taking several research trips to England to visit sites, scholars, and Eliot's long-time friend George Every; and publishing "A New Kind of Intellectual: Eliot's Contemplative Withdrawal."[2] Throughout this "rite of passage," the spiritual substance of *Four Quartets*, Eliot's "words I never thought to speak" echo again and again in my mind with startling clarity.

What continued drawing me to Eliot's *Quartets* as I matured in my reading of them was the intellectual and spiritual nourishment that can be derived from engaging Eliot's meditation on four secluded, spirit-charged landscapes. Moving between lyrical and prosaic speech, the poem takes place in four literal and metaphorical worlds: *Burnt Norton's* mythic First World of original innocence, whispered through the medium of *air*; *East Coker's* Old World of ancestral roots, grounded in the dust of the *earth*; *The Dry Salvages'* New World of youthful discoveries, buoyed by the endless oscillations of *water*; and *Little Gidding's* necessary choice Between Two Worlds, one of consuming desire and one of refining fire.[3] Each quartet is named after the place indicated in its title, and each landscape, as the poet describes it, portrays the interior gazes of an individual soul in pursuit of the "highest spiritual mysteries."

Four Quartets		
Burnt Norton (1935)	Air	Our First World
East Coker (1940)	Earth	The Old World
The Dry Salvages (1941)	Water	The New World
Little Gidding (1942)	Fire	Between Two Worlds

The book's thesis is both provocative and practical. *Four Quartets* contemplates, through idea and word, how timeless moments—of redeeming reciprocity, of graced consciousness—shine through physical landscapes and release the poet from temporal enchainments. In meditating on these landscapes, the poet discovers that spiritual substance cannot be found fully in himself or in the totality of his experiences. Rather, it emerges from unsought, unforeseen moments of redeeming reciprocity (divine-human mutual contact) that interrupt time briefly in places entered by chance, and that are then retrieved and appropriated through an interplay of detached memory and disciplined imagination. In *Four Quartets*, therefore, a continual back and forth movement occurs between ordinary time—a field of relentless distractions, struggle, and toil—and redeeming time—a graced elevation of ordinary consciousness arising from a genuinely mutual, giving-and-receiving engagement between poet and world that generates "inner freedom from the practical desire" and "release from action and suffering" (BN II).

Two interrelated key terms—"grace" and "redemption"—

reappear throughout this reading of the *Four Quartets*. For Eliot, "grace" is an empowering spirit that freely initiates and guides specific human actions, without effort or self-awareness, a gift that happens not in a person but to a person from a transcendent source. That is, a person is seized by a presence that recasts him or her in the shape of spontaneous mutuality emerging between humans and the divine. "Redemption" is not an isolated goal toward which to aspire. Rather, it involves events and acts awakening one from exile, suffering, and separation into liberating relationships with others and renewing relationships with the world. Redeeming time, accordingly, embodies an existential partnership between human action (attempts to eliminate self-reinforcing distractions) and divine grace (an empowering spirit that breaks into the temporal process with love beyond desire).[4]

Four types of redeeming reciprocities converge throughout Eliot's *Quartets*: (1) between poet and nature in *Burnt Norton*, (2) between poet and sacramental ritual in *East Coker*, (3) between poet and sacred text in *The Dry Salvages*, and (4) between poet and the stranger in *Little Gidding*. These four kinds of genuine reciprocity, in which one enters into direct, personal, spontaneous relationship with what is encountered, are interconnected in a particular way—namely, by the indwelling divine presence emerging from and irrigating (giving redemptive meaning to) the parched landscapes of our own private waste lands.[5] In his spiritual journey, the poet comes to recognize a new kind of spiritual chemistry—not the realization of an inner truth but experiencing a relational connection to God's presence hidden in the world. Emancipating reciprocities are discovered in the temporal flow that were before invisible; one can act in time without being attached to fruitless desires that lead toward suffering.

This book's organization is easy to follow. The introduction focuses first on relationships between the meditative poem and the contemplative spirituality of the poet. Drawn from Eliot's life experiences and influenced especially by his 1927 conversion to the Anglican church, the central focus of *Four Quartets* (four individual quartets, each with five movements) embodies the soul's resolute longing and search for the divine. To clarify what most commentators agree is a complex and difficult poem, and aware that readers should have a sense of the whole poem in order to understand its parts, this dialogic reading provides a network of theme words that help readers to map the entire poem while moving through individual scenes. These theme words, or word complexes, embody key spiritual motives that inhere in individual passages and are repeated throughout the poem's twenty movements. Responding to the *Quartets* through the theme-word interpretive code leads us through the five movements of each quartet and highlights the significant parallels among its primary spiritual wisdoms and practices.

Chapter 1, "*Burnt Norton*: Entering Our First World," begins at a spacious, seventeenth-century, ivy-covered manor house and formal English rose garden (located in Gloucestershire, near the town of Chipping Campden) with the poet's completely unexpected, timeless reciprocity between himself and its rose garden. The ensuing reflection on his experience, in the second movement, evokes an "inner freedom from practical desire" and through "a grace of sense" brings release from temporal suffering. The poet then, in the third movement, descends into a spiritual place of darkness and not-knowing thus preparing his soul, in the fourth movement, to receive the silent light at the still point of the turning world. He concludes *Burnt Norton* with the "timeless and undesiring" coexistence of words and stillness in language that continues to crack and break.

Chapter 2, "*East Coker*: Adopting the Old World," begins at a rural English village with several dozen thatch-roofed cottages (in southeast Somerset, from which Eliot's ancestors had immigrated to America) with the poet's encountering sacramental dancing around a bonfire at a wedding. In the second movement, he illumines lessons learned from his ancestors and recognizes both the limited value of the elders' wisdom and the "new and shocking / Valuation" of the wisdom of humility. Then, in the third movement, he enters stillness and waits in the darkness of God, which sensitizes him, in the fourth movement, to a seventeenth-century, metaphysical practice of Eucharist. The poet concludes *East Coker* by searching for a "further union, a deeper communion" both with transcendent presence and with language used to describe it.

Chapter 3, "*The Dry Salvages*: Rediscovering the New World," begins at a treacherous ledge of rocks projecting fifteen feet above low tide (located off the northeast coast of Cape Ann, in Gloucester, Massachusetts) with images and memories from the poet's childhood in New England and at the Mississippi River. He then recognizes, in the second movement, the "sudden illumination" that the meaning of his life experience involves the torment of others spread across many generations. In the third movement, the poet engages and is engaged by Krishna's teaching of yogic action in the *Bhagavad Gita*, of faring forward with an equal mind, which is then complemented, in the fourth movement, by his prayerful request to the mother of God. He concludes *The Dry Salvages* by becoming open to the "selflessness and self-surrender" necessary to apprehend the impossible union of Incarnation.

Chapter 4, "*Little Gidding*: Choosing Between Two Worlds," begins in a remote village with a few cottages, a farmhouse, and a medieval church (in Huntingdonshire, near Cambridge, where Nicholas Ferrar founded an Anglican religious community in 1625, during the English Civil War), with prayer that is tongued with fire. In the second movement, the poet "assumes a double part" and enters a mutual dialogue with the "compound ghost" of his former teachers about the craft of poetry. He then, in the third movement, values detachment by "purifying the motive" in the ground of his most fundamental strivings, which prepare him for the necessary choice, in the fourth movement, between the destructive fire of desire and the redemptive fire of the Holy Spirit. The poet concludes both *Little Gidding* and *Four Quartets* by bringing the complete consort of themes together and arriving where he started, only now knowing "the place for the first time."

We cannot, I believe, comprehend the fuller significance of these passages selected from *Four Quartets* without addressing the practical question of how they can nourish our spiritual life. *Redeeming Time* concludes by considering a practical question, "What specific practices can be appropriated from *Four Quartets* that open fresh possibilities for redeeming time?" Eliot highlights four spiritual paths (both to himself and to "you") that embody contemplative action in combination with the gift of divine grace. *Burnt Norton* offers the "way of darkness," a purgative path that empties one of self-will and opens one to God. *East Coker* fosters the "way of stillness," a method of withdrawing from the whirl of the senses to an inner tranquility. *The Dry Salvages* proposes the "way of yogic action," a mode of acting in the world without selfishly grasping. *Little Gidding* explores the "way of purification," a focus on humility and a generous-hearted trust before God.

Journeying back and forth between unredeemed and redeeming time, Eliot often brings us to the frontier beyond which words and images and even inspired thoughts falter. In *Four Quartets*, for instance, mystic flashes "tongued with flame" pierce through the horrific shadows and clanking routines of "the turning world," which otherwise allow "but a little consciousness." For this reason, readers are put in a difficult position—beyond a certain point one needs to avoid saying too much. This calls for a particular kind of discretion and restraint. Therefore, I have placed a rich array of additional biographical, literary-critical, and bibliographical details in the notes. This supplemental material will help clarify distinctions and comparisons that, in turn, encourage the reader to come to a deeper understanding of both the text as spoken word and its literary-critical context.

This book, then, is written for anyone who resists being trapped by mass culture's time-conditioned, high-decibel messages. In light of more than thirty years of reading, pondering, teaching, and discussing the poem, I have experienced how valuable *Four Quartets* can become for encouraging acts of spiritual resistance. On the one hand, this book is addressed to Eliot aficionados who, grasped by the vitality of his unforgettable wrestling with words and meanings, are repeatedly drawn back to what instigates the "new and shocking / Valuation of all we have been" (EC II). How many of us there are—in all occupations, in all cultures, in all ages, in all temperaments—who read the poem again and again to "reach / Into the silence" (BN V) of "a new beginning, a raid on the inarticulate" (EC V), to discover "the sudden illumination" (DS II) that makes "the soul's sap quiver" (LG I).

On the other hand, Eliot's *Quartets* can become an invaluable guide for quieting the mind and nourishing the soul for those on a spiritual journey or for those involved in interreligious dialogue who are interested in the relationship between Hindu and Christian mysticisms, or for seminarians studying innovative expressions of Christian spirituality. In fact, *Redeeming Time* is intended for anyone who, though not yet deeply acquainted with *Four Quartets*, might be curious enough to explore how Eliot's poetry can open fresh, adaptable, ecumenical paths for deepening and exhilarating our spiritual lives.

Summer 2006
Santa Cruz, California

Acknowledgments

Because I know not where to end, I will name only a few friends, colleagues, and students who have encouraged me over the years in the writing of this book. I am particularly grateful to Cleanth Brooks and Don Saliers, with whom I first took "backward half-looks" at the *Quartets*; Maurice Friedman, who introduced me to Martin Buber's dialogical approach to literature and who directed my doctoral dissertation on Eliot's *Quartets*; Keji Nishitani for suggesting a Buddhist reading of *East Coker*; Brother George Every, who advised me about the wisdom of bringing Eliot's *Quartets* into "something else"; A. David Moody for insights into Eliot's "poetic voice" in the *Quartets*; Cleo McNelly Kearns for detailing correlations between the *Quartets* and the Indic traditions; Lyndall Gordon for sensitizing me to issues involving the women in Eliot's life and poetry; Todd Perreira for his invaluable critical and cocreative responses to various stages of the manuscript; James Brown for his attentive and clarifying editorial reconfigurations of my language; Bruno Barnhart, O.S.B., for his generous and detailed reconstructive comments in response to the penultimate version of the book; my daughters, Leila Ann and Yvonne Rose, for their unconditional love; Zan Ceeley at Trio Bookworks, who encouraged me to recreate my last words; the T. S. Eliot Society for inviting me to speak at their twelfth annual meeting (1991); and my typists—Linda Garcia Young, Nancee Little, Michelle Cole, and Keren Holt for assisting me with the beginning, middle, and end of this eighteen-year project.

I especially wish to express grateful appreciation to Valerie Eliot for permission to examine her husband's unpublished letters, notebooks, and lectures. I also would like to thank the staff of the following libraries for making available Eliot's correspondence, which they hold in their collections: the Houghton Library at Harvard University; the Beinecke Rare Book and Manuscript Library at Yale University; the Manuscript Division of Princeton University Library; the Berg Collection of the New York Public Library; and the Huntington Library in Pasadena, California.

Several brief sections in the introduction and in the fourth section of each chapter first appeared in "A New Type of Intellectual: Contemplative Withdrawal and *Four Quartets*" in *Religion and Literature* 31, no. 3 (Autumn 1999): 43–75. The cover photograph of Eliot is used by permission of the Houghton Library, Harvard University. The photos were taken by the author and edited by Leila Kramer.

The author and the publisher wish to thank Valerie Eliot, Faber and Faber Ltd., and Harcourt Brace Jovanovich, Inc., for permission to quote excerpts from *Collected Poems 1909–1962* by T. S. Eliot, copyright 1964 by T. S. Eliot.

A Selective Chronology
of T. S. Eliot's Life

Ancestry

1670   Andrew Eliot leaves East Coker, Somerset, to settle in Massachusetts

1834   Reverend William Greenleaf Eliot (Eliot's grandfather) leaves Massachusetts to settle in St. Louis, Missouri

Early Years (1888–1914)

1888   Born September 26, St. Louis, Missouri

1896   Eliot's father, Henry Ware Eliot, builds summer house in Gloucester, Massachusetts

1897   Composes first poem (four verses) about the sadness of having to start school again every Monday morning; attends Smith Academy, St. Louis, until 1905

1905   Earliest poetry published in *Smith Academy Record*

1906–1910   Harvard University (studies comparative literature and Western philosophy)

Early poetry appears in *The Harvard Advocate*, which Eliot edited

1910–1911   Visits Paris; studies French literature and philosophy at the Sorbonne

Attends Henri Bergson's weekly lectures at the Collège de France; visits London, Munich

"Prufrock" completed

1911–1914   Attends Harvard Graduate School (studies Sanskrit and Indic philosophy)

1914   Travels to Europe; studies at University of Marburg; settles in London; meets Ezra Pound

World War I begins

Middle Years (1915–1944)

1915   "The Love Song of J. Alfred Prufrock" published in Chicago (June)

Becomes resident of London

Marries Vivienne Haigh-Wood (June 26)

1916   Teaches at Highgate Junior School for four terms

Lectures on Modern French and English Literature, extension courses at Oxford and London Universities

Completes dissertation on F. H. Bradley

1917   Joins the Colonial and Foreign Department of Lloyds Bank

Prufrock and Other Observations published in London

Assistant editor of *The Egoist* (until 1919)

1918   World War I ends

1919   Eliot's father dies (January)

"Gerontion" published in London (August)

1920   *The Sacred Wood*

Selected Poems published in London

1921   Suffers from nervous breakdown

1922   London correspondent for *The Dial*

The Waste Land published in London (October) in *The Criterion* (edited by Eliot until 1939)

Eliot wins Dial Award for *The Waste Land*

1925   Joins Board of Directors of Faber and Gwyer Publishers (later Faber & Faber)

Poems 1909-1925 published in London and New York

1926   Gives the Clark Lectures at Cambridge

1927   Baptized into Church of England (June 29)

Becomes a naturalized British citizen (November)

"Journey of the Magi" published in London (August)

1928   *Lancelot Andrewes*

1929   Eliot's mother (Charlotte Champe Eliot) dies

1930   *Ash-Wednesday* published in London and New York

1931   *Thoughts after Lambeth*

1932–1933   Visits America for the first time since 1914

Charles Eliot Norton Professor of Poetry at Harvard; lectures published as *The Use of Poetry and the Use of Criticism Selected Essays, 1917–1932*, including most of *The Sacred Wood.*

1933   Legal separation from Vivienne

1934   Visits Burnt Norton

After Strange Gods and *The Rock: A Pageant Play*

1935   *Murder in the Cathedral*

1936   *Collected Poems 1909–1935*

Burnt Norton published in London (as final poem in *Collected Poems*)

Visits the Medieval Church at Little Gidding

1937   Visits East Coker

1939   World War II begins; Vivienne suffers final breakdown

The Idea of a Christian Society

The Family Reunion

Old Possum's Book of Practical Cats

1940   *East Coker* published in London

1941   *The Dry Salvages* published in London

1942   *Little Gidding* published in London

1943   *Four Quartets* published in New York (1944 in London)

Later Years (1945–1965)

1945   World War II ends

1947   Vivienne dies

        Receives honorary degree from Harvard

1948   Awarded Nobel Prize for Literature

        Order of Merit from King George VI

        Notes towards the Definition of Culture

1949   *The Cocktail Party*

1953   *The Confidential Clerk*

1957   Marries Valerie Fletcher (January 10)

        On Poetry and Poets

1958   *The Elder Statesman*

1963   Visits New York with Valerie

        Collected Poems 1909–1962 published in London and New York

1964   *Knowledge and Experience in the Philosophy of F. H. Bradley*

1965   Dies January 4, London

        Ashes interred in St. Michael's parish church at East Coker

1969   *Complete Poems and Plays* published in London and New York

////

REDEEMING TIME

Introduction

THEME-WORD DESIGN

> When a poet's mind is perfectly equipped for its
> work, it is constantly amalgamating disparate expe-
> riences; the ordinary man's experience is chaotic,
> irregular, fragmentary. The latter falls in love, or reads
> Spinoza, and these two experiences have nothing to
> do with each other, or with the noise of the typewriter
> or the smell of cooking; in the mind of the poet these
> experiences are always forming new wholes.[1]
>
> —T. S. ELIOT

Four Quartets was initially published as separate pamphlets—
Burnt Norton in April 1936, *East Coker* in March 1940, *The Dry
Salvages* in February 1941, and *Little Gidding* in October 1942—
and first appeared collected in one volume in May 1943. Each secluded landscape, three in England and one in the United States,
is drawn from Eliot's life experiences and influenced especially
by his conversion to the Anglican church.

As if anticipating *Four Quartets*, in a letter to William Force
Stead, Eliot mentioned his long-cherished intention to explore a
mode of writing "between the usual subjects of poetry and 'devotional' verse." Like spiritual autobiography, this style of writing involves the experience of searching for God and "trying to
explain to himself his intenser human feelings in terms of the
divine goal."[2] For this reason, before turning to the currents of
Four Quartets, it is important to recount Eliot's 1927 conversion to the Church of England, which shifted the style of both

his life and his art. Then, to elucidate the immediate subject of this book—redeeming time in Eliot's *Quartets*—I will briefly examine two organizing components, or interpretive keys, that support the poem's rhetorical design: (1) its meditative voice and (2) its musical form. The interplay between these components generates a network of twenty theme words that map what Eliot called, in *Little Gidding,* "the complete consort dancing together" (LG V).

Eliot's Conversion

On June 29, 1927, T. S. Eliot, who thought of himself at the time as a "skeptic with a taste for mysticism," was received into the Church of England by William Force Stead, chaplain of Worcester College, Oxford. In the afternoon quiet of St. Peter's Day, Eliot entered the inconspicuous Finstock parish church in the Cotswolds. The doors remained locked behind him, and a verger was posted in the vestry to guarantee the privacy of the proceedings. His wife, Vivienne, was not present. Since the Unitarian church of Eliot's birth does not recognize or practice the sacraments, Eliot had first to be baptized to enjoy full membership in the Church of England. Stead, who performed the baptism, later noted that "it seemed odd to have such a large, though infant, Christian at the baptismal font."[3]

On the following day, the bishop of Oxford confirmed Eliot as an "Anglo-Catholic," and when Eliot announced his conversion and began describing himself as "anglo-catholic in religion" (refusing at first to capitalize the title) it surprised and even alienated many of his admirers, particularly those who had come to associate him with *The Waste Land.* Ezra Pound wrote a caustic couplet to describe his reaction: "In any case, let us lament the psychosis / Of all those who abandon the Muses for Moses."[4] While Pound expressed here the suspicion of many intellectuals of his generation that religion was an opiate, a dogma, or a mere manifestation of private ecstasy, Eliot departed from this view, writing to Paul More (August 3, 1929) that instead of settling "in an easy chair" of religion, he had "just begun a long journey afoot."[5] To experience his sensibilities with sympathy, then, one needs to realize that, for Eliot, religious traditions mattered because they addressed the deep and recurring longing within human beings for a redemptive, timeless presence.

Since Eliot's shifting spiritual attentions, evident throughout his career and culminating in his conversion, resulted from forces that intermixed over a long period of time, the spiritual biography behind Eliot's decision to become a member of the Church of England can never be fully apprehended. Even Eliot was unable to account for it completely. Suggestively, he once remarked after his conversion that the "Christian thinker—and I mean the man who is trying consciously and conscientiously to explain to himself the sequence which culminates in faith, rather than the public apologist—proceeds by rejection and elimination." Every person "who thinks and lives by thought must have his own skepticism, that which stops at the questions, that which ends in denial, or that which leads to faith and is somehow integrated into a faith which transcends it."[6] Through a process of spiritual and intellectual elimination and evaluation, Eliot joined the Church of England with the belief that he had chosen a faith that was "less false" and that balanced his "profound skepticism with the deepest faith."[7]

To trace Eliot's spiritual development and sensibilities from his liberal Unitarian family background, through his years of philosophical skepticism and Indic metaphysics, his move to England and unsuccessful marriage to Vivienne Haigh-Wood, his ten-year period of mental stress and depression, to his conversion, requires a broad collection of biographical information beyond the immediate scope of this introduction. We know, for example, that Eliot considered the Church of England a middle ground between undogmatic Unitarianism and overly dogmatic Catholicism, but at the same time his request that no official biography of his life be written makes tracing the psychology of his conversion difficult.

Eliot's lifelong resistance to public exposure is humorously reflected by the youthful self-incriminating braggadocio:

> How unpleasant to meet Mr. Eliot!
> With his features of clerical cut,
> *And his brow so grim*
> And his mouth so prim
> And his conversations, so nicely
> Restricted to What Precisely
> And If and Perhaps and But. . . .
> How unpleasant to meet Mr. Eliot!
> (Whether his mouth be open or shut). (CPP 93)

Yet in spite of Eliot's resistance to seeing his biography written in his lifetime, it is fruitful to wonder what Eliot's life was tending toward prior to his conversion and in what ways it may have influenced *Four Quartets*.

Several biographers, including Lyndall Gordon, indicate that the twenty-two-year-old Eliot passed through a period of deep emotional and spiritual turmoil. Representing Eliot as a tireless seeker of perfection who bore a "solitary burden of the soul," Gordon states that Eliot "began to measure his life by the divine goal as far back as his student days, in 1910 and 1911."[8] In a poem called "Silence," written during this period, he described an ecstatic visionary experience of the kind which, he later said, may be had only once or twice in a lifetime:

Silence

> Along the city streets
> It is still high tide,
> Yet the garrulous waves of life
> Shrink and divide
> With a thousand incidents

Vexed and debated:—
This is the hour for which we waited—

This is the ultimate hour
When life is justified.
The seas of experience
That were so broad and deep
So immediate and steep,
Are suddenly still.
You may say what you will,
At such peace I am terrified.
There is nothing else beside.[9]

A sense of communion with the divine is expressed here through a momentary illumination of the mind. The arresting power of the timeless presence of the divine is amassed in progressively inter-related symbols of human powerlessness: the city streets, garrulous waves, a thousand incidents, the ultimate hour, the seas of experience, broad and deep, immediate and steep. Though the poem records a visionary moment penetrating temporality with hints of ultimacy, it also records the poet's terror in the face of the transcendent presence it elicits. In Eliot's writing from this period appear both the optimism of a wavering faith and the sense of urban decay and spiritual disillusionment that eventually made its way into *The Waste Land*. From this period onward, Eliot's poetry would continue to mix atemporal moments of ecstasy with moments of temporal horror.

At the same time, there were other foreshadowings of Eliot's shift in spiritual sensibility. Perhaps the foremost among them was the significance of his relationship (or lack thereof) with his wife, Vivienne. In 1914, having completed his postgraduate studies at Harvard in philosophy, Eliot decided to accept a traveling fellowship to spend a year at Merton College, Oxford, to study Aristotle. There, he met Vivienne (she abbreviated it to Vivien and was commonly known as Viv), who was quite unlike any of the women he knew at Harvard. Those who knew her at the time described her as vivacious, romantic, self-conscious, and sharp-witted, a graceful dancer, a smart dresser, sensitive, the embodiment of spontaneity. Certainly Eliot was attracted by her exuberant though somewhat brash high spirits and by her ability to engage him in stimulating and creative conversations about his writing.

Almost from the start, their marriage began to disintegrate. In a way, each of them wanted something opposite—Eliot wanted to enter more deeply into the fabric of English culture, and Vivienne wanted to escape it. Raised in the Church of England from birth, she had become disinterested in its rituals, participating at most in weddings and funerals. Without a doubt, they contributed mutually to each other's unhappiness: her neuroses and frequent illnesses stymied his creativity and distanced him from the relationship; his neuroses and frequent exhaustion blunted her fragile exuberance. To cope with her condition, she sought medical remedies that included morphine-based depressants, bromides, and ether. As the marriage wore on, Eliot would spend more weekends away without her. It is likely, therefore, that Eliot's turn to the church was in part a turn toward the sacrament of confession. Gordon writes: "The sense of damnation, the remorse and the guilt that Vivienne evoked were essential to Eliot's long, purgatorial journey" and directed him to the "ascetic way of the Catholic mystics."[10]

A New Type of Intellectual

Eliot's biographers suggest guideposts leading toward Eliot's "conversion": his dissatisfaction with his Puritan background; his guilt over a failed marriage with Vivienne; his attraction to the conservative religious thought of Irving Babbitt, Charles Maurras, and other cultural authorities; and his varying degrees of interest in Indic mysticism, the void of the Buddhist *dharma*, and his skeptical humanism. And yet the most compelling ingredient informing his new spiritual sensibilities, usually undervalued by Eliot's biographers, was his discovery that he required a degree of "contemplative withdrawal" to clarify and deepen his inter-spiritual meditations.[11] One can glean insights into Eliot's con-version by reading through his correspondence, especially with Princeton professor Paul Elmer More. According to Eliot, the correspondence gave him much pleasure and allowed him to discuss matters of theology and literature.

Just two years after joining the church, Eliot wrote:

> What I should like to see is the creation of a new type of intellectual, combining the intellectual and the devotional—a new species which cannot be created hurriedly. I don't like either the purely intellectual Christian or the purely emotional Christian—both forms of snobbism. The co-ordination of thought and feeling—without either debauch-ery or repression—seems to me what is needed.[12]

Though tempting, it would be too simplistic to conclude that Eliot himself was "a new type of intellectual." I will, however, make the less risky assertion that "combining the intellectual and the devotional" remained a goal toward which Eliot aimed, and a compelling possibility glimpsed in *Four Quartets*.

At least three examples support the assertion that Eliot, in his life and art, strove to combine the intellectual and the de-votional. Eliot's eight lectures on metaphysical poetry at Trinity College, Cambridge, in the first three months of 1926, for in-stance, exemplify his interest in the interaction between intel-lectual activity and the mystical impulse. With their publication as the Clark Lectures, Eliot's attraction to the contemplative mo-nastic tradition came into clearer focus. In these lectures he dis-tinguished between the classical philosophical mysticisms of the twelfth and thirteenth centuries (e.g., Saint Thomas Aquinas and Dante) and the psychological romanticism of the later Spaniards (e.g., St. John of the Cross), and he devoted special attention to the twelfth-century mystic Richard of St. Victor. Central to this discussion, Eliot quoted a long passage from Richard in which he distinguished among *cogitation* (intellectual activity without devotion), *meditation* (sustained focus on a spiritual goal), and *contemplation* (freely gazing beyond reason and imagination).[13] For Eliot, as for Richard, contemplation was an attitude of mind, a proclivity of soul, a process of perceiving (and communicating), a "more penetrating gaze of mind."

Two other examples are experiential. Confirming the depths of Eliot's spiritual life, Wallace Fowlie provides a rare and privileged eye-witness account of Eliot's devotional practice. He writes that in the early 1930s, when Eliot was the Charles Eliot Norton lecturer at Harvard University, he often attended Mass at the Episcopal church of St. John the Evangelist on Beacon Hill in Boston. Eliot was drawn there in part because the church was served by the Cowley Fathers, whose monastery was in Cambridge. During his time at Harvard, Eliot was a daily communicant at the monastery chapel. At one Mass, attended by Eliot and only two others (including Fowlie), after Eliot received the Eucharist and returned to his place, he seemed to fall "flat on his face in the aisle, with his arms stretched out." But Fowlie adds, "it was obvious at a glance he had not fallen." Indeed, when Fowlie helped Eliot to his feet, almost no physical effort was required. Fowlie continues, "I realized that Eliot had just undergone a mystical experience."[14]

The third, and perhaps most compelling, example is Eliot's relationship to the monastic community at Kelham in England. In September 1933, he paid the first of many visits to the Society of the Sacred Mission at Kelham, an Anglo-Catholic religious community near Newark in Nottinghamshire, to which he retreated from his work two or three times a year until World War II. At Kelham, along with monastic companionship, he enjoyed periods of profound quietude. According to George Every, who entered the community in 1930 as a novice, liturgical activity was understood as the expression of our will to live and work together in obedience to Christ and in accordance with traditions derived from monasticism. Each student participated in manual labor in one of these departments: the house department (i.e., sweeping, polishing, dusting); the chapel department (i.e., cleansing, polishing); and the grub department (i.e., preparing food, washing dishes, setting tables). Much of this work was done in silence.[15]

Indeed, motivated in part by the distinction he consistently made between "natural love" and "divine love," Eliot became, for a period after separating from his wife, a kind of lay monk, feeling at times like a hermit without a hermitage. It would not lead us too far afield, therefore, to intimate that the root and branches of Eliot's conversion gradually grew out of the silent depths of contemplative life as he studied it intellectually and later practiced it.[16]

For Eliot, religious and spiritual life finally came to mean understanding and practicing a degree of monastic life. Arguably, what attracted Eliot to Kelham was not the thought of becoming a monk within the communal practice of contemplative Christianity, as has been suggested, but his attempt to get in touch with the "monk" within himself and to express it concretely in the world. In short visits, Kelham provided Eliot with the enjoyment of the company of lay brothers and students, a community that worked and studied in complete silence. These monastic silences echo through the moods and voices of *Four Quartets*, bringing readers to the frontiers of what cannot be spoken.

Eliot's intellectual proclivities developed in the academic study of written religious traditions and combined with a devotional spirit. Both study and devotion nourished his conversion and became a compelling influence behind the composition of *Four Quartets*. To apprehend "the point of intersection of the timeless / With time" (DS V), as Eliot expressed the contemplative experience in *The Dry Salvages*, an interplay among cognition, meditation, and contemplation capable of quieting the clatter of undisciplined thoughts was required. Indeed, following St. John of the Cross, in the third movement of *East Coker* the poet underscores the point that "In order to arrive at what you do not know, / You must go by a way which is the way of ignorance," for "what you do not know is the only thing you know." Coordinating the intellectual and the devotional allowed Eliot, as he wrote to Stead, to cross "a very wide and deep river . . . and *that* in itself gives one a very extraordinary sense of surrender and gain."[17]

Emerging Pattern

While I do not want to suggest that *Four Quartets* are primarily biographical, Ronald Schuchard's point that "if we cannot look to the biographer to explore and map the planes and intersections where life and art meet, then the job of constructing the interactive dynamic falls to the biographical critic" is compelling in Eliot's case.[18] Peter Ackroyd, for instance, has noted that "throughout Eliot's work, the idea of pattern or ordering becomes the *informing principle*. It can be found everywhere; in literary tradition, in ritual, in political myth, and in English history,"[19] and as Eliot once noted, a design emerges in great poetry "which reinforces and is one with the dramatic movement," a design that has "checked and accelerated the pulse of our emotion without our knowing it."[20]

Considering the possibility that the spirit of Eliot's Anglo-Catholic frame of reference was written into his late poetry, what might this tell us about the pattern of *Four Quartets*? Further, addressing the question of Eliot's design for the *Quartets* must recognize the unity of their parts, which, at the same time, like the contemplative sensibility that engendered them, are always becoming new in each reader's individual encounter with them.

The more familiar readers become with the whole of *Four Quartets*, the clearer the importance of its pattern of sequences, both within each quartet and as each quartet relates to the whole poem. A reader's initial feelings of appreciation for a poem, Eliot felt, needed to become enlarged through the reading into a greater self-understanding, and this called for acts of personal reorganization. Reading poetry was thus not simply the process of accumulating the sum of one's experience with the text but also of renewing the poem "in another pattern." For this reason, it would become important for Eliot that the ideal reader apprehends the *Quartets* in its totality, finding "a new pattern of poetry arranging itself in consequence."[21]

At the same time, Eliot's overall logic of imagery is controlled enough to remind us of the need for, and the danger of, forging a pattern out of the chaotic, irregular, and fragmentary moments of everyday temporal experience. In Eliot's words,

> Only by the form, the pattern,
> Can words or music reach
> The stillness (BN IV)

and yet

> knowledge imposes a pattern, and falsifies,
> For the pattern is new in every moment
> And every moment is a new and shocking
> Valuation of all we have been. (EC II)

Attempting to balance this tension between discovering a rhetorical pattern through which words can almost touch the unsayable and the ever-newness of the form that grants unforeseen meanings, Eliot writes of the need "to become renewed, transfigured, in another pattern" (LG III).[22] By what means, though, does Eliot express this always-forming, always-transfiguring rhetorical design? To put it another way, in the words of Elizabeth Drew, "What *designs upon us* does he have?"[23] Responding to this question, I believe, leads to identifying two interrelated components of the poem's overall design—its meditative voice and its musical form—that generate a network of twenty theme words that serve to unlock the importance of the poem's rhetorical goals.

Meditative Voice

The question of how *Four Quartets* was formed, in this case, involves the complementary question of how the poem is to be received by the reader. In a letter to Stead, Eliot provides a clue that helps us begin to answer these parallel questions: "A theory I have nourished for a long time, that between the usual subjects of poetry and 'devotional' verse there is a very important field still very unexplored by modern poets—the experience of man in search of God, and trying to explain to himself his intenser human feelings in terms of the divine goal."[24] Eliot concluded his 1930 letter by adding that he had "tried to do something of that in *Ash Wednesday*." Like *Ash-Wednesday*, *Four Quartets* takes the form of an unhurried conversation unfolding through the process of mining essential memories, sudden illuminations, and reanimated timeless moments. Fittingly, throughout the interior drama of Eliot's postconversion poetry, the way out of the "Waste Land" involves sinking deeper into it, becoming still, and waiting, since—to paraphrase Heraclitus and John of the Cross— "the way up and the way down are the same."

Following the path laid out from the bleak psychological death depicted in *The Waste Land* to the search for rebirth and renewal, accentuated in "Journey of the Magi" and *Ash-Wednesday*, the poet in *Four Quartets* meditates through two constituent human conditions—a deep *dissatisfaction* with the temporal limitations of life and its antithesis, and the soul's resolute *longing* to apprehend the eternally unlimited redemptive presence of the divine. In the process of examining these constituent human conditions, the poet's intenser human feelings are awakened by stillness and nurtured by a spirit of silence for the purpose of prying open inner doors to the soul.

To put it more simply, *Four Quartets* is a new mode of meditative poetry. For Eliot, as for John Donne and George Herbert, while the practice of meditation began with cognition, it often led to devotion and, at times, to a state of mystical contemplation. What makes Eliot's meditative style new is the interaction between its mystical substance and its musical form. Many commentators on Eliot's *Quartets* have noted its mystical impulse, and Eliot once remarked that while writing the *Quartets*, "he was seeking to express equivalents for small experiences he had had, as well as for mystical insights derived from his reading."[25] Indeed, Paul Murray has remarked that "the poet's essential method and the poet's mysticism have become one and the same thing."[26] While this assertion bears some merit, it is also important to recall Eliot's reservations with regard to what he perceived as the "warm fog" of false or feeling-oriented mysticism.

At the same time, for Eliot, mystical spirit without intellectual activity lacks creativity, self-reflection, and meaning, and intellectual activity without mystical spirit lacks fullness and depth. The mystical impulse that holds the various meditational movements of the *Quartets* together combines what Evelyn Underhill describes, in her classic study *Mysticism* (which Eliot once studied), "recollection of mind," "quieting of will," and "contemplation of heart." According to Underhill, spiritual life and practice require both "conversion," a shifting away from ordinary world concerns, and "introspection," or a deepening degree of spiritual interiority. While the complete path toward unitive awareness can be described in paired stages, the design of *Four Quartets* draws upon the preparatory process of recollecting spirit-charged landscapes, quieting will and imagination, and then passing into the unitive state of contemplation.[27]

Recollection commonly begins with concentration or meditation and develops into inward silence or quiet, which, as it becomes deeper, passes into contemplative union. Of these three introspective stages, contemplation—distinct from meditation, which is governed by a limiting set of psychic conditions—is the highest. Contemplation is an intuitive act of relational union

The Mystic Way	
Conversion: Turning from Appearances	Introspection: Turning toward Reality
Awakening of Self	Recollection of Mind
Purification of Self	Quieting of Will
Illumination of Self	Contemplation of Heart

with the divine that embraces and apprehends that which is most hidden. Neither purely intellectual nor purely mystical, Eliot's meditative poetry joins recollection, quieting, and contemplation and, in the process, is sustained by creative interactions among them. Intellectual activity without a taste for mysticism lacks fullness and emptiness, surprise and gratefulness. On the other hand, mystical awakening void of intellectual reflection tends to lose its capacity for being integrated into life.

As in the meditational experience, the poet's process depends upon interactions between a "projected, dramatized part of the self" (e.g., introspective self-examination) and the whole mind of the mediator (e.g., an illumined self-knowing). Meditation, especially as it was understood by the metaphysical and devotional poets of the seventeenth century, proceeds by stages from memory and imagination to a vision of spiritual union and then to a devotional response to that vision. Louis Martz writes that a meditative poem "creates an interior drama of mind . . . by some form of self-address, in which the mind grasps firmly a problem or situation deliberately evoked by the memory, brings it forward toward the full light of consciousness, and concludes with a moment of illumination."[28] The significance of Eliot's meditative self-address—"I said to my soul, be still, and wait" (EC III)—both as a process in spiritual life and as an organizing impulse within

Four Quartets provides an openness toward mystery leading to a new grounding in what is most meaningful for the poet.

This component of the poem's rhetorical design is found clearly in Eliot's meditative voice, which, according to A. David Moody, speaks with words that might be thought of as "instrumentalities" or "modes of mind" through which the "mind of the poem" itself speaks.[29] Yet we can ask if the narrator (the "I") of *Quartets* is Eliot's autobiographical voice or the voice of a created persona with a life of its own? Or is it more accurate to suggest that the poem's "I" is more specifically the inward interactions between the two—both the voice of the late 1940s to early 1950s Anglo-Catholicism *and* of the meditative persona? The question of who speaks in *Four Quartets*, especially when the "I" speaks, is central to apprehending Eliot's contemplative grain.

A pivotal moment in the fourth quartet, *Little Gidding*, suggests the validity of a "both/and" understanding of the poem's voice. For ten months during 1940–41, as London was bombed night after night, Eliot walked the streets as an air raid warden. In the midst of this biographical experience, at an early hour, in the second movement of *Little Gidding*, the poet "meets" a shadowy figure, a stranger with "brown baked features" and "the eyes of a familiar compound ghost." At this point in the poem, the poet says, "So I assumed a double part, and cried / And heard another's voice cry: 'What! Are *you* here?'" D. W. Harding has described this strange meeting and ghostly conversation as "the *logical* starting-point of the whole poem,"[30] explaining that the poet's "double part" unlocks the *Quartets'* continuity. By this sleight of hand, the narrator assumes the double part of his old self (who "met one walking") and new self (who was blown toward him to compel recognition). The "What! Are *you* here?" question thus invites readers into the text to engage and be engaged by the meditative voice.

Hugh Kenner, commenting on the colloquial intimacy and meditative deliberation of the *Quartets*, speaks about Eliot's voice as his last feat of technical innovation: "Of this Voice we may remark first of all its selflessness. . . . No *persona*, Prufrock,

Gerontion, and Tiresias or the Magus, is any longer needed. The
words appear to be writing themselves."[31] That is, it is not central to reading the poem that the first person pronoun hoard
the reader's attention. Instead, what comes to the fore is the first
person's almost complete disappearance—"I can only say, *there*
we have been: but I cannot say where" (BN II). Indeed, Dante's
journey up the mountain of Purgation dramatically presents
this need for self-purification. Along the way, Eliot's chief poetic
mentor views lost souls covered with the rust of self-love. For
the poet of the *Quartets*, detachment from this self-love—what
Richard of Saint Victor called self-simplification and St. John
of the Cross called self-emptying—takes the form of spiritual
poverty that overcomes desires and attachments. Ironically, the
poet's temporary disappearances only serve to intensify the impact and meaning of his words.

Musical Form

The poem's second organizing component, interrelating to the
first, is its musical form. In the context of Eliot's deep appreciation for music as the highest form of aesthetic sensibility, his use
of the classical string quartet as the appropriate musical analogy
for his poem takes on a translinguistic coloring. In a 1933 lecture,
Eliot said that he wanted to create poetry "so transparent that in
reading it we are intent on what the poetry *points at,* and not on
the poetry." To accomplish this would be "to get *beyond poetry* as
Beethoven, in his later works, strove to get *beyond music.*"[32]

Along similar lines, Eliot wrote to his good friend John Hayward that the *Four Quartets* "are all in a particular set form which
I have elaborated, and the word 'quartet' does seem to me to
start people on the right track for understanding them ('sonata'
in any case is *too* musical). It suggests to me the notion of making a poem by weaving in together three or four superficially unrelated themes: the 'poem' being the degree of success in making
a new whole out of them."[33]

While a musical analogy to the way in which Eliot's themes echo and interweave should not be insisted upon too rigidly, it does suggest ways that time and timelessness unfold in *Four Quartets*. In a 1942 essay, "The Music of Poetry," Eliot wrote that the properties of music that most concern the poet are "the sense of rhythm and the sense of structure" and that "there are possibilities" within this structure "of contrapuntal arrangement of subject-matter."[34] Drawing from Underhill's tripartite mapping, each quartet's five movements can be arranged into three divisions—preparatory recollections, interior quietude, and unitive contemplation—in order to track how each movement contributes to the divine goal. In light of Eliot's admiration for Beethoven's later quartets—"I should like to get something of that into verse before I die," he wrote—it is not surprising that a dynamic five-part movement forms the structural basis of each poetic quartet.[35]

Contemplative Pattern in *Four Quartets*

PREPARATORY RECOLLECTIONS

First Movement   **Landscape Meditation**
Composition of Place
Second Movement   **Temporal Illumination**
Interior Geography of Soul

INTERIOR QUIETUDE

Third Movement   **Spiritual Direction**
Via Negativa / Positiva
Fourth Movement   **Purification**
Via Purgativa

UNITIVE CONTEMPLATION

Fifth Movement   **Reconciliation**
Middle Way Immediacy

The first movement of each quartet presents a landscape meditation in which philosophical/spiritual tensions between time and timelessness are evoked and pondered. The second movements offer a lyrical and then a colloquial interior geography of the soul, reflecting and illuminating images from the first movements. The third and centering movement of each quartet offers an interspiritual discipline meant to move toward retrieving the intersection of timeless moments. This discipline involves multifaceted interactions between self-surrender and transforming one's will. All of the fourth movements dramatically shift the tone of each quartet by presenting a short purgative lyric. The final movement of each quartet consists of a colloquial then a lyrical reconciliation of that quartet's central themes. The apprehended wisdom of the Preparatory Recollections (first two movements) and the spiritual action of this wisdom expressed through Interior Quietude (in the third and fourth movements) are included and transmuted in the final movement's Unitive Contemplation, which binds time's distractions and timeless immediacy. Together, the five movements of each quartet—(1) a meditative landscape; (2) a temporal illumination; (3) a descending/ascending spiritual practice; (4) a purgative lyric; and (5) a unitive reconciliation—continually form "new wholes" so that the pattern in each movement is fresh yet contains echoes of previous movements.

Dialogic Motive

The power of Eliot's words, phrases, images, idiosyncrasies, and metaphors draws readers into meaningful dialogues with the poem such that *Quartets* articulates us (intensifying our awareness as readers) as we articulate it (intensifying our awareness of text/author). Herein lies the motive behind this reading. I agree with the dialogical hermeneutics of Martin Buber (1878–1965), for whom poetry does not originate *in* the senses responding to the world but arises from the oscillating realm of the *between*, whose interaction embraces the whole being of both text and reader.[36] According to Buber, when employing a dialogic approach to literature, the nature of our inquiry becomes an existential one occurring between a living text (in which one can hear the author's voice) and a reader who is vitally interested in understanding and applying its meaning. The artist, Buber affirmed, beholds the "whole embodied form" of what is encountered, and leads its inspirited form into language, where it can be categorized and viewed by others. Yet the languaged form that can be brought back into life, can "blaze up into presentness and enter the elemental state from which it came, to be looked on and lived in the present by [readers]."[37]

In thus engaging and being engaged, the reader makes the words immediately present, as if hearing the voice of the author by turning receptively toward the speaker with one's whole being, receiving the indivisible wholeness of something spoken, and lifting written words into the sphere of living words. The invigorating renewal of this approach to poetry, which continues to break through intellectual boundaries, transforms both text and reader/hearer because, as another dialogical interpreter, Mikhail Bakhtin, suggests: "there is neither a first nor a last word and there are no limits to the dialogic context (it extends into the boundless past and the boundless future)."[38]

This excursus into the matter of textual interpretation is particularly salient because what I discover about the world and myself is always discovered and animated anew. That is, reading *Four Quartets* through a dialogic lens, one continues to discover and respond to links between personal life and textual insights. The activity of reading takes place then in a conversational field and involves reciprocal and reciprocating interactions between author and poem, author and reader, and reader and poem. For this reason, *Quartets* is not just a soliloquy or a monologue, nor can the poem be reduced to any single understanding or interpretation. Rather, a fruitful mutuality exists among *Four Quartets*, T. S. Eliot, and the reader, with the meaning and value of Eliot's figuration located in their interplay. Entering into real dialogues with the poem finally necessitates, for Buber, both applying the text's message to the reader's life and sharing the resulting interpretation with a community of inquiry.[39] Rather than projecting subjective presuppositions onto the text, my reading of *Four Quartets*, accordingly, is situated in open-ended, disclosing exchanges between the horizon of Eliot's poetry—itself constructed in the rhetoric of address-response language—and the horizon of constructive response to its voices.

In this fashion, one's interactions with Eliot's poetry become individually—if not also socially—meaningful each time something the poet says penetrates and then supplements the reader's situation from within, revealing or clarifying his or her motives, thoughts, or behaviors in new ways. Moreover, and what bears immediate significance again and again throughout *Quartets*, Buber wrote that the poem's spokenness, "if one does not mean by that the subject of a biography and the author of many works, but just the living speaker of this very poem,"[40] discloses dimensions of reality of which a reader is unaware. The successful poem, for Buber, is an extension of the spoken word (both its present continuance and its potential possession) in that it challenges readers into give-and-take interactions with the text/ author. For this reason, when the poem's embodied spokenness addresses me wholly, calls me out of my concrete situation, to make a personal response to its newly awakened meanings, then, Buber wrote, "will its unfamiliarity not become merely an alienating oddness."[41]

Theme Words

We now approach the distinctive design of this reading: the main components of a dialogic motive (self/other, author/text, silence/speech, address/response) can all be seen as tools for the interpretive relationship. What concerned Eliot in structuring *Four Quartets* was the way that the poem supported intersections between ideas and themes appearing in each movement. Indeed, Eliot wrote that the "music of a word" arises at such points of intersection: "from its relation first to the words immediately preceding and following it, and indefinitely to the rest of its context; and from another relation, that of its immediate meaning in that context to all the other meanings which it has had in other contexts, to its greater or less wealth of association."[42] It is possible, with this in mind, to form a comprehensive figure of the poem, presented through twenty theme words that correspond to the poem's twenty movements, no one of which can be understood without reference to the unified structure of the whole. Through this distinctive interpretive technique, which highlights the essential spokenness of the poem, a unity of style and content can be found. Each poetic movement, that is, can be characterized by its leading "word complex" or phrase. These theme words, embodying the poem's key motives and intenser feelings, provide hermeneutical nodes for grasping the poem's primary interspiritual wisdoms and practices.[43]

By "theme words," I mean unitive metaphors that give focus to the section in which they occur and that are then (explicitly or analogously) repeated in the same movement and/or throughout the poem. These central words or phrases serve a double function. First, read individually, they reflect the unique theme and mood of each movement; second, taken together, they form a unitive yet polyphonous backdrop within which the inner rhythm of the poem unfolds. These guiding words suggest that Eliot used key utterances to arouse the reader's attention to music-like connections between stages in the poetic narrative. Moreover, they provide an interpretative code that illumines levels of meaning not at first apparent—namely, the soul's resolute longing and search for divine presence. Though assembling and arranging the network of theme words is not the ultimate point of reading the *Quartets*, and while this arrangement only makes sense in the context of reading the poem as a whole, doing so, in this instance, uniquely highlights the poem's overall rhetorical design.

Eliot hints at this verbal strategy when he writes, in the first movement of *Burnt Norton*, "my words echo / Thus, in your mind." This echoing needs to be attended to because "the full meaning of Eliot's key words is gathered only when one catches in a given context the overtones that the word carries from its use at other points in the poem, and may of course be further enriched when one catches overtones carried from outside the poem."[44]

Simultaneously, consecutively, and cross-consecutively, the poet's words interrelate with other words, images with images, symbols with symbols, and the poem becomes more meaningful through repetition and recontextualization of these guiding words.[45] The poem incorporates two interrelated design unities, side-by-side in a continuing embrace. Read consecutively, each individual quartet's narrative unity passes from an opening meditative landscape, through interior regions of the mind and a new awareness borne by a temporal illumination, through centering spiritual and purgative renunciations; it then opens into a unitive vision reconciling the prior themes and moods. Readers enter the "first world" of *Burnt Norton*, for instance, through the first movement's opening meditative landscape (the rose garden) and are led from there to the second movement's sudden illumination (the still point) generated by the landscape. We are then brought through the interspiritual disciplines of the third movement (descend lower), to the purgative lyricism of the fourth movement (the kingfisher's wing). The coexistence of words and silence, beginning and end, then culminate in the last movement's gathering unitive vision.

Simultaneous with the *consecutive* movement, a *cross-consecutive* movement shifts attention from chronological narrative to comparative, self-referential sections. The transitions among the four meditative landscapes of the first movements (i.e., the rose garden, the open field, the river and sea, and finally inside *Little Gidding*'s chapel) lead to Indic and Anglo-Catholic images of spiritual practice. Reading cross-consecutively, each of

Theme Words

FOUR QUARTETS	Preparatory Recollections		Interior Quietude		Unitive Contemplation
BURNT NORTON	I. Lotos Rose		III. Descend Lower		V. The Co-existence
	II. Still Point		IV. Kingfisher's Wing		
EAST COKER	I. Open Field		III. Be Still		V. Union and Communion
	II. Wisdom of Humility		IV. Wounded Surgeon		
THE DRY SALVAGES	I. River and Sea		III. Fare Forward		V. Impossible Union
	II. Sudden Illumination		IV. Queen of Heaven		
LITTLE GIDDING	I. Tongued with Fire		III. Purify the Motive		V. Dancing Together
	II. Compound Ghost		IV. Pyre or Pyre		

the third movements offers a different yet compatible interspiritual practice: *Burnt Norton* and the way of darkness (descend lower), *East Coker* and the way of stillness (be still), *The Dry Salvages* and the way of yogic action (fare forward), and *Little Gidding* and the way of purification (purify the motive). Understanding the interior structure of the poem thus embodies significant interactions between the first movements and third movements, wherein the *consecutive* pattern is incomplete without the simultaneous implications of the *cross-consecutive* pattern, and vice versa.

The poem's whole existing order, as Eliot noted in his essay "Tradition and the Individual Talent," accommodates itself uniquely to each reader, in ways that "ever so slightly alter" both text and reader.[46] This double alteration achieves richer implications for readers in relation to *Four Quartets* than in relation to others of his poems because of Eliot's juxtaposing a conversational style (repeatedly using personal pronouns like "we," "you," "us," "our") and his discovery of contemplative silence, which influenced both the way he read spiritual texts and his later poetry. For this reason, Eliot spoke of reading spiritual texts not only with the mind but with the whole being (advice that also serves readers of the *Quartets*).

In a preface to an anthology of texts drawn from devotional literature across a variety of religious traditions, Eliot made the startling claim that very few people really know how to read spiritual literature. Devotional reading, he wrote, "is the most difficult of all, because it requires an application not only of the mind, not only of the sensibility, but of the whole being." Moreover, after affirming the importance of examining the work as a whole, Eliot wrote of the need to "read two or three passages (at first, choosing passages in the same section), to attend closely to every word, to ponder on the quotations read for a little while and try to fix them in my mind, so that they may continue to affect me while my attention is engrossed with the affairs of the day."[47] Eliot addressed here not only the method to be employed for reading devotional texts but also the spirit in which such texts are to be read. The correct way to read a spiritual text, Eliot insisted, is to abandon some of our usual motives for reading (e.g., delighting in the language of the poetry or in the poet's life) and to remain directed toward the love of God, which is the true destination intended.[48] Perhaps it was his renewed ability to attend to the "whispered incantation" of this destination that enabled Eliot to hold *Four Quartets* up as his greatest poetic achievement.

1 ////

Burnt Norton

ENTERING OUR FIRST WORLD

Although the Logos is common to all
We live as if by our own wisdom;

The way up and the way down are the same.

—HERACLITUS

In the years after Eliot's 1927 conversion to the Church of England, a period of reflection and realignment, he plunged wholeheartedly into minute details of the Anglo-Catholic tradition and liturgy. In September 1929, barely two years after he had abandoned his family's Unitarian faith and his own American nationality, Eliot's mother, Charlotte Champe Eliot (née Stearns), died. The possibility that she had not really understood his marital choice, much less his poetry, left him feeling guilty and deeply disappointed. Emerging from this loss, in 1930 he published *Ash-Wednesday*, which drew largely upon images from scripture, the liturgy of the Mass, and Dante. Weaving together personal experiences and memories, the poem marks a turning point in Eliot's life. What was new in *Ash-Wednesday* was the poet's point of departure: there, he began with his decision not to turn back to the false deceptions of life but to explore faithfully the irreversible act of conversion. The themes of spiritual wisdom and ascesis, or self-denial—central to that poem—would continue to guide his search for divine presence.

Upon returning from the United States in 1933 (after his first visit in seventeen years), Eliot did not return to his wife,

Vivienne. Rather, he took residence in a boarding house in Kensington, near St. Stephen's Church, and adopted, with some difficulty, a self-imposed vow of celibacy. This vow, for him, was one of the many meditative practices that represented part of a profound struggle to avoid becoming trapped by the relativity of private experience. Soon thereafter, Eliot became warden of that church (in 1934), and Father Eric Cheetham, the vicar, offered him boarding in his presbytery at 9 Grenville Place. Eliot readily and gratefully accepted. The situation was ideal. It offered him a dependable spiritual companion, and Father Cheetham's homilies were to Eliot's liking. The room gave him privacy, the company of priests, and space to work without interruption on the pageant drama "Choruses from *The Rock*" (published and performed in 1934), and *Murder in the Cathedral* (commissioned in May 1934 and performed in June 1935). For the first time in his life, Eliot saw a wide audience responding positively to his writing.

Written in the autumn of 1935, the genesis of *Burnt Norton* lay in Eliot's 1934 visit to a vacant country manor house and formal rose garden, which are set apart from the rest of the world on a high hill overlooking a verdant English countryside in Chipping Camden, near Gloucestershire. *Burnt Norton* was first published independently as the final poem in T. S. Eliot's *Collected Poems 1909–1935*. *East Coker*, *The Dry Salvages*, and *Little Gidding* would follow in 1940, 1941, and 1942. According to Eliot, *Burnt Norton* might have remained by itself had it not been for World War II, which diverted Eliot from writing for the stage and turned him in on himself. It was only in writing *East Coker*, Eliot said, "that I began to see the Quartets as a set of four."[1]

Before reading a word of the poem itself, at the beginning of *Burnt Norton*, the reader faces the problem of understanding two fragments from the pre-Socratic philosopher Heraclitus, which are left untranslated. These aphorisms announce thematic notes that echo throughout the poem:

Although the Logos is common to all, the majority live as
though by a private wisdom of their own.

The way up and the way down are one and the same.²

These fragments, now appearing as an epigraph for the whole
poem, provide an interpretative lens through which the narrator's personal religious experience may be clarified and enriched.
Aside from the question of what these fragments mean individually, it is equally important to recognize what implications the
connection or disconnection between the two fragments make.
That is, in choosing these lines, Eliot highlighted a liberating relationship between the timeless pattern common to all and the
transient flux of daily life. The first fragment points to the *logos*
("one end" or goal of life that is common to all), which is recognized and explored especially in each quartet's first two movements. The second points to its associated path (the "one way"
or spiritual practice up and down), which is recognized and explored especially in each quartet's third and fourth movements.
Through "a grace of sense," the *logos* and its paths are then drawn
into a deeper communion in each quartet's fifth movement.

The key term *logos*, as used by Heraclitus, and by Plato, Philo,
and John, presents many problems for translators and has been
rendered Universal Law, Word, or Truth. In each case, the need
to capitalize the word chosen to define *logos* indicates a tendency in philosophy and theology to view it as a uniquely universal or transcendent reality, the realized knowledge of which
brings liberation into the world. Eliot quoted from his own copy
of Hermann Diels's arrangement of the Greek fragments (1901),
and it is likely that he would have agreed with Diels's translation of *logos* as "Word," especially since this translation includes
a creative interplay between philosophical renderings and its
Christocentric use in the Gospel of John. The poststructuralist
critic William Spanos rightly challenges modernist commentaries

that give privileged authority to a logocentric vantage point—of a fully established concept of eternal being, ontologically prior to contingency—from which to interpret *logos*.[3]

While I agree with Spanos that reading the *Quartets* cannot be based on oversimplified interpretations that assume an onto-theological, centered, or closed understanding of the universe, I disagree with his privileging Martin Heidegger's understanding of *logos*. Unlike Heidegger, for whom the *logos* of Heraclitus names not an unchanging truth but an individual disclosure of being as it emerges in existence, Martin Buber claimed that the ever-changing *logos* can be understood only in relation to meaningfully spoken words that are common to everyone. Buber argues that while each soul has its *logos* deeply within itself, "the logos does not attain to its fullness *in* us but rather *between* us; for it means the eternal chance for [human speech-with-meaning] to become true between [persons]."[4] What constitutes *logos*, for Buber, and I would suggest for Heraclitus and Eliot as well, is born of reciprocal and reciprocating sharing of knowledge—a "genuine We." It is this communal speaking that generates and is generated by a common cosmos, the shaped order of what is experienced. Eliot placed this Heraclitian fragment at the beginning of *Four Quartets* to situate the poems in the realm of a common *logos*: the immediate presence of unreserved, spontaneous mutuality common to each person, yet reaching beyond the sphere of either. Impossible to objectify, this unifying presence of reciprocal sharing (e.g., a memorable common fruitfulness between poet and readers) comes alive through common speech-with-meaning from which the uniquely human arises ever anew.

The second Heraclitian fragment embodies an existential demand that a person become disengaged from those satisfactions in life that curtail our ability to engage the common *logos*. Heraclitus affirms that "the way up" (the *via positiva*) and "the way down" (the *via negativa*) are both necessary and, in moments, complementary paths toward the common *logos* of meaningful speech between persons. The poet begins the second quartet, *East*

Coker, with a line that is applicable here: "In my beginning is my end." That is, life's goal (to apprehend "the point of intersection of the timeless / With time" [DS V]) and its associated path (to descend lower into spiritual darkness, and to fare forward with purified motives) become reconciled in moments of genuine reciprocity with life. Therefore, *Burnt Norton,* and *Four Quartets* as a whole, continually challenges individual wisdoms (including the poet's own), or private insights limited to one's own experience, and proposes instead the practice of endless humility from which genuine commonness can emerge. To move toward this dynamic goal, Eliot emphasizes returning again and again from temporal confusion and disharmony to interspiritual values both in one's present situation and in relationship with tradition.

The Lotos Rose (*Burnt Norton* I)

Burnt Norton's spacious manor, built in the seventeenth century, sits secluded on the edge of the Cotswolds, ninety miles northwest of London, overlooking the Vale of Evesham and the Malvern and Welch Hills. The grounds are located far from the main road, a mile and a quarter north of Chipping Campden, Oxford.[5] The manor house, which was once a home for boys, was named Burnt Norton because it was built on the site of a house that had burned to the ground in the eighteenth century.[6] The Burnt Norton garden is approached by way of a long private road that runs over a cattle grid and leads beyond a caretaker's house. Partially covered with ivy, the manor itself is relatively unimposing. Surrounded by a brick wall, a large formal garden lies to one side of the house. A gate opens to a rose-bordered walkway leading to another bed of roses. Two sets of stone steps descend to the lower level of the garden. To the left are two empty pools: one larger and rectangular; the other smaller and semicircular. From a knoll to the right, one can look out over the expansive and rolling valleys of Evesham.[7]

Landscapes in English poetry, especially English Romantic

The entrance to the garden at Burnt Norton.

poetry, often reflect elusive, spiritual, and emotional sensibilities.[8] According to Marshall McLuhan, Eliot's principle poetic innovation was that of *le paysage intérieur* or the "psychological landscape." That is, Eliot's "objective correlative" (a physical expression of the poet's state of mind) becomes "the places and things which utter themselves."[9] Moreover, according to Nancy Duvall Hargrove, five major "landscape clusters" representing five major psychological states can be located throughout Eliot's poetry: "The city (boredom, triviality, sterility), the country (release, fertility, rebirth), the desert (chaos, terror, emptiness), the garden (ecstasy, innocence, serenity), and the sea or river. . . ."[10] Each of these landscapes and states of mind appears in *Four Quartets*.

Prior to entering the serenity of the rose garden, however, we hear a philosophical meditation on time, which directs reader, poet, and poem toward contemplation of what is always present. *Burnt Norton* opens in a relaxed atmosphere of internal inquiry. In Eliot's oral reading of these lines, the word "time" is intoned meditatively in a way that clothes it with an importance beyond its ordinary usage. *Burnt Norton* begins with ten lines that frame not only *Burnt Norton* but the entire *Four Quartets* in the context of time and timelessness.

> Time present and time past
> Are both perhaps present in time future,
> And time future contained in time past.
> If all time is eternally present
> All time is unredeemable.
> What might have been is an abstraction
> Remaining a perpetual possibility
> Only in a world of speculation.
> What might have been and what has been
> Point to one end, which is always present.[11]

A central subject of the poem, as well as the ground of its discourse, is the ever-changing relationship between the timeless *logos* and the field of time. In these opening ten lines, the poet interweaves four distinct senses of time: chronological, eternal, speculative, and "always present."[12] First, time is presented as a chronological series of events, stretching between past and future. The first three lines present the possibility that present, past, and future "perhaps" coexist, each present in time past and time future. Second, time is imaged as eternally present. In such an eternal present, however, the future is already determined and thus unredeemable. Third, time is pondered as a series of unfulfilled potentialities that might have been realized differently. Abstracting one's self from the present moment to consider "what might have been," however desirable it may seem, remains an unrealizable speculation. Finally, all these possible manifestations of time point to the "one end" (the *logos* common to all), which is "always present." The fuller significance of the interplay between these distinct senses of time, only hinted at here, unfolds throughout the poem's spirit-charged landscapes.

Many commentators have noted that the specter of time and the presentation of its various "enchainments" haunt much of Eliot's verse. Prufrock's repeated "There will be time, there will be time," for instance, only allows "for a hundred indecisions / And for a hundred visions and revisions" (CPP 4) within which time itself is lost. The futility of time-bound existence is again explored in *The Waste Land*. In "A Game of Chess," for instance, a voice repeats: "What shall I do now? What shall I do?" Magnifying the underlying futility of the question, the voice repeats, "What shall we do to-morrow? / What shall we ever do?" (CPP 41) but finds no answer to this question. Later, however, in the Ariel poems, the poet's voice, though still distracted by the temporal process, begins to evoke hints of a timeless design that, when directly experienced and then recalled with a disciplined imagination, temporarily releases him from being trapped in the temporal flux.

Determined neither to succumb to time's enchainments nor to escape into his own imagination, the poet in *Ash-Wednesday* (1930) draws inspiration from the Lady (a compound figure embodying the Virgin Mary, Dante's Beatrice, and perhaps the mythic Isis) who wears "white light folded, sheathed about her" and whose presence restores Eden's innocence. With a "new years walk," she brings with her a "new verse" that transforms "ancient rhyme" with a liberating message:

> . . . Redeem
> The time. Redeem
> The unread vision in the higher dream. (CPP 64)

Adapting the biblical metaphor of "turning" (*teshuva*), redeeming time embodies a double movement: turning away from self-centered orientations and toward becoming reconciled with the world. In other words, redeeming acts involve release from self-imprisonment and meaningful implications of the soul's awakening toward God. This liberating message is taken into *Four Quartets*, where, as we will see, the poet addresses readers in ways that include them in the poet's situation and glimpses,[13] in the process, that the whole created order is in need of redemption.

Eliot's poetic imagery, in *Four Quartets*, divides itself between the ceaselessly restricting repetitions of "time before and time after" (BN III) and the echoed ecstasies of "movement / Timeless, and undesiring" (BN V). Remembered ecstasies, recollected in detachment and appropriated in different forms, prove liberating to the poet in unforeseen ways. Time is first *restored* to its original, undivided innocence (e.g., "you are the music / While the music lasts" [DS V]), and second, it is *renewed*, or filled with new immediacy (e.g., "I am here / Or there, or elsewhere. In my beginning" [EC I]). This double emphasis on restoring and renewing time will be reinforced and expanded, for instance, toward the end of *Little Gidding*, where the poet says,

> . . . A people without history
> Is not redeemed from time, for history is a pattern
> Of timeless moments. (LG V)

Four Quartets, accordingly, is characterized by a necessary back and forth movement between unredeemed and redeeming time. Being redeemed in time, we will discover, is a transforming condition that brings "inner freedom from practical desire" and "release from action and suffering" (BN II). It is a "condition of complete simplicity / (Costing not less than everything)" (LG V), which results from the reciprocal relationship between unpredictable grace and an undistracted openness to the fullness of the moment.

In this light, the significance of *Burnt Norton*'s opening passage consists both in what is said about time and its restoration and renewal as well as the meditative form of discourse that Eliot introduces. Looking through a contemplative prism, the pluralities of time (present, past, and future) reflect and co-implicate one another. The unredeemable "eternal present" (a perpetually speculative possibility) and the always present "one end" (timeless moments *in* time yet not *of* time) visually conflict with, though at times complement, one another. Chronological time, eternal time, speculative time, and the "always present" intertwine, especially as the poet evokes the power of memory, with varying degrees of significance throughout the poem. Reconstructions of remembered experiences and of images drawn from earlier poems, themselves remembered, traverse the poet's terrain.

Burnt Norton thus begins with speculation on the possibility of experiencing and retrieving timeless moments in the endless flux of temporal existence. Reverberating in time,

> Footfalls echo in the memory
> Down the passage which we did not take
> Towards the door we never opened
> Into the rose-garden. My words echo
> Thus, in your mind.

The rose garden is filled with echoes—both earthly and mythic, personal and universal, from the present situation and from inner recesses of his memory. A feeling of excitement enters the poem. The sound of birds fills the rose garden and urges the poet to risk the terror and ecstasy of entering a new world. Initially, the thrush's call—"Quick said the bird, find them, find them"—is deceptive, and we follow it only as an act of trust. Is the bird's call, "in response to / The unheard music hidden in the shrubbery," reliable? Will it lead us to Edenic redemption? Adding to the excitement, he notes: "And the unseen eyebeam crossed, for the roses / Had the look of flowers that are looked at" (BN I). As we will see in each quartet, repetition (whether of a rhetorical pattern or of one's own experience) alters, in the echoing, the meaning formally attributed to what is recalled. The power of memory, for the poet, did not simply involve recalling the details of past events. From Augustine, Eliot recalled that memory is the seat of both self-consciousness (*memoria sui*) leading to self-transcendence and the intuitive awareness of God's presence (*memoria Dei*). And from Dante, Eliot learned "to consider memory not simply as the repository for images of the past, but as a power that allows us to reshape and interpret past experiences into a new and different form."[14]

The poet's "we" and "your," meanwhile, suggest the presence of another person.[15] On the one hand, the disposition of the poet to engage his audience in the address-response spirit of dialogue becomes evident in his desire to create an ethos of intimacy and trust. In each quartet, the poet uses "we" or "us" or "our" (BN I, II; EC II, III, IV, V; DS I, II, V; LG II, III, IV, V) to draw readers more deeply into his intense reciprocities with spirit-charged landscapes. Moreover, the poet's use of "you" (EC I, III; DS III, V; LG I, II) challenges readers not only to enter into the landscape but also to consider turning away from time-conditioned, unthinking phatic chatter and toward the "still point of the turning world" (BN II). The poet thus reaches out to the minds and hearts of readers and urges us to participate with him through meaningfully encountering the *logos* common to all.

At the same time it is likely that Eliot had first visited Burnt Norton in 1934 with his longtime American friend Emily Hale (1891–1969), who was visiting her aunt and uncle in Chipping Camden at the time.[16] Beside his mother, Charlotte, who proudly admired him, Hale, whom he had met in his junior year at Harvard, was one of the few significant women in Eliot's early life.[17] What drew her to him, aside from their family circles, was their shared literary tastes, especially their mutual interest in religious poetry. A correspondence between them ensued and deepened. Starting in 1923, Eliot would send her inscribed copies of his works, including his conversion poem "Journey of the Magi" and all four of the *Quartets*.[18]

Emily visited Tom (as she called him) in England every summer between 1934 and 1938, except the summer of 1936. He felt very much at ease with her, and, in that spirit, they would often take long walks together. According to her American friends, after Eliot's separation from his wife, Vivienne, she felt unofficially engaged to him. Indeed, one of her friends in Chipping Camden remarked that Emily was "incurably and most uncomfortably in love for so many frustrated years, always believing that if she were patient long enough, her moment of glory would assuredly arrive."[19] It is safe to assume that, in addition to "we" as readers, Emily Hale is the other person of the "we" and "us" in the garden appearing as an idealized, faceless companion instead of as a unique woman.

The unfolding drama, signaled by the poet's repetition of "first"—"through the first gate / Into our first world"—takes us further back, biographically, to Eliot's childhood, mythically to the garden of Eden, and contemplatively to the primal senses of consciousness. Commentators have pointed out that these lines refer to Milton's account of Adam and Eve, who "were dignified, invisible."[20] The stress on invisibility in the garden—unheard music from unseen sources, disembodied voices echoing, and the "unseen eyebeam crossed"—suggests the presence of spirits diffused in the garden. In the midst of the autumn heat and vibrant air, arrestingly, the "unheard music" and the "unseen eyebeam" in "our first world" bring new life to the roses as well as the poet himself. Rounding the corner of the concrete wall that opens into the garden of "our first world" represents, from a contemplative viewpoint, a "return to the primal senses of consciousness, [where] the scenes enacted in 'our first world,' provide both a first destination for the 'strategic withdrawal' into inwardness and the starting point in the reconstitution of identity on a new footing."[21] This withdrawal into inwardness, as Eliot indicated,

A view of the lower-level garden at Burnt Norton.

temporarily at least, is necessary for the poet to then maximize his interactions in the world.

Lined with box hedges, the formal garden at Burnt Norton is rectangular and crowned with a half-circle. A drained pool sits next to a smaller, semicircular pool, at the center of the garden. The garden's shape is reminiscent of a mandala (meditational pattern), at the center of which is an empty pool, or "bindu point" (into which mediators disappear in contemplation).[22] When the thrush call leads the visitors past the flowers and out from the entrance walkway into the contemplative midpoint of the garden, we come to the pool.

> There they were as our guests, accepted and accepting.
> So we moved, and they, in a formal pattern,
> Along the empty alley, into the box circle,
> To look down into the drained pool.

The dry pool at Burnt Norton.

But who are "they" in this passage? As intimate, invisible presences, "they" (perhaps the innocent children of Eliot's youth
whose laughter is heard in the leaves) are also dignified and accepting guests in the "First World" garden.

Out of nowhere, the poet is overtaken by a visionary experience:

> Dry the pool, dry concrete, brown edged,
> And the pool was filled with water out of sunlight,
> And the lotos rose, quietly, quietly,
> The surface glittered out of heart of light,
> And they were behind us, reflected in the pool.
> Then a cloud passed, and the pool was empty.

In these six lines—which Martin Scofield called "as close to perfection as poetry has reached in [the twentieth] century"[23]—a
gray-brown desolate empty pool becomes transfigured by a glit-

tering light. Flanked on one side by a large tree and on the other by a smaller, shallower half-circle pool (that may at one time have surrounded a fountain), the central pool's walls are cracked from neglect, a reminder of time passed. Yet the empty pool has an almost hypnotic effect on the poet. Chronological time empties into an illumined moment of new birth as, suddenly, the pool's bottom (littered with moss and leaves) is filled with the sun's light through which he sees "the lotos rose." As the poet struggles to speak of this invisible light, he captures only its reflection at the surface, where his words end.[24]

What happened to the poet here (commentators have suggested a wide range of interpretations from a mystical experience to a hallucination) cannot finally be determined or understood. However, the metaphors he uses to describe the event open up provocative possibilities. The "lotos rose," for instance, joins Eastern and Western spiritual symbols in ways that transfigure the intended meanings of each. As a graduate student at Harvard University, Eliot had studied the "lotos" symbol in relation to both the Hindu true self (*atman*) and the Buddhist absolute emptiness (*shunyata*). In each of these traditions, it is said that heart-mind transforms through direct realization of one's true identity, symbolized by the lotus.

In the *Bhagavad Gita*, for instance, Krishna teaches Arjuna about the yoga of actionless action (*karma yoga*). When Arjuna asks to see Krishna's bodily form, Krishna reveals his dual (material and spiritual) nature. Krishna's infinite brilliance manifests, in response, as a thousand suns. Upon seeing Krishna's infinite form, Arjuna's first words are: "Brahma, the Lord [I see], throned on the lotus seat."[25] Analogously, in the Buddhist tradition, rooted in but not limited to the mud of temporal and physical reality, the pure "lotos" of the true self rises out of the muddy water of experience. According to Eliot's lecture notes from Masaharu Anesaki's Harvard seminar, "Schools of Religious and Philosophical Thought of Japan," the lotus can be distinguished from other plants by its flower and its fruit. Some flowers bear no fruit, while others (like the poppy) bear many fruits. And sometimes, as in the case of the peach or the plum, it takes many flowers to bear one fruit.[26] The lotus, in other words, *is* the fruit it bears.

Just as the lotus functions as a central symbol in Hindu and Buddhist traditions, the rose has come to occupy a central place in traditional Christian poetry. Indeed, the poet's epiphany in the garden parallels the radiance of Dante's Empyrean—"The heaven of pure light." In *Paradiso*, Dante (like Arjuna), after seeing the final and only true heaven, is momentarily blinded by its divine effulgence. Dante's "multifoliate rose," in Canto XXX, radiates "the heaven of pure light. And in Canto XXXIII, the Supreme Light of God is so dazzling that Dante has to turn immediately away.

> I saw within its depth how it conceives
> All things in a single volume bound by Love,
> Of which the universe is the scattered leaves.[27]

Here, the Book of God and the Rose of earthly existence are metaphorically one, and the conflict between Word and immanent reality is resolved. When asked about the significance of roses in *Four Quartets*, Eliot once remarked, "There are really three roses in the set of poems; the sensuous rose, the social-political Rose [always spelled with a capital letter] and the spiritual rose; and the three have got to be in some way identified as one."[28] The "lotos rose," it can be said, becomes a fourth kind of rose in the *Quartets*, acting as both a noun (a lotus and a rose that are united) and a verb (a lotus that "rose" from the pool). Subtle yet profound interactions generated by including and transmuting symbols from these two spiritual traditions—"the lotos" (emptiness, or true self) and "the rose" (fullness of the divine)—reverberate through the poem.

Yet what happened to the poet in the rose garden happened between time-conditioned, self-reflective consciousness and the consciousness that transcends time. What happened emerged from the reciprocal and reciprocating relationship between poet and garden. For this reason, the event cannot be reduced to the private wisdom of his own experience, no matter how remarkable that experience was. Instead, having already been seized by the spirit of the garden, the poet then becomes drawn into direct, exclusive relationship with the empty pool. The pool now becomes no longer pool. In this transfiguring occurrence, the poet experiences himself addressed by a unique presence beyond ordinary words. More than the sum of its qualities (color, texture, setting), the illuminating wholeness of this structure addresses him with a full presence that cannot be detached from his relationship to the pool. The poet receives what he did not have before—the elevating power of full mutuality stirs his soul with an inexpressible confirmation of meaning. Analogous to the poet's glittering "heart of light," Martin Buber, following Plato's Seventh Epistle, likens this "betweenness" of spontaneous mutuality to light that is kindled from "leaping fire."[29] Situated in these reciprocities (between poet and garden, between poet and reader) a new quality of communication leaps forth. Our ways of understanding become communal.

In light of Eliot's dissertation on the philosophy of F. H. Bradley, it has been suggested that the "lotos rose" represents the poet's "immediate experience," that is, experience of timeless unity prior to the distinction between perceiver and perceived, which is not an object of nature or thought any*where* present to any*one*, yet which cannot be analyzed away.[30] Yet, Bradley's term, whether intentionally or not, still seems to emphasize the content of one's own experience, no matter how transcendent that experience is perceived to be. In light of his understanding of the Heraclitian *logos*, Buber, on the other hand, speaks of "the between"—a genuine third alternative between inner and outer, subjective and objective, that is, the presence of spontaneous mutuality that comes alive in and through powerful moments of relational grace. Beyond "immediate experience," in the redeeming

reciprocity between poet and the fully sensible, unique wholeness of the rose garden, common to each yet reaching out beyond either, poet and garden affirm each other's unpredictable
uniqueness and simultaneously surrender to each other's innermost wholeness.[31]

Further, Charles Taylor has argued that the modernists like
Pound and Eliot have articulated epiphanies not of being but of
that which "comes from *between* the words and images." Taylor
therefore indicates that it is appropriate to speak of an "intertemporal epiphany," for "only when we recall it in memory can we
see behind it to what was revealed through it," and "the epiphany
can't be seen *in* an object but has to be framed *between* an event
and its recurrence through memory."[32] It is important to add, I
believe, another interdependent reciprocity to this frame—what
is between the poet's address and the reader's intelligent response.
Without the interpretive grasp of my voice "the lotos rose" loses
its meaning-bearing value. The "leaping fire" that opens heart and
mind is extinguished. Just at this "moment," though, as suddenly
as his awareness of time ceased, a cloud passes over what "has
been," and the timeless vision disappears into memory. *Burnt
Norton's* "heart of light" is hidden again in the empty pool.

The bird that initially invited the visitors into the garden
("quick, said the bird, find them, find them") suddenly and ur-
gently calls them to leave their "first world."

> Go, said the bird, for the leaves were full of children,
> Hidden excitedly, containing laughter.
> Go, go, go, said the bird: human kind
> Cannot bear very much reality.

The intense vision—the rising pulsing light—disappears into
emptiness. It is here that the poet records a glimpse into the overwhelming significance of the timeless moment. The sublime moment in which the "lotos rose quietly, quietly," apprehended not
in the poet but emerging from the vital reciprocity between him

and the "heart of light" from which it issued, cannot be sustained. Indeed, the bird's call necessarily brings us back from the perilous frontier of ultimacy and back into the things of this earth. Restating and recapitulating the heart of the opening mediation, the last three lines of the first movement of *Burnt Norton* remind us, however, that the always-present "one end," is now hidden, or forgotten.

> Time past and time future
> What might have been and what has been
> Point to one end, which is always present.

As it will continue to do, the poet's meditative voice concentrates upon this "always present" redemptive possibility of being released, temporarily at least, from the restrictive effects of the temporal process.

The Still Point (*Burnt Norton* II)

As each quartet shifts from the first to its associated second movement, the initial landscape meditation unfolds into a deeper rumination, which, through "a grace of sense," brings release from temporal suffering. In the meditative tradition of the seventeenth-century English metaphysical poets—who sought, as Eliot emphasized in his 1926 Clark Lectures, to balance the intellect, the emotions, and spiritual sensibility—the soul, longing for union with the divine and attempting to bring focus to its spiritual journey, projects itself through "interior dramatization."[33] Speaking of Eliot's interests in the metaphysical poets, Louis Martz's comments describe *Four Quartets* as well:

> A meditative poem is a work that creates an interior drama of mind; this dramatic action is usually (though not always) created by some form of self-address, in which the mind grasps firmly a problem or situation deliberately evoked by

the memory, brings it forward toward the full light of consciousness, and concludes with a moment of illumination, where the poet's self has, for a time, found an answer to its conflicts.[34]

In composition of place in *Burnt Norton,* self-examination takes the form of interior mindfulness pictured in exterior scenery, a pattern that is repeated throughout *Four Quartets.* Here the poet moves from a description of the external landscape to an internally oriented expression of the contemplative truths that it reveals.

The second movement of *Burnt Norton* begins with a fifteen-line lyric in which the "lotos rose" of the garden is transmuted into an earth-bound metaphor: "Garlic and sapphires in the mud / Clot the bedded axle-tree." Provocatively echoing the Buddhist wheel of samsara, as well as the manger and the cross, the "bedded axle-tree" reconciles above and below. Below, hunter and hunted in the round of daily existence "pursue their pattern as before"; above, our earthly movements are "reconciled" in the heavens. Opposing elements—the "garlic" is a white, pungent-smelling transmution of the lotus warring against the "sapphire," a blue mineral signifying stars glistening—are sunken into dark mud.[35] These seemingly different images manifest in two planes at once: dancing "along the artery" and "figured in the drift of stars." The axle-tree—or axis of the world, symbolically equated with the Tree of Life—reconciles them, becoming a fixed point at the center of the turning world. When one draws a circle and bisects it horizontally and vertically, as Northrop Frye has pointed out, the horizontal line represents linear time or the Heraclitean flux, whereas the vertical line represents the presence of the divine entering time.[36]

Garlic and sapphire, artery and boar, heaven and earth gather together

> At the still point of the turning world. Neither flesh nor
>   fleshless;
> Neither from nor towards; at the still point, there the dance is,

But neither arrest nor movement. And do not call it fixity,
Where the past and future are gathered. Neither movement
   from nor towards,
Neither ascent nor decline. Except for the point, the still point,
There would be no dance, and there is only the dance.

Suddenly, we are brought into the realization that except for the still point—a moment of timelessness within time—there could not be genuine reciprocity. One glimpses the poet's struggle here to recognize the *logos* common to all, arising from a multiplicity of consequent sensibilities and behaviors, arising from presence as well as absence.[37] To make some sense of these conflicting temporalities, the poet, like Heraclitus before him, relies on paradox. This rhetorical act of negation/affirmation allows him, by pushing language beyond its immediate boundaries, to enter his experience more deeply and opens fresh possibilities for understanding the *logos*.

It should be remembered that when Eliot left the Harvard philosophy department in the summer of 1914, after three years of study, he was awarded a travel fellowship to spend the academic year 1914–15 at Oxford studying Aristotle's philosophy with Professor Harold Joachim. Though Eliot was never to return to Harvard's philosophy department as a teacher, the work of Aristotle continued to interest him, especially the *De anima*, in which Aristotle, quite rationally, presents an image of the good, which both moves desire and attracts desire to the unmoved center of a wheel (III.10).

Viewed through overlapping philosophical and spiritual traditions that interested Eliot, the "still point" echoes the stillness alluded to in *Ash-Wednesday*. In the 1930 poem, the poet prayed to the "Blessed sister, holy mother, spirit of the fountain, spirit of the garden": "Teach us to care and not to care / Teach us to sit still" (CPP 67). In a sense, the entire dance of the poem revolves around the intertextual image of stillness. The stillness of "the still point," essential to the dance of life as well as to graceful interaction between people, does not refer, as one may too quickly assume, to the opposite of motion or to doing nothing. Nor does it identify a state of peace within the poet. It refers, instead, to an altogether different kind of inaction-in-action, which is why, in *Ash-Wednesday*, the poet asked to be taught how to care without caring. The "still point" refers to the oscillating sphere of genuine reciprocity between poet and rose garden, for example, or between poet and the kingfisher of the fourth movement. Beyond the sum total of poet and rose garden, a reciprocal and reciprocating mutuality—the "still point"—joins them briefly in a spontaneous mutuality that only later can be spoken as a timeless presence. As we have and will see, just as the poet ruminates on the varieties of time-bound existence framing our lives—its frenzies, distractions, and enchainments—he also repeatedly evokes moments of grace that restore a necessary balance between activity and stillness.

The significance of the next eleven lines sets them apart.

> I can only say, *there* we have been: but I cannot say where.
> And I cannot say, how long, for that is to place it in time.
>
>   The inner freedom from the practical desire,
> The release from action and suffering, release from the inner
> And the outer compulsion, yet surrounded
> By a grace of sense, a white light still and moving,
> *Erhebung* without motion, concentration
> Without elimination, both a new world
> And the old made explicit, understood
> In the completion of its partial ecstasy,
> The resolution of its partial horror.

These lines bear behavioral consequences of his recognition in the rose garden that "only through time is time conquered." From spatial and temporal images, the poet now evokes ascetical tensions. Intuitive sensations release him from temporal compulsion. Remembering moments of immediate connection with his environment—not moments measured in time, but timeless moments—his spiritual history reactivates the "inner freedom" of these moments. Two things occur. First, he "must be still and still moving," and second, he must become "surrounded / By a grace of sense." The immediate sensation of renewal lies outside sense experience as we know it, and the words "I cannot say" point to the fact that extraordinary meaning cannot be contained in time-determined words. Pushing beyond speech, the intensely contemplative experience overcomes subject-verb-object relationships through genuinely reciprocal relationships with the world in the midst of the *logos* common to all.

What is made explicit here, or is understood in a new way, are the behavioral effects arising from entering a genuine reciprocal relationship with nature, or persons, or art. He likens this experience to being at a physical and metaphysical still point, which, at the same time, is moving like the hub of a wheel that does not seem to move at all as the wheel turns. While he intuitively realizes that the still point does not release him from the limits of time-bound existence, the evocation of "inner freedom" ("surrounded / By a grace of sense") suggests positive behavioral consequences of the still point. The poet's experience of "inner freedom" can be understood in a redemptive sense in that, on the one hand, it brings release from attachments to desire and action, suffering and compulsion, and, on the other hand, it brings exultation (*Erhebung*) to consciousness. Beyond yet within time, supported by a "grace of sense," the intuition of a new "first world" includes and transmutes the old such that the old is revealed in a new light.

Though the all-important phrase "a grace of sense" reads easily, apparent contradictions—"*Erhebung* [lifting up, exultation] without motion," and "concentration [gathering together at the center] / Without elimination"—strain old vocabularies beyond their normal capacities. The poet's renewed imagination gains him access to previously unapparent similarities-in-differences and differences-in-similarities. "First world" states of soul are glimpsed where contradictory actions are neither one nor two, rendering the limitations of old world attitudes (one, not two) more deeply explicit. Resulting from the event of real mutuality in the rose garden, contrary views, voices, styles, and goals both challenge and reify each other. Fittingly, just a year after publishing *Burnt Norton,* Eliot wrote: "The human mind is perpetually driven between two desires, between two dreams each of which may be either a vision or a nightmare: the vision and nightmare of the material world, and the vision and nightmare of the immaterial. Each may be in turn, or for different minds, a refuge to which to fly, or a horror from which to escape."[38] Such feelings of ecstasy and horror are, in *Burnt Norton,* held in fruitful tension: horror (fear and trembling before the divine) is connaturally a part of life's ever-unique, ever-surprising ecstasies.

In a gripping image, the poet concludes this movement by necessarily juxtaposing the positive, even redemptive, effects of genuine reciprocity by acknowledging that restrictive limitations are endemic to fleshly existence:

> Yet the enchainment of past and future
> Woven in the weakness of the changing body,
> Protects mankind from heaven and damnation
> Which flesh cannot endure.

In these lines, separating disincarnated contemplation from genuine contemplation, the poet distinguishes between contemplation that excludes everything, and contemplation that includes everything, especially the body. Since past and future are woven into the flesh, one is at least "protected" from being overwhelmed by "too much reality." At the same time, it is precisely because of, and within, temporal "enchainments" that the poet can say,

> Time past and time future
> Allow but a little consciousness.
> To be conscious is not to be in time
> But only in time can the moment in the rose-garden,

The moment in the arbour where the rain beat,
The moment in the draughty church at smokefall
Be remembered; involved with past and future.
Only through time time is conquered.

Memory—moving both backward into the past and forward into the present—is now introduced as an agency for retrieving redemptive moments from unliberated temporality. As it becomes a major theme in the poem, *remembering* (through smells, sounds, sights) both recollects special places and moments of past experiences (now altered and transfigured) and integrates their transfigurations into the present moment. The "moment in the rose-garden," the "moment in the arbour," and the "moment in the draughty church," are retrieved from time past and become a spirit-infused lens through which to engage the present. By restoring these moments of "immediate experience," in which the enchainments of past and future are broken, if only temporarily, the soul, burdened by temporal limitations, is awakened to new life. After timeless moments are directly, albeit briefly, experienced, then later retrieved from memory, when revivified *in* time through a disciplined imagination, the poet is liberated from himself. For this reason, the poet, throughout the *Quartets*, attempts to distance himself from the deleterious distractions of his personal, historic, and artistic life, in order to pass back into life with maximum potency.

Descend Lower (*Burnt Norton* III)

If the first movement presents a meditation on the poet's immediate experience in the rose garden, and the associated second movement evokes a temporal illumination by which the inner freedom of the still point is glimpsed, the third movement elicits the spiritual discipline necessary to purify the soul in its journey toward union with the divine. The third and centering movement of each quartet evokes a descending-ascending spiritual practice, oriented toward redeeming moments of time. In *Burnt Norton*, this core movement has two parts: acknowledging weary routines of the "twittering world" and yet, in response, describing the necessity of practicing traditional ascetic paths.

The first half of the third movement shifts the poem's atmosphere from the light-filled garden of our "first world" down into the darkness of the London Underground. (Eliot often took the train from Glouster Road Station to work.) Before we can realize it, we descend into the contemptible underworld of Dantesque half-light that is neither the full light of day ("investing form with lucid stillness / Turning shadow into transient beauty / With slow rotation suggesting permanence"), nor the true darkness of the soul's dark night, nor the true darkness that purifies the soul ("emptying the sensual with deprivation / Cleansing affection from the temporal"). Underworld dwellers, those who have passed from elevation into a twilight world, are dominated by distracted, empty, tumid, unwholesome, faded, and torpid consciousness. In this time-bound world, "time before and time after," there is neither daylight nor darkness, neither "lucid stillness" nor the darkness of the physical world that lies at the entrance to a mystical darkness purifying the soul. Here, there is neither plentitude of meaning and value nor vacancy of sensual attachments. Here, in these dark moments, there are only "strained time-ridden faces."

The death-undone faces that flowed over the London Bridge in *The Waste Land* echo here: frightened, troubled, confused, dull, sweaty, almost dead. These masks for human faces recall the head-pieces "filled with straw" in "The Hollow Men," where "between the motion / And the act / Falls the shadow" and where we confront the horror of eyes that cannot see, ears that cannot hear. The unhealthy atmosphere also recalls the yellow, putrid fog in "Prufrock" that settles in the tedious streets, "the burnt-out ends of smoky days," the "dull head among windy spaces." The "chilled delirium" of "Gerontion" and the twisted faces tossed up from the bottom of the street by waves of fog in "Morning at the

Window" also make their way into the underground's "teetering world." One of Eliot's most memorable phrases—"Distracted from distraction by distraction"—effectively encapsulates the negative power of this "twittering world," where there is only "tumid apathy."

But the third movement of *Burnt Norton* does not only denounce the lesser darkness of clockwork time. The next stanza opens by juxtaposing a redemptive possibility in the midst of a more radical darkness. A central realization of *Ash-Wednesday* resurfaces: overcoming the impact of the "Waste Land" on the human soul involves sinking downward more deeply into the darkness. John Senior notes that "since the central meaning of the poem is the idea that the way out is down and through, as if the answer to all questions could be found by pulling the questions inside out like a sock, Eliot [at this point] pulls the poem inside out."[39] Echoing the writings of Pseudo-Dionysius the Areopagite, Aquinas, and especially St. John of the Cross, the poet introduces the way of darkness (*via negativa*) and proposes that the way up and the way down are, mystically, the same.

> Descend lower, descend only
> Into the world of perpetual solitude,
> World not world, but that which is not world,
> Internal darkness, deprivation
> And destitution of all property,
> Desiccation of the world of sense,
> Evacuation of the world of fancy,
> Inoperancy of the world of spirit

The poet especially echoes here a profoundly mystical, contemplative theologian, Carmelite reformer, and poet, St. John of the Cross (1542–1591), best known for *The Ascent of Mount Carmel, The Dark Night of the Soul,* and *The Living Flame of Love.* According to St. John, toward whom Eliot's intenser spiritual sensibilities often turned, one's faith journey must pass through a "dark night of the soul."

St. John, in his often-studied mystical writings, describes the "dark night" as an episode of emptying the self of desires and passions. Forsaking the time-conditioned, time-restrained ego, choosing to renounce temporal gratifications—it is suggested— opens up possible liberation from this world's "metalled ways" by reconnecting the soul to its source.

Then, the poet brings forward a compatible path

> This is the one way, and the other
> Is the same, not in movement
> But abstention from movement; while the world moves
> In appetency, on its metalled ways
> Of time past and time future.

One of St. John's major themes involves a radical shift in our ordinary habits of thought by choosing forms of detachment and depravation that lead through purgation to illumination and encountering the divine. For St. John, the negative way of "deprivation" and "internal darkness"—if deliberately chosen—involves becoming reduced to a state of emptiness, poverty, and abandonment, for the sensual part is purified in emptiness and the spirit is purified in darkness.

St. John also emphasized that both the active path of prayer and the passive path of waiting on God remain in creative tension with one another and are mutually necessary:

> This first night is the lot of beginners, at the time God commences to introduce them into the state of contemplation; it is a night in which the spirit of man also participates. . . . The second night of purification takes place in those who are already proficient, at the time God desires to lead them into a state of divine union. This purgation, of course, is more obscure, dark and dreadful.[40]

One path necessarily resonates and is implicated by the effects of practicing the other. The poet's most important phrase in the passage quoted above ("and the other / Is the same") suggests that each path—the one of movement (practiced by beginners on the spiritual path), and the one of abstention from movement (practiced by more experienced contemplatives)—is sufficient and complementary.[41] Each way can become a means for finding reconciliation with ultimate reality, and each can move the practitioner (metaphorically) both upward and downward.

That his darkness is reoriented toward awareness of God becomes clearer if one juxtaposes the spiritual discipline of each third and centering movement. In the third movement of *East Coker*, after the poet takes a Miltonic descent into the darkness of death, a meditative voice will resurface: "I said to my soul, be still, and let the dark come upon you / Which shall be the darkness of God." In the third movement of *The Dry Salvages*, after beginning with Krishna's teaching that the future is futureless (since we are not the same people in the future), the poet is brought to consider past and future with "equal mind." And in the third movement of *Little Gidding*, after meditating on the three conditions of attachment, detachment, and indifference, the poet will speak about becoming "transfigured, in another pattern." The images in each of these centering passages move from the external world into inner silence, from what we can know to what is unknown, and from descent to purification. By holding each of these third movements together, the poet's interspiritual path moves from self-disappearance into darkness, from self-transfiguration into actionless action.

Kingfisher's Wing (*Burnt Norton* IV)

Burnt Norton began with a "heart of light" vision "at the still point of the turning world," then descended into a "world of perpetual solitude," where the spiritual practice offered is characterized by destitution of property, desiccation of senses, evacuation of fancy, inoperancy of spirit, and "abstention from movement." In the fourth movement of each quartet, the poet's tone shifts, becomes more liturgical, even devotional. The brief lyrical interlude reflects the basic themes of the first two movements and deepens the spiritual practice related in the third. And while it may be too provocative to suggest that the whole meaning of the quartet is embodied in this movement, the possible implications of that suggestion do not become clear, or really useful, until we have read through the poem more than once.

Since the fourth movement of *Burnt Norton* is so compressed, it is helpful to read it in its entirety.

> Time and the bell have buried the day,
> The black cloud carries the sun away.
> Will the sunflower turn to us, will the clematis
> Stray down, bend to us; tendril and spray
> Clutch and cling?
> Chill
> Fingers of yew be curled
> Down on us? After the kingfisher's wing
> Has answered light to light, and is silent, the light is still
> At the still point of the turning world.[42]

This entire passage, it has been suggested, focuses on death and burial. But is that all? While the bell's clanging marks the disappearance of the sun, it would have reminded him of its monastic context, where the bell also signals a call to prayer, a call to break out of ordinary time. During the Mass (as Eliot knew it), a bell was rung at the moment when the bread and wine were consecrated and became the transubstantial body and blood of the risen Christ. A powerful ambiguity emerges: the bell announces the death of the day (and by implication hastens a necessary *kind* of dying) and yet is accompanied by images of new life and the hope that a sunflower will soon greet the new dawn. The sense of this interlude is evoked by a single, isolated word—"Chill"—

around which sunflower, clematis, and fingers of yew intertwine. The single, monosyllabic sound achieves more than just a linguistic effect. It seizes his spirit. One emerges from the darkness of the preceding section with a double sensation: the cold extinction of death and the delicate warmth of nature's light. It is helpful here to note that Eliot associated the yew tree, often found in English churchyard burial sites, with both death and new life in resurrection.

In response to the redemptive question—will the sunflower, will the clematis turn to us?—the kingfisher answers "light to light." As perceived in the rose garden, yet uniquely here, a visionary light breaks through the clouds. From a grave darkness, light beyond light glances off the kingfisher's wing. The contrast between "has" and "is still" pulls us into a present heading toward a redeemed future. At the same time, the "still point" arises from the reciprocity between poet and kingfisher and radiates the cusp between present and future, where seeming opposites are held in creative tensions. While some commentators emphasize that the kingfisher in folklore represents Christ (the fisher of men, whose light reflects the divine light and defeats the powers of darkness), the poetic stress is not only on the "kingfisher," or on the "light" reflected off the kingfisher's wing,[43] but on their relationship. One commentator has suggested that "the light of the kingfisher passage is the light of the illuminative way. The logic of this is simple. If the darkness of the first lines of this passage represents the night of the senses, which lies at the entrance of the illuminative way, the light . . . is part of the total characterization of the illuminative way that also involves the yew."[44]

At the same time, it is important to keep in mind that these disclosures are occasional and relational rather than progressive and individual. "They occur as sudden and discontinuous eruptions generated by encounter, which are subsequently covered over or subsumed under the poet's restatement in the old metaphysical language."[45] At the same time, our understanding of the disclosures can be enriched through comparisons. In devotional stillness, the light "is still / At the still point of the turning world," shattering the darkness of the soul. The rose garden's "heart of light" becomes a visible reminder of the Invisible Light of God. In moments like these, at the center of the rose garden and here at the center of the turning world, a "heart of light" still point quickens the contemplative's soul.[46]

The Coexistence (*Burnt Norton* V)

The fifth movement of each quartet brings forth the "one-end/one-way" unitive awareness hinted at throughout that quartet. The poet now attempts to reconcile, albeit provisionally, the apprehended wisdoms and spiritual practices already introduced. Poetic and purgative movements have activated a sanctuary for the soul and, in the midst of an intellectual and emotional struggle deep within the self, a unitive presence emerges. Concurrently, it begins to feel as if the conflict between time and the timeless has been reconciled. Still, as it will continue, the poet reflects on the troubling question of how words can evoke redemptive possibility drawn from immediate experience.

Recalling the rhetorical difficulties of his own verbal process, he says:

> Words move, music moves
> Only in time; but that which is only living
> Can only die. Words, after speech, reach
> Into the silence.

The poet's only hope, since he must work with language, lies in discovering verbal patterns that can glimpse, if only briefly, the deeper insights arising from silence. Throughout the *Quartets*, poetry arises from this silence and ultimately—contemplatively—evokes and embodies its deeper significances.[47] Using words to "reach / The stillness, as a Chinese jar still / Moves perpetually in its stillness," becomes a spiritual practice. A classical spatial form gives the poet a metaphor of indwelling opposites—stillness and movement. This stillness is not just the absence of sound,

> Not the stillness of the violin, while the note lasts,
> Not that only, but the co-existence,
> Or say that the end precedes the beginning,
> And the end and the beginning were always there
> Before the beginning and after the end.
> And all is always now.

The dynamic image of "the co-existence"—like the images of "a further union, a deeper communion" in *East Coker* V, the "impossible union" in *The Dry Salvages* V, and "the fire and the rose are one" in *Little Gidding* V—juxtaposes seemingly differing elements in ways that allow the joined differences to fructify in the poet's imagination. Here, light and darkness, words and silence, music and stillness, end and beginning are, temporarily at least, engaged. Simultaneously, their differences become included and transmuted in the poet's unitive recognition.

What Eliot affirms here, although tentatively, is both the impossibility of transcending the limits of language and the drive to do so despite that impossibility. Eliot reflected on this urge to write poetry that transcended itself in an unpublished lecture called "English Letter Writers." He wrote that he aimed

> to write poetry which should be essentially poetry, with nothing poetic about it, poetry standing naked in its bare bones, or poetry so transparent that we should not see the poetry, but that which we are meant to see through the poetry, poetry so transparent that in reading it we are intent on what the poem points at, and not on the poetry, this seems to me the thing to try for. To get beyond poetry, as Beethoven, in his later works, strove to get beyond music.[48]

In fact, this may well serve as a partial "statement of intent" for the *Quartets*. No longer just poet, the spiritual pilgrim descends into inner stillness, into the quietude of the soul, and returns to articulate the practices of renunciation, purgation, devotion, and faith. While rhythms of stillness and silence perpetually move beneath the verbal patterns of *Burnt Norton*,

> . . . Words strain,
> Crack and sometimes break, under the burden,
> Under the tension, slip, slide, perish,
> Decay with imprecision, will not stay in place,
> Will not stay still. Shrieking voices
> Scolding, mocking, or merely chattering,
> Always assail them. The Word in the desert
> Is most attacked by voices of temptation,
> The crying shadow in the funeral dance,
> The loud lament of the disconsolate chimera.

While continuing to lament the intrinsic limitation of words, in the midst of this apprehension he shifts focus from the mutability of words to "the Word," an interplay between the incarnate *logos* of the Greek (Heraclitus) and Christian (St. John) traditions. Recalling closely analogous lines from *Ash-Wednesday*— "Where will the Word / Resound? Not here, there is not enough silence" (CPP 65)—enriches an understanding of this section. Interior silence, it is implied, the quiet force of contemplative practice, is here called for as an antidote to the absence of the transforming Word. The Word—both the Heraclitian speech-with-meaning rising dialogically from the "genuine we" that is common to all and the incarnation of divine wisdom and compassion in the historical person of Jesus—is attacked in the parched desert by illusions of the individual's mind. It is significant here to remember that the teachings of Jesus as incarnate Word are formed from the preserved nucleus of authentic conversations that once took place between Jesus and his disciples as well as his enemies. One can infer that Jesus taught and was always willing to enter into unconditional, situation-specific dialogues with others, which are embodied in his parables and his life. For this reason, one realizes the importance of reciprocal relationships for Jesus, as exemplified in his saying, "Where two or three are gathered in my name, I am there among them" (Matthew 18:20). That is, Jesus both recognized and embodied the spirit of the *logos*.

In the poet's spiritual quest, restimulated by *Burnt Norton's* "first world" rose garden epiphany, Eliot discovers, or comes to the threshold of discovering, that remembering and retrieving in his life "the still point of the turning world" (BN II)—the Word (*logos*)—will liberate him from the attachments and sufferings of temporal existence. In the process, and here I disagree with William Spanos and others who argue for "absence" rather than "presence" at the still point, the poet recognizes the liberating coexistence of absence (timelessness) in presence ("the end and the beginning were always there"). The poet realizes that escaping the life-diminishing limitations of remaining caught in "the aspect of time" is quickened by retrieving remembered moments ("timeless and undesiring")—themselves temporal, and therefore in need of "a grace of sense," of "concentration / Without elimination" (BN II)—and in the process allowing the fractious splinters of one's thoughts, feelings, dissatisfactions, insights to disappear at the still point.

Ironically, by virtue of the threatening voices of temptation and destruction, self-pity, existential doubt, and mistrust, that populate clockwork time, the spiritual quest is deepened. Following his attestation of the redemptive Word, the poet shifts to dynamically short, discursive lines to exemplify its associated behavioral consequences.

> The detail of the pattern is movement,
> As in the figure of the ten stairs.
> Desire itself is movement
> Not in itself desirable;
> Love is itself unmoving,

Only the cause and end of movement,
Timeless, and undesiring
Except in the aspect of time
Caught in the form of limitation
Between un-being and being.

In his continual search for the rhetorical pattern's detail that matches his intenser feelings, the poet recalls St. John of the Cross's "figure of the ten stairs," or ten rungs, of the mystical ladder of love, representing spiritual ascent in our temporal lives. The first five stages toward contemplative realization of divine love are stages of the Dark Night of Faith:

1. Love which causes the soul to languish in desire.
2. Love which actively seeks God.
3. Love which works fervently toward union with God.
4. Love which causes habitual suffering for God, without weariness.
5. Love which desires God.

The second five are those stages on the illuminative way toward becoming united with God:

6. The soul runs to God and touches him again and again.
7. Love which is vehement, without judgment or restraint.
8. The soul grasps and holds fast to God.
9. The soul is burned with sweetness in God.
10. Whole assimilation/clear immediate vision of God/ going forth from the flesh/becoming like God.[49]

Involving faith, hope, and union, the secret of the ladder, according to St. John, refers to the spiritual fact that it may be used for both ascending and descending, that descending is ascending and ascending is descending, since, to paraphrase the Beatitudes, one who humbles oneself is exalted. When ascending-and-descending in ecstasy-and-humiliation, the soul is not caught by desire but perfected by love that is "timeless and undesiring." "The tenth and last step of this secret ladder of love causes the soul to become wholly assimilated to God, by reason of the clear and immediate vision of God which it then possesses; when, having ascended in this life to the ninth step, it goes from the flesh."[50] Contemplation of God in stillness only seems to leave the contemplative within the limitations of temporal existence "between un-being and being." God's unconditional love, however, is beyond time, and Eliot's vision of perfect love in *Burnt Norton* assimilates the soul to this love.

Reflecting the ecstasy and terror of contemplative union, the last lines of *Burnt Norton* reaffirm manifestations of the still point.

> Sudden in a shaft of sunlight
> Even while the dust moves
> There rises the hidden laughter
> Of children in the foliage
> Quick now, here, now, always—
> Ridiculous the waste sad time
> Stretching before and after.

From a time-bound "shaft of sunlight," there rises in memory— briefly and passingly—a poignant recollection of a timeless moment ("Quick now, here, now, always") marked by children's laughter.[51] This recalled glimpse of the rose garden event intuits redemptive life, to begin with, by reminding him to become fully present in the succession of nows. "What might have been" (i.e., the mythic garden of Eden) and "what has been" (i.e., the mystical adventure of the soul) "point to one end, which is always present." In the "first world" of inner stillness, time past and time present in-fold and transmute into Edenic experience and are subsequently recalled through intuitive apprehension and then brought, in a different form, back into life. How ridiculous, in contrast, the sad and spiritless time that is wasted day to day.

2

East Coker

ADOPTING THE OLD WORLD

After completing *Burnt Norton,* Eliot turned his attention to political and social problems related to Christian activism and to the theatre, which increasingly interested him. His 1935 play *Murder in the Cathedral* became far more successful than he could have hoped, and it provided him with a revived sense of creative accomplishment. Meanwhile, his daily life was taken up with routine duties, church responsibilities, various memberships and social engagements, publishing and editing deadlines, and endless correspondences. He delivered numerous lectures and, along the way, collected several honorary doctorates. Indeed, during the period from 1936 to 1939, he became increasingly visible as a prominent Church of England layperson who, like Ezra Pound and other American exiled writers, had adopted and adapted European culture "before the possibility of a transfigured return [could] be imagined."[1]

Nine months before Germany invaded Poland, Europeans were beginning to feel the foreboding anxiety that war was immanent, and the Chamberlain-Hitler pact, signed at Munich in September 1938, deepened Eliot's gathering sense that the demise of Western civilization was near at hand.[2] After war was declared in October 1939, the conditions of Eliot's life changed dramatically, and he directed himself to the immediate cause of England's national defense, becoming an air raid warden for the Kensington area. In the meantime, his writing suffered, and he feared he would never again write anything of consequence. Beginning in August of 1938, Vivienne took up residence in a mental hospital, and although her institutionalization continued to depress him, to his friends Eliot seemed somewhat revived, at times even playful. Partially as a result of feeling deeply guilty about Vivienne's internment, Eliot's interest in continued meetings with Father Cheetham, his spiritual adviser, diminished.[3]

Despite his social duties and church obligations, Eliot managed to write a second theater piece, *The Family Reunion*, a tragicomic verse melodrama, which was first performed in 1939. Like *Murder in the Cathedral*, the play encompasses two worlds, the "normal" world and the "spiritual" world, with its leading character, Harry (Lord Monchensey), struggling for answers to religious as well as mundane problems.[4] *The Family Reunion* opened at the Westminster Theater in March 1939, coinciding not only with the onset of the second world war but also with Eliot's January 1939 announcement that the *Criterion* (the literary review he had edited since 1922) would be discontinued. In the last editorial that Eliot wrote for the review, he pointed to the worsening worldwide political situation: "In the present state of public affairs—which had induced in myself a depression of spirits so different from any other experience of fifty years as to be a new emotion—I no longer feel the enthusiasm necessary to make a literary review what it should be."[5]

Following *The Family Reunion*, Eliot in *East Coker* returns to his ancestral home, bringing with him an ever-awakening acceptance, which was reenergized by his 1932–33 sojourn in America, that his writing continued to embody the co-implicating movement of setting forth from eroding traditions (whether European or American, whether theologic or aesthetic) and returning with revitalized meanings. In August 1937, Eliot visited St. Michael's Church in East Coker, where Eliot's ashes are interred today and from which his ancestors had migrated to the New World around 1669 in search of religious freedom. The road to East Coker is situated in the midst of a lush countryside in Somerset, west of London and not far from Stonehenge. While visiting East Coker, Eliot photographed the tiny village, where the Eliots (or Elyots,

The road to the village of East Coker.

as the family name was once spelled) had lived for several centuries. The village itself is comprised of one main road and several dozen thatch-roofed cottages. On a hill that overlooks the village houses sits St. Michael's Church, from which the Eliot family records can be traced.[6]

It is important to recall that the same year in which Eliot joined the "English Catholic Church" as he called it (1927), he also adopted British citizenship, which embodied, for him, the principles of the Church of England exemplified in and by the values of his English ancestors, not to mention the finest spirit of European tradition. Nonetheless, Eliot recognized that the highest goal of a civilized, or mature, spirituality, grounded as it was in an ever-developing interplay between the Old and the New

World, combined the "profoundest skepticism" with the "deepest faith." For this reason, in *East Coker*, recognizing himself "in the middle way" (EC V)—between beginning and end, each present at the beginning—Eliot will discover that the goal of spiritual life is not "arriving" or "achieving" but exploring and still moving "into another intensity / For a further union, a deeper communion" (EC V). Whether in the Old World or the New, the real heart of the matter becomes what is most required to participate in the sacramentality of all existence—real humility, and "humility is endless" (EC II).

By the time he began writing *East Coker*, Eliot had searched out a *Sketch of the Eliot Family* at the British Museum and traced his earliest recorded ancestry to the village that would name his second quartet. Among the Eliots' ancestral line, T. S. Eliot identified most with Sir Thomas Elyot, the Tudor moralist. Through 1939 and into 1940, feeling increasingly forced in upon himself, Eliot was a middle-aged introvert living mostly by and within himself. It was only in the course of writing the second quartet in this period that, as he told his close friend John Hayward—whom Eliot acknowledged at the beginning of *Four Quartets* "for improvements of phrase and construction" and with whom Eliot shared a large flat in Chelsea from early 1946 until his marriage to Valerie in January 1957—he began to conceive a suite of four poems organized around the basic Heraclitian elements: air, earth, water, and fire. As Eliot remarked in a 1953 interview,

> Burnt Norton might have remained by itself if it hadn't been for the war, because I had become very much absorbed in the problems of writing for the stage and might have gone straight on from *The Family Reunion* to another play. The war destroyed that interest for a time: you remember how the conditions of our lives changed, how much we were thrown in on ourselves in the early days? East Coker was the result—and it was only in writing East Coker that I began to see the Quartets as a set of four.[7]

St. Michael's Church.

Indeed, Eliot's phrase "thrown in on ourselves" suggests the quality of interiority heard throughout the poem.

Open Field (*East Coker* I)

East Coker was published in the *New English Weekly* on Good Friday 1940, about five years after the publication of *Burnt Norton,* and it immediately met with a favorable reception. Within a few months it was republished in book form, selling nearly twelve thousand copies within a year. The poem was written as regular evening bombing raids ransacked London and as Eliot suffered from chronic viral infections (that would later lead to serious bronchial problems and emphysema, exacerbated by his smoking). His energy was deflated to such an extent that he confessed to Bonamy Dobrée that "he was abandoning the writing of poems" because "he did not want to repeat himself."[8] Nevertheless, with memories of his 1937 visit to East Coker in mind, he began, near the end of 1939, to write another meditative poem in which a brooding darkness replaced the "heart of light" of the preceding quartet. If *Burnt Norton* was a confident, visionary, even mystically illumined poem, *East Coker* is initially dubious about mystical insight and the ability of poetry to speak meaningfully about experiences of transcendence.[9] *East Coker* is both more concrete and more personal than *Burnt Norton*, reflecting the reality of England at war and calling on the ghosts of Eliot's own seventeenth-century ancestors.

Though the differences, influenced by world events, between the first and second quartets are notable, their similarities underscore his motive for writing them—"trying to explain to himself his intenser human feelings in terms of the divine goal."[10] In *East Coker*, Eliot returned to the characteristic pattern he had developed in *Burnt Norton*, bringing us from the opening meditative landscape of the first movement (the Open Field) to the temporary illumination of the second movement (Wisdom of Humility), from which we enter into the spiritual discipline of the third movement (Be Still) and the purgative lyric of the fourth movement (the Wounded Surgeon), finally arriving at the unitive vision of the fifth movement (Union and Communion). In other words, like *Burnt Norton*, *East Coker* proceeds through (1) a landscape meditation, (2) a sudden temporal illumination, (3) spiritual practices, (4) a brief lyric interlude, and (5) a middle way vision embracing the coexistence of wisdom and practice.

Whereas in *Burnt Norton* the contemplative poet begins by ruminating on the simultaneity of timelessness and the flux of time, here the poet turns his attention to the seemingly purposeless, repetitive cycle of birth and death, creation and destruction. Nothing endures; everything changes. The opening phrase "in my beginning is my end," repeated several times in *East Coker*, situ-

Sequential Pattern					
	I	II	III	IV	V
BN: (Air)	Lotos Rose	Still Point	Descend Lower	Kingfisher's Wing	The Co-existence
EC: (Earth)	Open Field	Wisdom of Humility	Be Still	Wounded Surgeon	Union and Communion

ates this quartet in both historical and personal contexts. This phrase reverses the famous motto of Mary Queen of Scots on her martyrdom: "*en ma fin est mon commencement*" (in my end is my beginning). "Beginning" and "end," with manifold co-implications, interact here and throughout the poem in ways that deepen and enrich the meaning of each term for the poet's life. For example, "beginning" marks the poetic origins of a new quartet, the familial origins of Eliot's personal life, the theological origins of the soul, the anthropological origins of humankind imprisoned within fixed cycles of birth and death, and his historical existence in this moment of time. The phrase "my end"—indwelling each "beginning"—refers to both a direction of movement and a goal that is sought after. It also refers to the thread of death (with its many faces, many appropriations), which flows just beneath the poem's surface, emerging for a time, then disappearing only to resurface later. Thus, already in his beginning "houses rise and fall, crumble, are extended / Are removed, destroyed" as, at the same time, "old stone to new building, old timber to new fires / Old fires to ashes, and ashes to the earth" (EC I).

As we will see, the pivot of death has several faces for the poet—physical, psychological, emotional, and spiritual—that intertwine throughout the suite of poems. Most notably, like fourth- and fifth-century desert fathers, Eliot's solitary nature embraced an ascetic way of meditating on death in which death becomes a metaphor for the disappearance of self-identity. Noting similarities among Christian ascetics, Indian Yogis, and Zen Buddhist monks, Thomas Merton explains the philosophy and practice of the desert fathers this way: "The only way to find solitude is by hunger and thirst and sorrow and poverty and desire, and the man who has found solitude is empty, as if he had been emptied by death."[11] Throughout this meditative vision, the poet-as-ascetic returns to the roots of his personal and natural history. Compare to the biblical rhythms from Ecclesiastes 3 ("A time to tear down, and a time to build") Eliot's lines "There is a time for building / And a time for living and for generation." The words imply a divine context for human experience and align the rhetoric of his meditation with biblical rhythms.[12] Stretching between birth and death, the mutability of successive temporal events is captured in the repeated conjunction "and": the new decays and becomes old and dies in due time and season.

Edward Lobb suggests, I think quite accurately, that Eliot's appeal to the biblical texts in the midst of an otherwise darkly ironic description is his way of maintaining a "double focus" (human and divine). Lobb writes that

> in Eliot's post-conversion perspective, the limitations of human perception are now accepted as part of the discipline of humility: with the recognition that our own perspective is limited comes the recognition that the two views of human activity in the first verse-paragraph—the ironists' and Ecclesiastes'—are perhaps not incompatible. Irony and vision can be reconciled.[13]

After reiterating "in my beginning is my end," the next stanza shifts focus from his opening meditation on an "open field" late one warm, dark afternoon:

> . . . Now the light falls
> Across the open field, leaving the deep lane
> Shuttered with branches, dark in the afternoon,

Where you lean against a bank while a van passes,
And the deep lane insists on the direction
Into the village, in the electric heat
Hypnotised.

It is easy to imagine yourself—indeed, the poet encourages readers to do just that by addressing us with "you"—standing on one side of a narrow road in the shadows of a fragrant afternoon, along with breathing in a silence that takes no note of itself. The imagery of "the deep lane," the dark afternoon, the "empty silence," and "the early owl" all suggest nightfall, conveying a transition from light to the absence of light. As the "empty alley" of *Burnt Norton* led to the rose garden, here "on a Summer midnight" in an open field, the poet comes upon a marriage dance.

> In that open field
> If you do not come too close, if you do not come too close,
> On a Summer midnight, you can hear the music
> Of the weak pipe and the little drum
> And see them dancing around the bonfire
> The association of man and woman
> In daunsinge, signifying matrimonie—
> A dignified and commodious sacrament.
> Two and two, necessarye coniunction,
> Holding eche other by the hand or the arm
> Whiche betokeneth concorde.

Repeating "you" three times (inviting readers into the common *logos*), his inclusive imagery in this passage, drawn from his readings and reanimated with a disciplined imagination, envisions the immediacy of a wedding ceremony. In *this* moment, the "one end" is intimately, even sacramentally, associated with *this* field, *this* earth, *this* music of pipe and drum, *this* dancing. There is no other time. The archaic spelling of words connects us to an older tradition's view of values and spiritual community in which an entire village participated in the sacramental celebration that joined two lives together permanently. Eliot drew the language for this passage from the annals of East Coker and from Eliot family history. In *The Boke Named the Gouvernour* (1531), Sir Thomas Elyot strongly associated marriage with dance: "And for as moche as by the association of a man and a woman in daunsinge may be signified matrimonic, I could in declarynge the dignitie and commoditie of that sacrament make intiere volumes, if it were not so commonly known to all men that almost every frere lymitour carieth it writen in his bosome."[14]

Eliot was well aware of the many similarities between two ancient traditions, pagan festivals and Christian rituals, through his study of Sir James George Frazer's *The Golden Bough*, which describes a wide range of seasonal folktales and agricultural and marital rituals. In Frazer's work the European Midsummer's Eve festivals, celebrated among agricultural communities, are said to commemorate the summer solstice.[15] Eliot, though, was less interested in Frazer's analysis of these rituals as "homeopathic or imitative magic," than he was with their sacramentality, that all reality is potentially the bearer of divine grace. The dance, for instance, is an external manifestation of what appears in *Burnt Norton* as the "dance along the artery"; the dance at the still point becomes a grace-manifesting sign of God's presence. This sacramental dance will be transfigured later in the poem, influenced by the high Eucharistic doctrine of the Anglican church.

Eliot once remarked to his longtime friend and most valuable critic, John Hayward, "It looks as if daunsinge and not matromonie was the sacrament" here.[16] Although in the Anglo-Catholic tradition marriage is a sacrament and dancing is not, like the pagan ritual of marriage, in which partners who trust each other enter a deeply bonded relationship embodying a past, present, and potential future, and in which each partner affirms and confirms the other, dancing too signifies a mutual presence (*logos*). In dancing and matrimony alike, the focus is on the reciprocity of relationship—the "necessarye coniunction . . . whiche betokenth concorde"—rather than on the act itself. Whereas in *Burnt Norton*, lotus and rose coexist, here male and female are joined in a meaning-giving relationship. In both instances, contraries are united (though not unified), but here in *East Coker* the primary emphasis is on reconciling the tension between the *sacramental* moment and the entirely personal moment.

To begin to grasp what Eliot intends here, it is important to realize that natural or pan-sacramental consecration is neither a traditional religious ritual nor a heightened or transcendent experience. In noninstitutional traditions, the sacramental life is lived by a person who wholly, naturally gives of herself or himself into the service of the moment. Natural sacramental existence, that is, does not follow an acquired set of rules, inherited techniques, or traditional value systems but is always new, always occurring for the first time. For example, according to Buber, "sacramental presence" emerges from inter-activity between persons or between persons and the world, in which the spirit of genuine reciprocity unfolds. Buber writes that sacramental existence "can be awakened and liberated in each object and in each action—not through any methods that one can somehow acquire but through the fulfilling presentness of the whole, wholly devoted [person]. . . ."[17] What makes sacramental reciprocity genuine—when the relationship between persons and ritual form is openly, honestly chosen by each partner who surrenders completely into it—involves mutual stand-taking and mutual self-giving. The spirit emerging from sacramental reciprocity, indeed generating it in the first place, embodies mutual trust and respect.

Buber indicates that the human task, in moments of sacramental existence, is to awaken a holy power laid in things as sparks, and in the process liberate from its isolating shell "the divine spark" living in everything and everyone. This happens when one's entire energy turns toward whatever engages one in the moment. Buber writes, "The people we live with or meet with, the animals that help us with our farm work, the soil we till, the materials we shape, the tools we use, they all contain a mysterious spiritual substance which depends on us for helping it towards its pure form, its perfection."[18] Accordingly, the necessary concord of which the poet speaks comes to fruition as the dancers enter a genuinely reciprocal relationship with each other. They dwell where divine presence dwells. Through the dynamic interchange between the divine presence and authentic reciprocity that exists in genuine relationships, the "mysterious spiritual substance" comes-into-being.

At this point, the poem intensifies into the sensual rhythms of the wedding dance:

> Round and round the fire
> Leaping through the flames, or joined in circles,
> Rustically solemn or in rustic laughter
> Lifting heavy feet in clumsy shoes,
> Earth feet, loam feet, lifted in country mirth
> Mirth of those long since under earth
> Nourishing the corn.

Here, *Burnt Norton*'s "heart of light" can be glimpsed in the fire at the center of the circling dancers. "Keeping time" through primitive rhythms—the dancer's steps "rising and falling" ("reconciled among the stars" in *Burnt Norton*)—now becomes incarnate and reconciled on earth. As the dancers circle round, man and woman, stillness and movement, joy and sadness are harmonized. The dance is rustic, tied to the earth; the dance is awkward, tied to the history of the village; the dance is in time, tied to the rhythms of life; the dance is sexual, tied to marital love.[19]

In the midst of new promise, the ever lurking reminder of death in human affairs—an inevitability that breeds both horror and fascination—surfaces. The poet's eye pulls back to another time of day, to other places.

> Dawn points, and another day
> Prepares for heat and silence. Out at sea the dawn wind
> Wrinkles and slides. I am here
> Or there, or elsewhere. In my beginning.

Subtle yet vital hope concludes this movement: "dawn points," on the one hand, to a new day and, simultaneously, toward the sea of *The Dry Salvages*. Though we remain landlocked in this quartet, which takes earth as its element, for a brief moment, we smell a breath from the ever-present sea. And in that brief moment the poet realizes a deep insight, which echoes mantra-like through the rest of the poem: "I am here / Or there, or elsewhere. In my beginning." That is, no matter where he is, he is always here, beginning to do what needs to be done in that moment and in the next. The phrase "in my beginning" does not refer just to a point in time, therefore, but to a new way of knowing, knowing with "a beginner's mind," a transformative awareness continually radiating in time. Each redeemed moment, therefore, is not a timeless now, but a unique moment full of surprise, replete with challenges—existing nowhere, and yet everywhere.

Wisdom of Humility (*East Coker* II)

The second movement of *East Coker* both echoes the immediate experience of the first movement and draws new and deeper insights from it. As in *Burnt Norton* II, the opening sequence of the second movement of *East Coker* begins with a series of abruptly short, irregularly rhymed lines. The orderly conduct of the first movement now becomes disorderly, and we are confronted with an unreconciled conflict between the seasons: "What is the late November doing / With the disturbance of the spring . . . ?" And the "late roses" are filled with "early snow." Apocalyptic images of disharmony whirl around: "Until the Sun and Moon go down" and "comets weep and Leonids fly." It is as if the traces of *Burnt*

Norton's serene vision have been eclipsed by "that destructive fire / Which burns before the ice-cap reigns" (EC II).

As powerful as this depiction of global disturbance and natural chaos may seem, the poet begins the next stanza (as he does in the fifth movements of *Burnt Norton*, *The Dry Salvages*, and *Little Gidding*) by expressing a recurring dissatisfaction with his own poetry:

> That was a way of putting it—not very satisfactory:
> A periphrastic study in a worn-out poetical fashion,
> Leaving one still with the intolerable wrestle
> With words and meanings. The poetry does not matter.
> It was not (to start again) what one had expected.

The outright concern about poetic language, at least about the kind just read, which typically does not surface until the end of each quartet, appears early in *East Coker*. As he did in *Burnt Norton* V, the poet now reflects "the intolerable wrestle / With words and meaning," words that both strive and fail to adequately articulate the power of the singular Word. If "the poetry does not matter"—a proposition that at first seems both surprising and puzzling spoken by a poet—this is because the "one way" is the way of reversal, the way downward and backward, and the poetry is only a vehicle. More important than the poetry itself, behind the words that the poet cannot speak lies the divine mystery, the *mysterium tremendum*. No matter how ingenious, no matter how descriptive, no matter how breathtaking a statement about God may be, it reveals nothing of God's relational presence.

Where *Burnt Norton* is filled with illuminating light, *East Coker* unfolds in the shadow of darkness: the darkness of the sky over the field; the darkness of the late November; the darkness into which Eliot's ancestors have peered before him; and the spiritual darkness into which the poet enters especially in the next movement. In spite of Eliot's latent admiration for the past,

A house in the village of East Coker.

now he wonders "what was to be the value of the long looked forward to / Long hoped for calm, the autumnal serenity / And the wisdom of age?" (EC II). Were Eliot's Puritan forbearers, the poet asks, wrong to assert that through diligent practice and patience one comes to glean wisdom? "Had they deceived us / Or deceived themselves"? Is their knowledge of now-dead secrets no longer of value? Were they, in fact, afraid to peer into the indefinable darkness that confronts those who seek meaning beyond the deception of mere precept? And was the knowledge they left "only the knowledge of dead secrets"? Questions like these fire the poet's impetus to arrive at wisdom beyond poetry. We are given both a warning and a realization. The wisdom derived from personal experience is falsified by the pattern that knowledge imposes on it.

> For the pattern is new in every moment
> And every moment is a new and shocking
> Valuation of all we have been. We are only undeceived
> Of that which, deceiving, could no longer harm.

Every real encounter with nature, every authentic meeting with unique persons is a new valuation of this moment and of an entire life. To be "shocked" includes a range of feelings (from elevation to terror), but more significantly, here it shakes the poet loose from old habits of mind.

Temporarily, the poet brackets the realization that "the pattern is new in every moment." In the repeated experience of retrieving remembered timeless moments and allowing that retrieval—always taking new forms—to reorient his life, this bracketing quickly dissipates. At this point, however, he reflects on his own situation.

> In the middle, not only in the middle of the way
> But all the way, in a dark wood, in a bramble,
> On the edge of a grimpen, where is no secure foothold,
> And menaced by monsters, fancy lights,
> Risking enchantment.

It is easy to associate these lines with *The Divine Comedy*, in which Dante begins:

> In the middle of the journey of our life
> I come to myself in a dark wood
> Where the straight [or right] way was lost.[20]

Yet, at the same time, Eliot's phrase "all the way" indicates his willingness to push through darkness, through bramble and grimpen (a bog), where one must risk confrontation with menacing monsters and such fanciful apparitions as the "fancy lights" appearing at the dance in the first movement.

Having recognized again, as he will continue to do, the sense of darkness implicit in the human condition, the poet turns to the central focus of the second movement. In *Burnt Norton*, the apprehension of wisdom leads to the "completion" of a "partial ecstasy" and the "resolution" of a "partial horror." Here, however, true wisdom is seen as humility, or, more succinctly, the way to true wisdom is through humility:

> . . . Do not let me hear
> Of the wisdom of old men, but rather of their folly,
> Their fear of fear and frenzy, their fear of possession,
> Of belonging to another, or to others, or to God.
> The only wisdom we can hope to acquire
> Is the wisdom of humility: humility is endless.

Aware of the ultimate futility of will power and the precepts it generates, and resolved to resist the pull of the past, the poet now recalls only his elders' folly, fear, frenzy. A main poetic argument becomes clearer. If the law of progress has proved itself illusory, as it certainly had by the outset of World War II, wisdom cannot be reduced to or contained by an accumulation of knowledge. Instead, he is directed toward "the wisdom of humility." But how does Eliot understand this image, especially since it can take on very different meanings?

At the end of his lectures on *The Idea of a Christian Society* (given at Cambridge in 1939), Eliot reflected that he was "deeply shaken" by the events that eventually led to war with Germany and argued that the gathering war demanded a personal "humiliation" and "an act of personal contrition, of humility, repentance and amendment."[21] Eliot spoke in this lecture from a deep sense of social and cultural responsibility wedded to a theological and spiritual commitment to working toward righting a profound human immorality. In Western contemplative traditions, appropriately, the practice of humility is seen as countering all forms of self-love and self-centeredness. As Eliot understood it, the perfection of humility brings the soul toward union with God through a selfless love, empty of the desire for its own way. True humility, therefore, as we will be told in the next movement, means not being concerned about one's self at all, but choosing to surrender oneself into ever-deepening relationships with the unique particulars of one's current situation.

Age, the poet now realizes, has brought (both to himself and to humankind) neither serenity nor mature wisdom. True wisdom, as distinct from ego-centered self-affirmation, begins with "endless humility." False wisdom, on the other hand, like false humility, desires the perfection of the self as a self-reflecting ego, unable to love. While the wisdom of humility does not permanently overcome "fear and frenzy," it does make real joy possible because it is grounded in grace-infused trust. The realization and practice of endless humility, as Edward Lobb has argued, "is the central drama of the *Quartets* generally, and of 'East Coker' in particular."[22] While it would be, I believe, difficult, if not impossible, to attribute the "central drama" of *Four Quartets* as a whole, or even of *East Coker*, to any single theme or motive, the wisdom of selfless humility does describe as the second movement's mood.

More ethical than mystical, more a deeply embodied attitude toward life than a principle to be learned, the poet's illumination that true wisdom is humility has deep roots in Christian monastic tradition. Practicing humility, in this context of human powerlessness, opens a person to the liberating possibilities of grace. In *The Rule of St. Benedict*, for instance, the three virtues of obedience, silence, and humility are closely linked. Though true humility, Benedict wrote, involves twelve steps, he does not ask monks to count but to climb. To illustrate his point, Benedict, like St. John, used the image of Jacob's ladder: "The ladder represents our life in the temporal world; the Lord has erected it for those of us possessing humility. We may think of the sides of the ladder as our body and soul, the rungs as the steps of humility and discipline we must climb in our religious vocation."[23] Fittingly, this image captures the endless wisdom of humility in that it combines not only body and soul but human and divine will as well. In the religious vocation, humbling oneself elevates one's soul, and the religious vocation of humility, the poet reminds us, is impossible without divine grace.

Be Still (*East Coker* III)

The third and centering movement of *East Coker*, like the central movements of *Burnt Norton* before it and *The Dry Salvages* and *Little Gidding* after it, transitions into an interspiritual discipline. And as in the other quartets, the signifying motive of this practice in *East Coker* is grounded in writings of the mystics. The closing lines of the first movement—"The houses are all gone under the sea. / The dancers are all gone under the hill"—have paved the way for this movement by reintroducing the threatening specter of mortality. Echoing Milton's *Samson Agonistes*, the third movement opens by meditating on the ever-present, mutually embodied fact of death (*memento mori*): "O dark dark dark. They all go into the dark, / The vacant interstellar spaces, the vacant into the vacant." "They," for the poet, are

> The captains, merchant bankers, eminent men of letters,
> The generous patrons of art, the statesmen and the rulers,
> Distinguished civil servants, chairmen of many committees,
> Industrial lords and petty contractors.

Not to be forgotten, the poet adds: "And we all go with them, into the silent funeral, / Nobody's funeral, for there is no one to bury" (EC III). All those just mentioned, plus the poet himself, plus you the reader, are included in the silent funeral's inevitable presence.

From "The Love Song of J. Alfred Prufrock" to *Four Quartets*,

Eliot consistently broods on the sudden disappearance of life into the night of final darkness. By the 1930s, he had become acutely suspicious of fame, especially in the face of death's inevitability, and he includes himself here among the "eminent men of letters" in this somewhat satirical catalogue of those who will die. At this point, however, we recall that in the third movement of *Burnt Norton,* darkness is not only the darkness of the temporal world, marked at every moment by the impending darkness of death, but also the yearned-for mystical darkness, the darkness of the mystical night, which is

> . . . darkness to purify the soul
> Emptying the sensual with deprivation
> Cleansing affection from the temporal. (BN III)

Like Saint John before him, the poet, in sending himself into darkness, voids himself from the sensual temptations of time.

Having accepted, first, the limitations of knowledge and, now, the limiting inevitability of death, the poet presents humility as intentional stillness (as he will again in *Little Gidding*). He begins by addressing his soul directly: "I said to my soul, be still, and let the dark come upon you / Which shall be the darkness of God." The impact of these two lines, crucial to the development of this movement, gains in significance if we juxtapose them with a relevant remark that Eliot once made in a 1937 letter to his friend Paul Elmer More: "I know a little what is the feeling of being alone—I will not say *with* God, but alone in the presence and under the observation of God—with the feeling of being stripped, as of frippery, of the qualifications that ordinarily most identify one: one's heredity, one's abilities, and one's *name*."[24] Ancestry and poetry, which have brought poem and poet to this place, are, in the balancing relation between death and eternal life, rendered irrelevant. According to Ronald Schuchard, "nowhere does Eliot describe more vividly the shadow of the dark angel coming upon him than in *East Coker*, but there he waits, at last, not in fear but in stillness, faithfully waiting for the darkness to become the light."[25] This darkness, to which the soul submits, is not vacancy but the "darkness of God," and the "darkness of God" is not just emptiness but a necessary stage in the soul's progress toward purification, the stripping away of self-satisfactions.

Eliot's key image of this necessary stage in the spiritual life, the "darkness of God," is envisioned through a three-fold simile: (1) it is like the movement of darkness upon darkness, when theater lights are extinguished; (2) it is like the mental emptiness behind faces when the underground train stops longer than usual and people are left with the terror of nothing to speak of or think about; and (3) it is like being etherized when "the mind is conscious of nothing." The image of the train ride in *Burnt Norton* that brought us "into a world of perpetual solitude" and "internal darkness" returns in these lines, as does Eliot's theological debt to St. John of the Cross (that of acquiring, as Eliot once noted, "the highest criteria"). St. John writes in *The Ascent of Mount Carmel* (I, ii, 1):

> We can offer three reasons for calling this journey toward union with God a night. The first has to do with the point of departure, because the individual must deprive himself of his appetite for worldly possessions. This denial and privation is like a night for all the senses.
>
> The second reason refers to the means or the road along which a person travels to this union. Now this road is faith, and for the intellect faith is also like a dark night.
>
> The third reason pertains to the point of arrival, namely God. And God is also a dark night to man in this life. These three nights pass through the soul, or better, the soul passes through them in order to reach divine union with God.[26]

This spiritual path into the darkness of God's night, in other words, introduces a new element, one that requires a deliberate withdrawal of sense, reason, and will.

The metaphor "the darkness of God" therefore refers, to paraphrase Wallace Stevens's poem "The Snowman," to the nothing that is there and the nothing that is not. Not only must temporal ambitions and comforts be rejected, but spiritual aspirations themselves must be discarded for the soul to advance along the ladder of faith. This is true not only of St. John's point of departure up the ladder (privation and denial) but of the entire road of faith. St. John's spiritual poverty—the poverty of emptiness, of desolation, and of total abandonment—is captured by his hyperbolic expression on his illustration of the path: "nothing, nothing, nothing, nothing, nothing, nothing." Yet it is unlike the corresponding section in the third movement of *Burnt Norton*, which spoke of acquiescing to a state of "internal darkness," deprivation, and

> ... Dessication of the world of sense,
> Evacuation of the world of fancy,
> Inoperancy of the world of spirit ...

Here, now, darkness associates with possibilities leading to moments of illumination. To enter fully into this process, to partake of the infinite beauty of the created universe that manifests its creator, one empties of finite attachments.

In the midst of this darkness, the poet's invocation takes on incantatory rhythms:

> I said to my soul, be still, and wait without hope
> For hope would be hope for the wrong thing; wait without love
> For love would be love of the wrong thing; there is yet faith
> But the faith and the love and the hope are all in the waiting.
> Wait without thought, for you are not ready for thought:
> So the darkness shall be the light, and the stillness the dancing.

The dialogue between the poet and his soul, which is similar, structurally, to Yeats's poem "A Dialogue of Self and Soul," is an exchange between two natures of the same person: the embodied, visible personality and the embodied, invisible, animating spirit. Unlike Yeats's poem, however, in which the soul summons the self "to set all your mind upon the steep ascent,"[27] the poet in *East Coker* asks the soul to refrain from acting (i.e., thinking, hoping, loving). It is only through stillness, through emptiness, that the soul can listen beyond personal preoccupation and projections and ascend, led by God, toward its source. Fittingly, Eliot's "dialogue of self and soul" echoes *The Ascent of Mount Carmel* by including three signs by which the spiritually awakened mind passes from reason to contemplation: (1) when one no longer takes pleasure in the reasoning-imagining process; (2) when one has no desire to fix one's attention on any particular object; and (3) when one is able to wait without performing any particular meditation. According to St. John, waiting without hope, love, and thought—that is, waiting in darkness—becomes a prerequisite for passing through contemplation toward inward peace and union with God. Beneath the desiring chatter of the mind, the contemplative spirit sinks to the deepest and most silent place of the soul.

The significance of this interior self-address can be understood more clearly if we position it in the context of Martin Heidegger's distinction in *Discourse on Thinking* between two kinds of waiting: "waiting for" and "waiting upon." "Waiting for" involves having a fixed and concrete result of that waiting in mind, a result that is not yet present but which, by human effort, can be made present. In other words, it involves an attempt to control the fulfillment of human desire. "Waiting upon," by contrast, involves allowing insight to emerge from the field of awareness without a prior desired result. Heidegger characterized this waiting as "releasement," an "openness" toward mystery that leads to a new grounding in that which is most meaningful.[28] Heidegger's distinction, applied to the *Quartets*, suggests the impassable difference between goal-oriented cognitive thinking and the open-minded meditative thinking that Eliot explores throughout the poem.

In this sense, waiting without thought does not mean waiting mindlessly or clearing the mind of impure thoughts by concentrating on some external object. It means, rather, a radical quieting of thoughts, even the thought of waiting without thought. If one already has an idea about the purpose and quality of waiting, or if one already has thoughts about its benefits, the source of that waiting, the divine presence, will remain eclipsed. Hope (not hope in an external reality), love (not the love of someone else), and faith (not the faith *in* or the faith *that*) are perfected as they dwell within the positive spiritual act of waiting. Throughout Eliot's later poetry, and particularly here in *East Coker*, meditative thinking gives form to an unmitigated surrender of self-control that remains attentive to life without imposing anything upon it. Rather than waiting for a specific end, the poet waits upon an as-of-yet undisclosed possibility and is willing to dwell in not knowing.

After the assurance that "the darkness shall be the light, and the stillness the dancing," the poet recalls past moments of vital reciprocity—moments in time, but not of time.

> Whisper of running streams, and winter lightning.
> The wild thyme unseen and the wild strawberry,
> The laughter in the garden, echoed ecstasy
> Not lost, but requiring, pointing to the agony
> Of death and birth.

As in *Burnt Norton* V and in the fifth movements of *The Dry Salvages* and *Little Gidding* as well, a recollected moment of immediate interrelational experience is retrieved by a disciplined imagination along with engaged humility. The significance of these timeless moments of elemental togetherness, both here and throughout *Four Quartets,* requires not an intuition or private insight or theological doctrine but retrieving and integrating its life-giving insights into the incessant struggle between "death and birth." What sense this coupling of death and birth makes becomes one of the most important questions addressing the reader.

We find a clue to this question in Eliot's 1927 poem "Journey of the Magi," published a month after his baptism. In it, the hardship of the soul's faith journey is symbolized, in its opening, by wise men making their way to find the infant Jesus: "'A cold coming we had of it, / Just the worst time of the year" (CPP 68). The next stanza, rehearsing a variety of distractions encountered along the way (sore-footed camels, cursing and grumbling men, a lack of shelter, dirty accommodations, and high prices), demonstrates the challenges to the Magi's faith. Despite temptations to abandon their journey, they continue and arrive "at evening, not a moment too soon / Finding the place; it was (you may say) satisfactory." Wrestling with the conflict between self-will and willed selflessness, the central dilemma for the Magi is the necessity of the soul's dying and being reborn in the presence of God:

> There was a Birth, certainly,
> We had evidence and no doubt. I had seen birth and death,
> But had thought they were different; this Birth was
> Hard and bitter agony for us, like Death, our death. (CPP 69)

The "hard and bitter agony" of "our death" and this "Birth" are joined in one necessary movement: Christian ecstasy (moments of drawing near to the divine presence) and agony (moments of spiritual dryness fueled by the eclipse of God) are inseparable. They both challenge and clarify one another. Most importantly, here and in the *Quartets*, practicing endless humility involves the voiding of self—the courage to become empty of habitual impulses that perpetuate self-serving attitudes.

In keeping with the spirit of this earlier poem, as we approach the end of *East Coker*, Eliot borrows from and alters the *via negativa* of St. John even more directly than he has already:

> You say I am repeating
> Something I have said before. I shall say it again.
> Shall I say it again? In order to arrive there,

> To arrive where you are, to get from where you are not,
>   You must go by a way wherein there is no ecstasy.
> In order to arrive at what you do not know
>   You must go by a way which is the way of ignorance.
> In order to possess what you do not possess
>   You must go by the way of dispossession.
> In order to arrive at what you are not
>   You must go through the way in which you are not.
> And what you do not know is the only thing you know
> And what you own is what you do not own
> And where you are is where you are not.

Some critics have suggested that in this passage the poet builds a construct to convince readers of the nobility and difficulty of his own craft. While the poet clearly attempts to engage readers with his descriptive elaboration of spiritual practice (using the inclusive pronoun "you" seventeen times), Eliot's words both express and exemplify the poet's method of repetition, of echoing passages from his own or others' writings. What repetition grants, at the intersection of time and memory—besides reanimation of an event—is, for the poet, the ability of one text to transfigure and be transfigured by another. "In subjecting his recollections to repetitions, Eliot frees himself to feel and express their new possibilities, to inhabit and orchestrate the coexistence of nostalgia, despair, faith, and skepticism in the unfolding remembrance that is his present."[29] Almost verbatim, in this passage, the poet paraphrases from St. John and points not to his particular poetic path but to the path of contemplative union. St. John writes:

> In order to arrive at that wherein thou hast no pleasure,
> Thou must go by a way wherein thou hast no pleasure.
> In order to arrive at which thou knowest not,
> Thou must go by a way that thou knowest not.
> In order to arrive at that which thou possesses not.

Thou must go by a way that thou possesses not.
In order to arrive at that which thou are not,
Thou must go through that which thou art not.[30]

In both Eliot's passage and St. John's, anything that can be imagined (by the inner or outer senses or thought about, or ritually recited) has nothing to do with the reality of God. Rather, as Paul Murray indicates, Eliot's "central and almost exclusive concern, *at this stage of the poem*, is with the purification and negation of the interior life of the spirit."[31]

In St. John's unrelenting insistence on a total self-emptying, Eliot recognized what he had earlier recognized in the Buddhist philosopher Nagarjuna, who wrote:

Since there is no dharma whatever originating independently,
No dharma whatever exists which is not empty.

He who is without possessiveness and no ego—He, also, does
   not exist. . . .
When I and mine have stopped, then also there is not outer nor
   an inner self.[32]

The road to attain wisdom, both Nagarjuna and St. John assert, must go through the way of negation. The annihilation of self was, for St. John, the foundational illumination: "this negation must be similar to a complete temporal, natural and spiritual death, that is, in reference to esteem of the will which is the source of all denial."[33] As much as it depends upon courageous intention and a willing self-surrender into not-knowing, spiritual death—dying before dying—finally involves the liberating gift of grace that reactivates the divine-human relationship. It is necessary, therefore, to recognize that the only thing we own is precisely that which we are most unwilling to surrender: the illusion of self. Clearly, Eliot's paraphrase of St. John was not the celebration of a craft, but recognizing practical implications of his faith, the expression of which, of course, is encumbered by an imperfect craft.

The Wounded Surgeon (*East Coker* IV)

After the landscape-inspired meditation of the first two movements of *East Coker* and the *via negativa* renunciation of the third movement, the fourth movement casts Christ's (and humankind's) suffering in a seventeenth-century verse form laced with metaphysical wit. Integrally connected to the interior quietude of the third movement, the fourth movement expresses a selfless appropriation of being still before the Eucharistic mystery. Eliot once remarked that the fourth movement of *East Coker*, a lyric revolving around the Christian themes of Good Friday, represents "the heart of the matter."[34] Elsewhere, however, Eliot wrote that "the poem as a whole—this five part form—is an attempt to weave several quite unrelated strands together in an emotional *whole*, so that really there isn't any heart of the matter" at all.[35] The phrase "emotional whole" clarifies the apparent contradiction between these two statements: for Eliot, the sacramental "heart of the matter," hinted at throughout each quartet, gains expressive efficacy by virtue of unexpected rhetorical and surprising associations.

The real "heart of the matter," it can be persuasively argued, especially in light of the first movement's marital dance, is grounded in Eliot's understanding and expression of sacramental existence, especially the interplay between its less traditional, primitive associations in the first movement and its more traditional, Anglo-Catholic associations here. From the pan-sacramental ritual of sacred marriage, in which the consecrated partners consummate a covenant with the Absolute, the poet discerns that sacramental consecration is not merely a celebratory experience but, even more, a participatory relationship in which partners are seized at their innermost core by the spontaneous spirit of reciprocity. Everything, in this view, all nature, all activity, is replete with sacramental substance ever ready to flash up with life-claiming power. And from the Anglo-Catholic ecclesiastical practice of sacramental consciousness, he discerns that the ritual of Eucharist does not cause grace automatically but involves a free gift of God joined by the participant's faith and devotion—a relationship that, in turn, disposes the recipient to grace. Like the poet's remembrance of timeless moments of vital reciprocity, Eucharist is a ritual act of remembrance (*anamnesis*), remembering the person of Christ in a way that makes Christ effectively present again. The "real presence" of Christ, therefore, does not rely upon the belief of individual participants but upon the redemptive power of mutual dependence between a believer's affirming faith and God's liberating presence.

These somewhat different views of holy contact, rather than illegitimizing or neutralizing each other, enlarge the sacramental province on the one hand and provide a historically repeated ritual form on the other. Further, each practice (pan-sacramentalism and Eucharist) in its own way centers on the necessary partnership between the Absolute and the human, between the spirit embodied in the consecrated forms and the spirit embodied in those who surrender into sacramental action. Analogously, as early as 1913, in Josiah Royce's advanced seminar in comparative methodologies, Eliot used the phrase "intuitive sympathy" to depict the meaning of primitive ritual behavior. And in 1928, just a year after his conversion, Eliot suggested that, unlike a person attending a drama, the devout person attending a Mass "is *participating*—and that makes all the difference."[36] "Intuitive sympathy," which is not individually controlled thought but the ability to assume both sides of the relationship, is similar to what Eliot means by "participating," the two-sided action of choosing and being chosen, of acting and surrendering. By participating, Eliot did not mean intensifying his own identity or defining the ritual itself more clearly. Rather, a sacrament draws participants into a deeper reciprocity with the sacred.[37]

Imitating the poetry of Donne and Crashaw, the intellectual and emotional structure of this movement is expressed through five stanzas of five lines each, which begin by linking Christ's redemptive task with that of a surgeon:

The wounded surgeon plies the steel
That questions the distempered part;
Beneath the bleeding hands we feel
The sharp compassion of the healer's art
Resolving the enigma of the fever chart.

The supreme archetype of the Lenten season is, as Grover Smith writes, the downward way—the death and burial of Christ—and the poem, inter-religiously woven until now, here becomes Christocentric.[38] In a major inspiration for these lines, John Donne's "Good Friday, 1613," the poet travels with his back facing eastward (toward the scene of Christ's crucifixion), haunted by the realization that Christ's death atones for sin, which "eternally benighted all." As both victim and savior, Christ, the wounded healer, here resolves the disease of the world through compassionate suffering. For Eliot, the soul's descent into darkness, like Christ's descent into the dark night of the tomb, unites the way up and the way down.

The "dying nurse" of the second stanza, "Whose constant care is not to please / But to remind of our, and Adam's curse," is a figure of the church. Here too, contrary images abound: "Our only health is disease," and to be restored from "Adam's curse," one must first accept the complete consequences of our original, or originating condition. "The whole earth is our hospital," the next stanza continues, "endowed by the ruined millionaire" [Adam]. Glaringly poignant paradoxes arise, the most difficult of which is: "to be restored, our sickness must grow worse." By dying to the disobedience that "prevents us everywhere" and by waking to Christ's redeeming message, one receives life-transforming grace. In the next stanza, in a pattern that will remain consistent through each of the quartets' fourth movements, a contradiction leads to a paradox. "The chill [of death] ascends from feet to knees," for to be warmed "I must freeze" and "quake in frigid purgatorial fires / Of which the flame is roses [eternal life], and the smoke is briars [the wounded savior's crown of thorns]." These lines point ahead to the fourth movement of *Little Gidding*, in which Eliot will write: "The only hope, or else despair" is to be "redeemed from fire by fire" (i.e., redeemed from the fire of damnation through the fire of divine love and purgatorial grace).

The final stanza of this movement culminates at the Eucharistic altar:

> The dripping blood our only drink,
> The bloody flesh our only food:
> In spite of which we like to think
> That we are sound, substantial flesh and blood—
> Again, in spite of that, we call this Friday good.

The celebration of the Eucharist, as Eliot knew it, was the central and most important sacrament of the church, bearing the full mystery of Jesus—his life, teaching, suffering, death, and resurrection. However, like Søren Kierkegaard before him—who emphasized Christianity's need to express its redemptive teachings in new, unusual, unexpected ways—Eliot expresses the "heart of the matter" in deliberately stark language. Spiritually poignant in its Eucharistic and sacrificial context, the "dripping blood" and the "bloody flesh" become our only sustenance through empathetic experience. That is, the Eucharist fulfills its sacrificial significance by inviting celebrants to participate by bringing their own self-sacrifice to the real presence of Jesus. In sacramental time, the past (the life/death/resurrection of Jesus) and the future (the redemption of the church community) are immediately present to the believer who is able to become empty of self.[39]

That is, the poet keeps us grounded in the metaphysical land-scape by emphasizing the devotional practice of the believer's sacrifice.

Both the formal and the symbolic structure of this lyric, written for Good Friday, at times seem strained, awkward, and primitivistic; however, this effect only serves to accentuate the spiritual values addressed. Through the atoning unity of suffering and action, the goodness of this Friday culminates in the death of Jesus, from which new life springs. Another *coincidentia oppositorum* flourishes. In the sacrament of Eucharist, God incarnates Jesus; Jesus becomes bread; death and resurrection become both the partaker and the partaken. Most important, spiritual comfort is offered to the ordinary believer for whom the mystical heights of Saint John, though desirable, remain an unattainable goal because they are, for most, impracticable. For the believer, at least, the Eucharist embodies the incarnate *logos*—the redemptive wisdom common to all—to whom the poet turns for spiritual sustenance and direction.

Union and Communion (*East Coker* V)

As in the fifth movement of *Burnt Norton,* the fifth movement of *East Coker* gathers the various motifs of the quartet together and reconciles the tensions generated between them—between beginning and end, death and birth, darkness and light—in metaphors of middle-way immediacy. At the same time, the multiple inner connections between "beginning" and "ending" deepens his discovery that the spiritual goal is not to be achieved by "arriving" but by ever-renewed striving. The final movement of *East Coker* begins by recalling the poet's earlier paraphrase of Dante's middle way:

> So here I am, in the middle way, having had twenty years—
> Twenty years largely wasted, the years of *l'entre deux guerres*
> Trying to learn to use words, and every attempt

Is a wholly new start, and a different kind of failure
Because one has only learnt to get the better of words
For the thing one no longer has to say, or the way in which
One is no longer disposed to say it.

This opening reference to the "middle way" achieves multiple effects. It is both candid and intimate; as if, in a relaxed and conversational style, the poet is taking the reader into his confidence. At the same time, his words are only tentatively conclusive; they reiterate the fifth movement's characteristic unitive reconciliation, underscoring the darkness of the poem with the depression felt as the poet recalls his largely wasted years.

When Eliot speaks of himself as *"entre deux guerres"* (between two wars), many interpreters have suggested that he was referring to the period between World War I and World War II. Yet the "middle way," for Eliot, included multiple voices and interpretive perspectives. Initially, the poet refers to the period between the wars and to his own biographical age. (Eliot was fifty-two at the time of writing these words.) On one level then, the "middle way" refers to his struggle with language, for he had spent twenty years trying to overcome the "intolerable wrestle / With words and meanings."[40] However, especially in light of Eliot's use of the battlefield story from the *Bhagavad Gita* that will appear in the third movement of the next quartet, a further possibility is worth considering. In the metaphysical structure of the *Bhagavad Gita*, the great war in which Krishna reveals himself to Arjuna as God incarnate takes place on two battlefields simultaneously: *kuru-keshetra*, the field of the Kuru (the literal place of the battle) and *dharma-keshetra,* the field of *dharma* (the spiritual battleground). The two wars here, then, could refer simultaneously to the outer war (World War II) and to the always-raging inner battle between acting and acting-without-acting (the *Gita's* main teaching).[41]

Looking back over the years between the wars, Eliot recognized a twofold pattern in his poetry: the finding that every moment is a fresh beginning and the realization that each new attempt is "a raid on the inarticulate / With shabby equipment." In *Burnt Norton* the poet struggled with the question of how to arrange words in time-bound patterns that could capture experiences of eternal dimensions. Single isolated moments of speech and action, with no real before or after, were reified and severed from experience after the fact. In *East Coker,* the question of how to get the better of words (as well of the difficulties along one's spiritual path) is intensified by his awareness that as soon as he speaks, his words are altered in and by time's passing. Therefore,

> There is only the fight to recover what has been lost
> And found and lost again and again: and now, under conditions
> That seem unpropitious. But perhaps neither gain nor loss.
> For us, there is only the trying. The rest is not our business.

The recognition that words embody only what has already been discovered in thought reminds him of a somewhat frustrating inevitability in his spiritual life—that his goal has shifted from achieving a transformation of consciousness to retrieving revealing reciprocities from events in which he had participated.

In this struggle—ours as well as his—he comes to a place where he must let go and give up his attachments to producing aesthetically or morally pleasing words. Back and forth, again and again—now striving to remember encounters with the *logos,* now disclosing an endless humility—the poet realizes, then forgets, then rediscovers that his goal is called forth only in the trying. These evolving and necessarily repeated realizations of the goal-less goal only accentuate his attention to the significance of sacramental existence as a practice (certainly not the only one) that elevates, even redeems the "trying" by introducing grace into the heart of its movement. A leading undercurrent of this fifth movement, therefore, hinted at in *Burnt Norton* and anticipating a central theme of *The Dry Salvages,* is personal detachment, which "may be thought of as the practical side of 'the wisdom of humility.'"[42]

The question of where to begin saying what the poet is struggling to express is resolved here in a return to the opening of *East Coker*: "Home is where one starts from." Yet growing older brings with it not only increased complications in the relationship between living and dying but, as well, the growing realization that

> Not the intense moment
> Isolated, with no before and after,
> But a lifetime burning in every moment

These relationships burn in every moment of awakened attention and not just those relationships occurring in this life only. The poet becomes more aware, growing older, of a community of persons to whom he is significantly related that stretches across the limitations of death and birth. With this realization comes another, more profound, recognition to which he will return in the next two quartets. Human love is most truly human—that is, completely for others—when it is not dependent on how he may feel either in this moment or at this place. For love to be genuine, these attachments to "here and now" must fall away.

Reminding us of images of that sea whose influence moved inland in the first movement, the meditation culminates in a brief passage that offers a somewhat encouraging, though difficult to practice, suggestion: the ever-present threat of becoming trapped in time's kingdom—which is annihilated "Not with a bang but a whimper"—elicits the need to be "still and still moving."

> Old men ought to be explorers
> Here and there does not matter
> We must be still and still moving
> Into another intensity
> For a further union, a deeper communion
> Through the dark cold and the empty desolation,
> The wave cry, the wind cry, the vast waters
> Of the petrel and the porpoise.   In my end is my beginning.

At the close of *East Coker* the poet urges those who would be explorers to enter into "a deeper communion"—a divine contemplation—whose goal ("a further union") and method ("being still and still moving") are essentially the same.[43] In this "deeper communion," time becomes redeemable as the temporal becomes immersed with the sacred.

The closing words, "In my end is my beginning," reverse the beginning of this quartet: "In my beginning is my end." Provocatively, William Spanos suggests that "the end, in all its senses—the 'termination' of the process of writing 'East Coker,' old age (of the poet, of the literary tradition, of Western civilization), and spiritual goal—does not bring the com-pletion, the ful-fillment, the satisfaction expected by 'old men,' but rather the imperative to explore in the midst, in the realm of difference."[44] Recognizing the implications arising from the awareness that each new beginning of the spiritual journey already, at least in some sense, embodies its "end" (or goal) is itself a spiritual practice. At the same time, recognizing that the "end" of one's journey is already embodied, in part at least, in the beginning returns the poet's focus to here and now, not as a goal to be achieved but as a "condition of complete simplicity" through which one becomes new. While this reversal, or nonlinear coupling of two phrases, reinforces a central paradox of the poem—the need to "be still and still moving," to travel *in search of* and to wait *in contemplation*—this closing passage points ahead to the "vast waters / Of the petrel [Peter] and the porpoise [Christ]" of *The Dry Salvages*.[45]

3 ////

The Dry Salvages

REDISCOVERING THE NEW WORLD

As *Burnt Norton* begins in an English manor and garden, and *East Coker* in an idyllic, almost medieval village, both of which Eliot visited as an adult, *The Dry Salvages* opens with two landscapes drawn from his childhood: the Mississippi River in St. Louis, where he spent his first years, and the coastal region of Cape Ann, Massachusetts, where he spent the better part of nineteen summers from 1893 through 1911 in a house built by his father, Henry Eliot. On June 20, 1930, the English Eliot wrote a revealing letter to William Force Stead (who received Eliot into the Church of England) that speaks of Eliot's relationship to the American landscape:

> I was a nomad even in America. You see, my real ancestral habitat is Massachusetts and my branch of my family only lived in the South for about fifteen years. Everything I remember about Missouri is now swept away in modern improvements; but, on the other hand, I was enough of a southerner to be something of an alien in Massachusetts; and even in my youth the New England of my associations existed more in Maine than in Massachusetts.[1]

Though he was born in St. Louis and attended Harvard University, Eliot did not fully identify with American culture because it did not offer him coherent literary, political, or religious traditions. It was only after Eliot had left the United States and had adopted Europe as his new home that he could look back—not to the possibility of a transfigured return as so many other artists had done, but to rediscover the value of his American roots for his poetry. Realizing that even in England he did not feel fully at home—indeed, he often signed himself with the Greek term *metoikos*, resident alien—further confirmed for him the revitalizing power of his American experience. In the 1930s, culminating with his visiting the United States for the first time since 1914 to become the Charles Eliot Norton Professor of Poetry at Harvard University (1932–33), Eliot reappraised the contours of his American heritage. This homeward movement, Gregory Jay rightly suggests, "sails through an exile in the old, recharts the ancestral isles, and re-discovers the first home as metaphor of perpetual pilgrimage."[2] Eliot discovered—or more accurately, rediscovered—that the great and terrible river running through the center of the New World, as well as in his veins, empties into the many-voiced primordial sea, which connected him to the Old World.

One of the most significant early influences on Eliot took the form of the two houses in which his family lived: a two-story frame house in St. Louis, where Eliot was born and spent his first sixteen years, and a summer house on Gloucester harbor in Massachusetts built by his father in 1896, where, in his youth, Eliot spent his summers and, lured by the shimmering Atlantic waters, learned to sail. On countless solitary afternoons, he would venture into the sea off the coast of Cape Ann. As he became proficient at navigating Cape Ann's unpredictable waters, Eliot often used the "distant rote in the granite teeth" (DS I) of the Dry Salvages' rock ledge as a seamark. Wandering the Gloucester shorelines in the sweet innocence of youth, he no-ticed, as he wrote in "Cape Ann," that the many birds (swamp sparrows, warblers, and purple martins) all resigned "to its true owner, the tough one, the sea-gull" (CPP 95). During those fam-ily summers at Cape Ann, Eliot also heard countless sea stories of storms and shipwrecks told by Gloucester fishermen. Photo-graphs show him in fishing garb at Gloucester harbor and sailing a small craft off the rocks in short sleeves beside a cigar-smoking friend. Not only was Eliot steeped in the lore of Cape Ann, he became familiar with the encompassing ocean. Indeed, cruising in college days with his friend Harold Peters, the Dry Salvages was the last seamark they passed outward bound, and the first they picked up homeward bound.[3]

While *East Coker* revisits Eliot's ancestral roots in England, *The Dry Salvages* evokes a companionable rediscovery of youthful ventures and educational awakenings in the New World. According to A. David Moody, the closing lines of *East Coker*—"The wave cry, the wind cry, the vast waters / Of the petrel and the porpoise"—tie the two poems together, making "of two *Quartets* a single, continuous work" or a "double-quartet: East Coker–The Dry Salvages."[4] Indeed, we can say that these two quartets connect the earth of the Old World to the sea of the New. That is, Eliot's adoption and adaptation of European history and tradition make possible his revision of and rapprochement with his American homeland. With delightful detail, *The Dry Salvages* draws upon the innocent joys of Eliot's personal memories of his childhood summers. As a child, Eliot would often wander along the granite rocks of Gloucester's beaches discovering "the starfish and the hermit crab" and hearing "the menace and caress of wave that breaks on water." Eliot addressed the ongoing power of these childhood experiences in a 1932 essay on "Wordsworth and Coleridge":

> There might be the experience of a child of ten, a small boy and peering through sea-water in a rock-pool, and finding a sea-anemone for the first time: the simple experience (not so simple, for an exceptional child, as it looks) might be dormant in his mind for twenty years, and to re-appear transformed in some verse-context charged with great imaginative pleasure.[5]

The Dry Salvages, then, like *Burnt Norton*, arises out of the depths of the poet's experiences and memories drawn imaginatively out of the past. Though Eliot gave up his American citizenship in 1927, throughout his life he called himself a Yankee and a "New England poet." When he visited America to receive the Emerson-Thoreau award from the American Academy of Arts and Sciences in the winter of 1959, he took as his subject "The Influence of Landscape upon the Poet." In these brief remarks he said,

> My urban imagery was that of St. Louis, upon which that of Paris and London have been superimposed. It was also, however, the Mississippi, as it passes between St. Louis and East St. Louis in Illinois: the Mississippi was the most powerful feature of Nature in that environment. My country landscape, on the other hand, is that of New England, of coastal New England, and New England from June to October. In St. Louis I never tasted an oyster or a Lobster—we were too far from sea. In Massachusetts, the small boy who was a devoted bird watcher never saw his birds of the season when they were making their nests.[6]

Before concluding this address with a reading of *The Dry Salvages*, he told his audience "you will notice . . . that this poem begins where I began, with the Mississippi; and that it ends where I and my [second] wife expect to end, at the parish church of a tiny village in Somerset."[7]

River and Sea (*The Dry Salvages* I)

In spite of regular evening bombing sorties over London and his ongoing viral infections, by January 1941, Eliot was able to send a draft of *The Dry Salvages* to his valued critic John Hayward, and, after exchanging responses to queries from Hayward and Geoffrey Faber, he saw it published in February. One of Eliot's chief concerns resurfaced during the composition of *The Dry Salvages*: he "did not want to repeat himself."[7] He did, however, repeat the pattern established in the first two quartets. Calling

Sequential Pattern					
	I	II	III	IV	V
BN: (Air)	Lotos Rose	Still Point	Descend Lower	Kingfisher's Wing	The Co-existence
EC: (Earth)	Open Field	Wisdom of Humility	Be Still	Wounded Surgeon	Union and Communion
DS: (Water)	River and Sea	Sudden Illumination	Fare Forward	Queen of Heaven	Impossible Union

on the basic five-part musical structure used in *Burnt Norton* and *East Coker*, *The Dry Salvages* reframes the central images and tropes of the earlier quartets. In *The Dry Salvages*, more than in any other quartet, the poet's themes become explicitly incarnate in shared archetypes or figures of the divine, especially in the profiles of Krishna and Christ, whose similarities-in-difference and differences-in-similarity provided Eliot with an efficacious interspiritual prism, as we will see, through which to understand each figure in new ways.

The opening meditative landscapes of the first movement (the river and the sea) and the related interior illumination of the second movement shift to the interspiritual discipline of the third movement (Krishna's yoga) before moving to the devotional lyric of the fourth movement (Mary's prayer) and culminating in the fifth movement's unitive vision of Incarnation.

In addition to being the only quartet set in America, *The Dry Salvages* is also the only poem of the four that begins with an explanatory note, which was added in response to a question from John Hayward—is *The Dry Salvages* a "place name" or the "name of a place?": "(The Dry Salvages—presumably *les trois sauvages*—is a small group of rocks, with a beacon, off the N.E. coast of Cape Ann, Massachusetts. *Salvages* is pronounced to rhyme with *assuages. Groaner:* A whistling buoy.)" In the official guide *United States Coast Pilot, Atlantic Coast, Section A: St. Charles River to Cape Cod* (4th edition, 1941), the Dry Salvages are described as "a bare ledge about 15 feet above high water near the middle of a reef about 500 yards long in a northerly direction."[8] The rock cluster lies about a mile from Straitsmouth Island and is straddled by a rock reef (called the Little Salvages) that is covered at high tide and forms a half-mile long rocky reef (Flat Ground). In the words of historian Rear-Admiral Samuel Eliot Morison, "when an easterly gale is raging the entire group—Dry Salvages, Little Salvages and Flat Ground—becomes a seething mass of foam, as heavy swells from the Atlantic break and roar over it."[9] Of the three formations, all a danger to ships, only the Dry Salvages is visible at high tide, and the partly hidden rocks came to serve as a safety marker for sailors.

Despite the title's emphasis on these rocks, the poem's opening meditation takes place by the Mississippi, a fact not surprising in light of comments Eliot made both before and after writing the poem. In a 1930 letter to the *St. Louis Post-Dispatch*, he provided a youthful picture that partly accounts for his opening lines.

> And I feel that there is something in having passed one's childhood beside the big river, which is incommunicable to these who have not. Of course my people were Northerners and New Englanders, and of course I have spent many years out of America altogether; but Missouri and the Mississippi have made a deeper impression on me than any other part of the world.[10]

Both for the young boy growing up in the once westernmost territory in the young nation and for the mature poet, the Mississippi river became "The River God."[11] The generative impulse that dominates this first movement interweaves two temporal images: that of the ocean (prehistoric time) and that of the river (personal time), which runs to the sea.

Given *East Coker*'s ending, which evokes "the vast waters," it is not surprising that *The Dry Salvages* begins with a boyhood memory from the New World.

> I do not know much about gods; but I think that the river
> Is a strong brown god—sullen, untamed and intractable,
> Patient to some degree, at first recognized as a frontier;
> Useful, untrustworthy, as a conveyor of commerce;
> Then only a problem confronting the builder of bridges.

The further a reader progresses into *Four Quartets*, the more important it becomes to periodically glance backward to similar movements in earlier quartets. Reviewing the opening lines of the other quartets underscores notable differences between *The Dry Salvages* and the first two quartets. The uniform line lengths at the opening of *Burnt Norton* situates that poem in a meditation on time that is speculative and highly prosaic:

> Time present and time past
> Are both perhaps present in time future,
> And time future contained in time past. (BN I)

More rhythmic and musical, the opening *East Coker* meditation again situates that poem in time's passage by calling attention to the inevitable cycle of change and decay through time: "In my beginning is my end. In succession / Houses rise and fall, crumble, are extended" (EC I). The opening verse paragraph of *The Dry Salvages*, evocatively recalling the implacable Mississippi River of Eliot's childhood is, by comparison, more elongated, more brooding. Physically and symbolically, the river flows with an accumulation of human experience moving through time into the endless flux of successive moments replacing one another.[12]

Like the river in *Huckleberry Finn*, the brown river god here embodies both a powerful natural force and an innocent, self-contained dignity. The intimate connection between human life and natural life is rhythmically reciprocal, and those who live beside the river in the flux of chronological time (builders of bridges, dwellers in cities, and worshipers of the machine) are reflected in the river's "waiting, watching and waiting." The river observes human life from its place in nature, yet is kinesthetically present in the human lives that dwell on its banks. Its rhythms flow through "the nursery bedroom," through youth, adulthood, and death, while marking steady seasonal changes of "the April dooryard," and "the autumn table," and "the winter gaslight." There is a sense of fear and awe in these lines, as the river god reminds us of the cycles of death and life that we choose to forget.

A contrapuntal balance exists between sea and river, which suggests the intersection between the lifeblood of nature's cycles bound up in time, and the boundless expanse of the sea's timelessness:

> The river is within us, the sea is all about us;
> The sea is the land's edge also, the granite
> Into which it reaches, the beaches where it tosses
> Its hints of earlier and other creation:
> The starfish, the horseshoe crab, the whale's backbone;
> The pools where it offers to our curiosity
> The more delicate algae and the sea anemone.
> It tosses up our losses, the torn seine,
> The shattered lobsterpot, the broken oar
> And the gear of foreign dead men. The sea has many voices,
> Many gods and many voices.

Notably, the line "The river is within us, the sea is all about us" is central to this movement. The river's flow, "sullen, untamed and intractable," courses through him with primitivistic urgency; the sea's immensity, hinting at earlier preconscious origins, surrounds him both geographically and ontologically. The poet stands at the continual confluence of the river into the sea, the one constantly influencing and being influenced by the other. This passage, shifting the poem's focus to the primordial, all-embracing sea, is one of the most melodious sections in all of *Four Quartets.* Resembling a nautical museum of death, the sea tosses up debris onto the beach for inspection, hints of earlier creation. If the river reminds us of commerce and seasons, of bridges and flooding, the sea reminds us of "ceaseless flux, an endless motion to no end, not the human time of chronometers, but the time of the ground swell or undulating movement caused by distant storms or earthquakes."[13]

As the ebb and flow of waves onto "the land's edge" continues, the assonance and dissonance of the sea's many voices move inland: "The salt is on the briar rose, / The fog is in the fir trees." In this and the following passage, which sustain a rhythmic undertow not unlike the ocean itself, the sea's primordial, unfathomable abyss interrupts the dwellers in chronological time. The different voices of the sea—the "sea howl" and the "sea yelp," and "the whine in the rigging" and "the wailing warning from the approaching headland"—powerfully evoke these threatening menaces of the vast body of water, which outshout an undercurrent of silence.

> And under the oppression of the silent fog
> The tolling bell
> Measures time not our time, rung by the unhurried
> Ground swell, a time
> Older than the time of chronometers, older
> Than time counted by anxious worried women
> Lying awake, calculating the future,
> Trying to unweave, unwind, unravel
> And piece together the past and the future,
> Between midnight and dawn, when the past is all deception,
> The future futureless, before the morning watch
> When time stops and time is never ending;

And the ground swell, that is and was from the beginning,
Clangs
The bell.

In this moment, human time is interwoven into, and emerges from, primordial time, which is "measured" by the focal sound of the "tolling bell." Against the background of primitive terror and the mechanical darkness of machines, anxious women (in a traditional seacoast community in New England) lie awake at night fearing the death of their loved ones, struggling to make sense of past events in light of future possibilities. But notice the difference between their anxious preoccupation of "counting" time (as if chronological temporality can be separated from infinite time) and the unhurried bell's "measuring" time (that is here and now present and also "was from the beginning"). Indicative of both this moment and the inexorable end of human time, the bell's "clang" also brings momentary silence. Recalling the clanging bell of the fourth movement of *Burnt Norton*, the "tolling bell" later in the fourth movement will become the Angelus bell harkening to the Angel Gabriel's annunciation and the birth of Christ, through which new life emerges from death.

Sudden Illumination (*The Dry Salvages* II)

Commenting on the influence of World War II on *Four Quartets*, A. David Moody notes that Eliot's poetry written after 1939 "is not so 'metaphysical' as that of 1925–35: its concern is rather to penetrate than to pass beyond the physical world." The main difference in this period, Moody argues, "can be indicated by observing that the mind of the wartime Quartets is not haunted by what might have been, but is concentrated upon what has been."[14] Even more than that, in the last three quartets (*East Coker*, *The Dry Salvages*, and *Little Gidding* take shape in 1939–42, against the background of the war), Eliot focuses here on the subtheme of death that flows beneath the more apparent motif of time and timelessness.

In the opening sestina of the second movement, the poet ponders three types of annunciation, which are associated with three senses of death. The horror of physical death marks the first annunciation. The habitual, repetitive, and apparently meaningless pattern of death seems to hasten the termination of any real possibility for redemption. Rather than seeing souls caught up in the clouds, we are given "the silent withering of autumn flowers / Dropping their petals and remaining motionless." In the overwhelming presence of physical death, there is no possibility for prayer. While the calamitous annunciation is the death of the body, the second or "last annunciation" corresponds to the failing vital powers of psychological death. Likened to drifting in a boat "with a slow leakage" that moves toward no fixed destination, this enunciation is accentuated by the drifting ennui of mindless habits and failing pride. Like fishermen lulled by the incessant rhythms of the sea—"failing," "sailing," "bailing"—into unknowing, in this condition one endures by "forever bailing," setting and hauling in a life that bears little self-examination.

Following the first and second annunciations, which correspond to the death of the body and the death of the psyche, the poet turns to the third, or "one Annunciation" of spiritual death and rebirth, as emphasized in the juxtaposition here between calamity and annunciation.

> There is no end of it, the voiceless wailing,
> No end to the withering of withered flowers,
> To the movement of pain that is painless and motionless,
> To the drift of the sea and the drifting wreckage,
> The bone's prayer to Death its God. Only the hardly, barely
>   prayable
> Prayer of the one Annunciation.

Unlike "the calamitous annunciation" and "the last annunciation," which are both conditions of and conditioned by repetitiously hollow moments of ordinary time, the "one Annunciation" (here alone the word is capitalized) announces the coming of divine incarnation. Like the "one end" and the "still point" in the previous quartets, the "one Annunciation" points toward a uniquely redemptive event, offering hope through intercessory words addressed to the Blessed Virgin Mary. That is, in the midst of "the drifting wreckage" of life, the presence and possibility of prayer distinguishes the one Annunciation (of the soul's glorious death-rebirth in the spirit) from the others and paves the way for the poet's "sudden illumination."

In the second section of the second movement, the poet's tone shifts, but not his inclusive voice. After using "us" and "our" in the first movement, he draws readers into his observation (about aging and popular notions of sequential time and even a "sudden illumination") by addressing us as "we." In longer, more discursive lines, the poet ponders the complex pattern to human history in a new light compared to those proposed in the earlier poems.

> It seems, as one becomes older,
> That the past has another pattern, and ceases to be a mere
>   sequence—
> Or even development: the latter a partial fallacy
> Encouraged by superficial notions of evolution,
> Which becomes, in the popular mind, a means of disowning the
>   past.
> The moments of happiness—not the sense of well-being,
> Fruition, fulfillment, security or affection,
> Or even a very good dinner, but the sudden illumination—
> We had the experience but missed the meaning,
> And approach to the meaning restores the experience
> In a different form, beyond any meaning
> We can assign to happiness.

But what is meant by "the sudden illumination"?

The mystical moment recorded in *Burnt Norton* is now retrieved "in a different form," one that includes and transmutes the present and the past as well. Situated in an open-ended time-consciousness, in which the poet weaves sequential and cyclic, historic and primordial, western and eastern visions together, the meaning of "illumination" doubles. On the one hand the "sudden illumination" embodies an emotionally infused recollection of immediately experienced moments, which are recalled in memory and restored in the present moment. On the other hand, beyond referring to a heightened moment or extraordinary event experienced in but not completely contained by time, the image also refers to a new meaning arising from immediate experience. He realizes that "the sudden illumination," by itself, often becomes nothing more than another form of time-bound experience, and that cognitive attempts to understand immediate experiences are doomed to fail since the cognitive faculty is temporarily suspended during the moment of intuitive awareness.

Moments of intensely profound clarification, on which the poet has focused since the rose garden, can no longer be regarded *by themselves* as capable of redeeming time. Evoked by the poet's repeated use of the inclusive pronoun "we," a new possibility for redeeming time opens up. The "I do not know much about gods, but I think . . .", with which the first movement began, now becomes "We had the experience but missed the meaning. . . ." Recalling Eliot's appropriation of Heraclitus' common *logos* and Buber's understanding that the fullness of this *logos* does not occur in us, but between us as "speech-with-meaning," Eliot's "we" invites our experiences into a colloquy with his. In our engaged response, like the poet we realize that the common *logos* joins us to the common cosmos from which, as Buber wrote, "we come and which comes from us," and from which we obtain "the shaped order of what is experienced by [us] and what is known as experienciable, a shape that grows and changes."[15] In his shaping and re-shaping of the cosmos, the poet engages not only his own past but also the past generations and cultures that enrich and deepen his realization. Redeeming time, as well, "embraces the dead who once took part in colloquy [reciprocal sharing of knowledge] and now take part in it through what they have handed down to posterity."[16] By what the past generations leave behind, Eliot especially would have had in mind written words, which according to Martin Buber become "living words" when we hear the voice of the one who wrote them.

Seeking to deepen this realization, when the poet attempts to "look behind" the veil of recorded history, he recognizes that both "moments of happiness" and "moments of agony" flow together in all "currents of action." Further, while personal moments of happiness and agony inform the uniqueness of individual human beings,

> . . . the meaning
> Is not the experience of one life only
> But of many generations.

Busy dwellers in cities have almost forgotten the strong brown river god, whose "primitive terror" remains obscure but always potentially threatening, while

> The backward look behind the assurance
> Of recorded history, the backward half-look
> Over the shoulder, towards the primitive terror

makes us aware of the agony of the "sea's wreckage." In its devastation, the wreckage becomes an objective correlative of the agony of physical and psychological death that permanently abides in the human condition. What catches our attention (and prepares us for the next movement) is his confession that this discovery is made clearer "in the agony of others." Unlike the torment of our own agony, which too quickly is covered over by subsequent actions, another's agonizing moments are more clearly perceivable. If a new possibility for redeeming time is to open up, that redemption must address and overcome whatever triggers distress and anguish.

Having recalled that past agonies necessarily abide in the present, the second movement concludes by recalling:

The bitter apple and the bite in the apple.
And the ragged rock in the restless waters,
Waves wash over it, fogs conceal it;
On a halcyon day it is merely a monument,
In navigable weather it is always a seamark
To lay a course by: but in the sombre season
Or the sudden fury, is what it always was.

Echoing the earlier line—"the river is within us, the sea is all about us" (DS I)—time, like the sea, both destroys and preserves. On the one hand, an abiding monument to the passage of time, the "ragged rock" in the restless waters off the coast of Cape Ann, is both a "seamark / To lay a course by" to passing ships in good weather and a hazard to those same ships in foggy weather. Waves of "original sin" ("the bite in the apple") wash over it, and at times it stands dangerously concealed by the fog of ignorance. On the other hand, it is around the figure of the "ragged rock" that the unfolding spirit of *The Dry Salvages* gathers.

The "ragged rock" (itself a kind of still point) echoes imagery from Eliot's 1934 "Choruses from *The Rock*,"[17] in which the Rock, who speaks as a character in the play, combines St. Peter ("You are Peter, and on this rock I will build my church" [Matthew 16:18]) with 2 Samuel 22:2, "the Lord is my rock, my fortress, and my deliverer." Identified as "The Witness. The Critic. The Stranger," the Rock invites listeners to "*make perfect your will*" (CPP 97) through the grace of the Son of Man in communion with the "soul of Man," which quickens to the creation of new life. As a directional marker, the ragged rock gives further dimension to his "sudden illumination." Its meaning cannot be limited to what happens in one lifetime or even to what occurs across many generations but involves, as well, the redeeming significance of incarnation (both Christian and Hindu) in the third and fifth movements.

Fare Forward (*The Dry Salvages* III)

The third and centering movement of *The Dry Salvages*, following the normal pattern of *Four Quartets*, explores the spiritual consequences for personal behavior suggested by the realization unfolded in movements I and II. Just as the poet retrieved moments from his American youth in the first movement, in the third movement he recovers an element of his Harvard education that deeply affected his spiritual sensibility—the drama of the *Bhagavad Gita*. In the parallel third movements of *Burnt Norton* and *East Coker*, the poet explored the spiritual value of negation, that is, of descending more deeply into the "darkness of God," and the value of being able to wait without hoping that the waiting will soon be transcended by a new relation to knowledge of God. What is now required is listening to the voice of Krishna's teachings on the limitations and liberation of one's action in time.

Redeeming reciprocity in *Burnt Norton* arises between the poet and the rose garden and in *East Coker* between poet and the sacramental ritual of marriage, each of which lead toward becoming emancipated from time's enchainments; here that liberation in and from time arises from the poet's engagement with a sacred text, the *Bhagavad Gita*. According to Buber, one instance in which redeeming reciprocity arises between poet and text occurs when, by virtue of its uniquely direct address, a text becomes person-like for the reader. Encountering a text from a Buberian perspective involves at least four dialogically oriented pointings. The first points to reading the text with open receptivity to hear the "living voice" of the author, which allows one to enter into active give-and-take dialogues with the author's voice. In the second, the otherness of the text reflects back the reader's own historical and cultural presuppositions. The third pointing invites one to reflect on values and meanings of the text. The reader then, through the fourth pointing, can apply the text by sharing interpretations with a larger community of readers. In this way, through faithful openness and by returning again to the text with new questions, one is able to grow through ever-new dialogues with the unique person's words, thoughts, and feelings addressing him or her.[18]

Analogous to Buber's textual hermeneutic, the movement opens (and closes) with an intertextual allusion to the Hindu classic the *Bhagavad Gita*, which helps to universalize the point he makes about nonattachment. In the midst of recapturing the experience of his American boyhood and youth, Eliot recalls his intellectual and spiritual voyage to India while at Harvard, where he studied Indian philology under Professor Charles Lanman, Indian philosophy with James Woods, and Buddhist traditions with Irving Babbitt and Masaharu Anesaki.[19] Although Eliot wrote somewhat negatively that his two-year study of Sanskrit and the metaphysics of Patanjali left him "in a state of enlightened mystification," his study of Indic philosophies affected him deeply.[20] At the same time, he indicated that his only hope for penetrating into Indian philosophy "would lie in forgetting how to think and feel as an American or a European; which, for practical as well as sentimental reasons, I did not wish to do."[21]

Of all the Indic texts he studied, he was most enthralled by the *Gita,* which he called "the next greatest philosophical poem to *The Divine Comedy* within my experience."[22] Indeed, the *Gita*'s opening line—"In the field of *dharma* (righteousness, law, virtue), in the field of Kuru (physical land belonging to the clan of Kuru)"—offers a contextual perspective analogous to that explored in *Four Quartets*, that is, alongside the field of *logos* (timeless moments of genuine reciprocity with the world, or the Word common to all) dwells the field of bounded time.

The third movement of *The Dry Salvages* begins:

I sometimes wonder if that is what Krishna meant—
Among other things—or one way of putting the same thing:
That the future is a faded song, a Royal Rose or a lavender spray
Of wistful regret for those who are not yet here to regret,

Pressed between yellow leaves of a book that has never been opened.

And the way up is the way down, the way forward is the way back.

These lines (which some commentators find awkward and pretentious) indicate, among other things, that the poet has wrestled with Krishna's teaching as its voice relates to temporal existence more than once.[23] Significantly, Eliot's profound attraction to Indic tradition reverberated in his life and writings long after his conversion to the Anglican church, and when Eliot introduced Krishna into *The Dry Salvages*, he was "availing himself of that allusive technique of using other poetic voices to widen the perspective of his insight."[24] These very different yet mutually completing voices also deepen the insight that their coupling evokes. Indeed, Eliot's intertextual approach makes explicit the interreligious spirit that has guided and shaped much of the poetry thus far. Appropriately, Raimundo Panikkar, an interreligious dialogian, has suggested that two principles can govern any sound interaction between different faiths—homogeneity and dialogue. Exclusive homogeneity, according to Panikkar, paralyzes real progress toward mutual understanding and dialogue, which is necessary both to promote understanding and to eliminate incongruous assumptions and unwarranted judgments. Panikkar writes:

> Only through an internal or external dialogue can we become aware of uncritical or unwarranted assumptions. This dialogue does not merely look for new sources of information, but leads to a deeper understanding of the other and of oneself. We are all learning to welcome light and criticism, even when it comes from foreign shores.[25]

It is as if the dialogue generated by listening carefully to the other's views, wrestling with them, and integrating what is most meaningful, allows the poet to look into his own point of view, only now through the eyes of the other. As a consequence of this process, one comes to unlearn the tendency, no matter how cleverly executed, of unilaterally affirming the correctness of one's own position. Listening to and considering deeply parallel elements in the Hindu tradition, and engaging others dialogically about the challenges of these elements, deepens his knowledge of that tradition so that he understands more precisely what is to be placed in dialogue with Christianity.[26]

This section of the poem in particular results from Eliot's internal dialogue with the Indic traditions generally, and with the soteriological implications of Krishna's teaching specifically. Rather than suggesting a mere journey through time, in this context Eliot's appropriation of Krishna's "fare forward" suggests movement toward awakening to fuller consciousness.[27] As well, the poem's image of the train (also used in *Burnt Norton* and in *East Coker*) is an urban counterpart to the image of moving into a deeper delusion. By introducing Krishna here, Eliot brings into dialogue with his Christian convictions a spiritual philosophy much different, on the surface, from his own. Yet for Eliot, the enriching value of Krishna's wisdom and spiritual practices was more important than theological differences between them and Christianity. In an extremely telling statement, Eliot once commented on conflicting religious traditions, saying that "of revealed religions, and of philosophical systems, we must believe that one is right and the others wrong." Wisdom, however, which is the same for all people everywhere, "is communicated on a deeper level than that of logical propositions; all language is inadequate, but probably the language of poetry is the language most capable of communicating wisdom."[28]

For this reason, an open-ended act of "wondering" characterizes Eliot's juxtaposition of the figure of Krishna with Christian figures like St. John of the Cross and Christ.[29] Indeed, the poet's "I wonder" reflects the depth of Arujuna's wonderment when he reveals to Krishna that his being is overcome with the question of how he should live his life: "My mind is confused as to my duty" (II:7), and it "runs / After the wondering senses, / Then it carries away one's understanding" (II:67). The spirit of wondering, in fact, is at the heart of the *Gita's* story.

As mentioned, in the initial narrative section of the *Gita*, Krishna, disguised as a charioteer, comes to aid the warrior Arjuna, who has been called into battle to recover land that is rightfully his.[30] Arjuna, for his part, does not desire victory or land if it means killing his relatives. He argues that killing will lead to the annihilation of family and the collapse of society and will only elicit caste-confusion. Surprisingly, in the "Holy Dialogue" Krishna urges Arjuna to "fare forward" in battle by pointing, among other reasons, to the futility of worrying about the future.[31] Like a modern-day Arjuna, the reader of *The Dry Salvages* too, is urged to "fare forward," into life's battles, not by "escaping from the past / Into different lives, or into any future" since "you are not the same people who left that station / Or who will arrive at any terminus." The poet warns that struggling to escape from the past in the future is futile: "You cannot face it steadily, but this thing is sure, / That time is no healer: the patient is no longer here."

In light of the poet's advice in the third movement of *East Coker* ("be still"), Eliot's "fare forward," meanwhile, seems to bring to the fore of the *Quartets* another apparent contradiction. Calling on Krishna's emphasis on the yoga of actionless action, of surrendering attachments to the outcomes of action (*karma yoga*), serves to resolve this contradiction between movement and stillness. The word "forward," that is, implies not just spatial direction but also equanimity of purpose and response. Drawing together elements already introduced, and creating an intrareligious dialogue that was ahead of its time, Eliot writes:

> At nightfall, in the rigging and the aerial,
> Is a voice descanting (though not to the ear,
> The murmuring shell of time, and not in any language)
> "Fare forward, you who think that you are voyaging;

You are not those who saw the harbour
Receding, or those who will disembark.
Here between the hither and the farther shore
While time is withdrawn, consider the future
And the past with an equal mind.

The way into the so-called future is also the way backward into the so-called past insofar as one considers future and past with "an equal mind." If "you" are to "fare forward," then "you" move (without the attaching action of the ego) into a new equanimity, a deeper communion (with self and with life). By reiterating Krishna's emphasis on an active spiritual discipline, one that integrates *karma yoga* (the renunciation of the fruits of action) and *bhakti yoga* (surrender and self-less devotion), the words "fare forward" include *Burnt Norton's* "descend lower" and *East Coker's* "be still" and transmute their descending inaction into ascending action without attachment to outcomes.

Central to the *Bhagavad Gita* in this context, for Eliot, was its teaching of the extremely difficult practice of nonattached action. The fire of one's passionate attachment to desires consumes all senses and keeps one from extinguishing karmic fires. Humans cannot be totally free from desires, but as Krishna teaches, one can be free from attachments to desires. Desires simply produce more desires, which are never satisfied even if they are attained, for attainment only produces more desires. Whether one suffers shipwreck or arrives safely at port, realizing life's destination demands "faring forward" with "an equal mind," that is, with actionless action made possible by one's intention, surrender, and divine grace. Therefore,

At the moment which is not of action or inaction
You can receive this: 'on whatever sphere of being
The mind of a man may be intent
At the time of death'—that is the one action
(And the time of death is every moment)

> Which shall fructify in the lives of others:
> And do not think of the fruit of action.
>> Fare forward. (DS III)

In Krishna's teaching of the art of dying, one's last words, last thoughts, last prayers can liberate one from rebirth if they are wholly concentrated upon and surrendered to Krishna. In this passage the poet recalls Krishna's pivotal reminder to Arjuna about dying the "good death":

> On whatever sphere of being
> The mind of man may be intent
> At the time of death
> There will he go in the next life. (XIII:5–6)

Since a person's last thoughts will naturally turn toward the objects of one's lifelong attachments, the poet adds "(And the time of death is every moment)." One should, therefore, as much as possible, become detached in every moment as if it were the last. The poet thus not only appropriates Krishna's insights but revitalizes Krishna's teaching by suggesting that—as he did in the beginning of *East Coker*: "In my end is my beginning"—personal actions bear fruit in the lives of others when our behavior is both ending (old habits of mine) and beginning (without attachments).[32]

Dialogically engaging the *Gita* in this way, the poet suggests that spiritual death—that is, the immediacy of death/rebirth—arises when one's whole being encounters divine presence.[33] It is not, as one critic argues, that Eliot "has changed the very completion of the *Gita* by shifting the emphasis from action to contemplation."[34] Rather, the poet discovers, or recovers, the significance for the spiritual pilgrim of questioning beliefs and teachings, especially from the perspective of another tradition, and remaining satisfied, temporarily at least, with having no finished answers. Eliot's placing two texts or two teachings from different traditions side by side and reading them in each other's light support his brooding skepticism yet deepen the ground in which his faith stands and develops. The poet juxtaposes Christian and Hindu traditions to highlight the fact that redeeming time is not brought about, as was thought before, by moments of illumination but rather the moment of engaged self-sacrifice. *This is the one action that continues to bear fruit in the lives of others.*[35]

The injunction to "fare forward" as it meant in the *Gita* now comes to mean an increasing sense of nonattachment from notions of the self coupled with an increasing openness to the divine admonishment.

> "... O voyagers, O seamen,
> You who come to port, and you whose bodies
> Will suffer the trial and judgement of the sea
> Or whatever event, this is your real destination."
> So Krishna, as when he admonished Arjuna
> On the field of battle.
>   Not fare well,
> But fare forward, voyagers.

The "real destination"—both for those who return to port and for those who suffer at sea—is discovering the unique liberation of nonattached action. Whether "you" are coming back from having traveled or are just setting forth on a new journey, "faring forward," in this spiritual sense, faces the horrors of the calamitous annunciation directly. Despite our resistance, for which we of course continue to have good reasons, if we are fortunate enough to receive divine admonishment—whether through a person or a text—we can discover that our "destination" is not a place toward which we travel but a transformation of awareness occurring in the traveling itself.

Queen of Heaven (*The Dry Salvages* IV)

The lyric prayer of the associated fourth movement of *The Dry Salvages* initially shifts attention from the cosmic avatar, Krishna, to the humble "handmaiden," Mary. Like the corresponding passages in *Burnt Norton* and *East Coker*, this brief interlude concentrates the spiritual discipline of the poem in a central purging image. From his earliest childhood, Eliot was familiar with Our Lady of Good Voyage Church in Gloucester, located on Prospect Street on a promontory overlooking the harbor. "Between the towers and facing the harbor is a large statue of Mary, her left arm holding a fishing vessel and her right arm raised in a gesture of blessing or peace."[36] The fourth movement opens with this image: "Lady, whose shrine stands on the promontory, / Pray for all those who are in ships." The Lady of the fourth movement, who prayed the "Prayer of the one Annunciation" in the second movement, is petitioned to intercede for all sea voyagers through time.[37]

At the time Eliot was writing these lines, Anglo-Catholics not only venerated Mary as Our Lady of the Rosary but participated in Eucharistic celebrations honoring her throughout the liturgical year: Mary Mother of God (January 1), Visitation (May 31), Assumption (August 15), Queenship of Mary (September 8), and Our Lady of the Rosary (October 7). It is not surprising, therefore, that the poet would address her here as "Queen of Heaven."

> Repeat a prayer also on behalf of
> Women who have seen their sons or husbands
> Setting forth, and not returning:
> Figlia del tuo figlio,
> Queen of Heaven.

What stands out here is the poet's reference to St. Bernard's mystical prayer for sailors, recorded in the last canto of Dante's *Paradiso*. In the *Paradiso*, Mary is addressed as both mother and daughter of Jesus—"Figlia del tuo figlio" (Daughter of thy son).[38] Together, these names for Mary suggest the cooperative role she plays in her son's redemptive mission. Although in the Anglo-Catholic tradition, the Blessed Virgin, "the single rose," is powerless to redeem time, she is elevated as one who intercedes between Christ and humankind.[39] At the same time, they underscore her necessary, self-reversing submission to that mission. That is, as Jesus flows forth from the body of Mary, Mary flows forth from the spiritual body of Jesus.

Echoes of Eliot's 1930 poem *Ash-Wednesday* enrich the texture and sharpen the spiritual significance of this movement. In *Ash-Wednesday* Eliot wrote,

> Blessèd sister, holy mother, spirit of the fountain, spirit
> of the garden
> Suffer us not to mock ourselves with falsehood
> Teach us to care and not to care
> Teach us to sit still
> Even among these rocks,
> Our peace is His will
> And even among these rocks
> Sister, mother
> And spirit of the river, spirit of the sea,
> Suffer me not to be separated
>
> And let my cry come unto Thee. (CPP 67)

Recalling Dante's exalted passage that elevates Mary as the Mother of God, the Lady here is a compound figure: Jewish virgin, the Greek *theotokis* (mother of God), and the animating spirit of the garden, the fountain, the river, and the sea in communion with one another.[40] By practicing stillness, he recognizes a divine-human reciprocity from which his peace grows. Caring, in this instance, and not caring become remembered and envisioned through a new innocence. Commensurate with Eliot's predilection for holding contraries together, these prayers are addressed to the "Lady of Silences" who is also "Calm and distressed / Torn and most whole."[41] Reiterating Mary's significance in Eliot's imagination, Ronald Schuchard has noted that "His Lady, no longer an object of physical desire, has become a figure of spiritual purity." It is clear in this movement the degree to which Eliot "reveres the Lady as his 'Rose of memory,' his 'Rose of Forgetfulness,' through whom his memory of natural objects may be raised to the supernatural and transformed in divine union."[42]

Eliot's most Anglo-Catholic stanza ends with an injunction on behalf of those unable to hear the bell that tolled in the opening movement of this quartet:

> Also pray for those who were in ships, and
> Ended their voyages on the sand, in the sea's lips
> Or in the dark throat which will not reject them
> Or wherever cannot reach them the sound of the sea bell's
> Perpetual angelus.

Whereas the first movement of *The Dry Salvages* closed with a ringing bell that announced the apocalyptic death of the first annunciation ("Time and the bell have buried the day"), here the sound of the bell ashore suggests the perpetual rebirth of the one Annunciation. In Helen Gardner's words: "The bell sounds a warning and a summons: it demands a response. Like the Angelus it is a call to prayer, and a commemoration of the mystery of the Incarnation; like the bell at the consecration it is a call to worship, and announces the presence of Christ; like the tolling bell it reminds us of our death, and calls us to die daily."[43] The word "angelus," meanwhile, recalls the morning, noon, and evening repetitions of the "Hail Mary" in Catholic devotions, often accompanied by the ringing of the cathedral bell in remembrance of the Incarnation.[44] Mary is asked to intercede on behalf of those who are vulnerable in a double sense: to the possibility of being shipwrecked spiritually and to the possibility of dying without apprehending the message of the Incarnate Word.

It should be asked, however, what we are meant to make of the seemingly strange juxtaposition between Lord Krishna of the third movement and the Virgin Mary here.[45] Why does the poem move from Krishna's India to Mary's Bethlehem? If in *Ash-*

Wednesday and here Mary represents selfless sacrifice, in that sense, Mary could be said to embody *bhakti yoga* (devotional surrender to God). Just as Krishna advises Arjuna to "fare forward" without fixating on the fruits of action, so Mary surrenders her will to God's intention. While Krishna's appeal to *karma yoga* and the Anglo-Catholic practice of "perpetual angelus" seem quite different, they are held together in this movement within a mutually inclusive spirit.

Perhaps, then, the poet's juxtaposition of contrary spiritual figures is not as radical as it at first appears to be. Krishna's message to Arjuna (surrender yourself to me) and Mary's response to the Annunciation ("Be it done unto me according to thy will") mirror each other in subtle yet fructifying and—on reflection—somewhat unsurprising ways. Mary's self-will (doubts, fears, confusions) dies; in its place, her "one action" (purified intention) is expressed. What Krishna teaches, Mary comes to embody, becoming the person Arjuna is called to be: (1) she is detached from the fruit of her actions, (2) she bears the one fruit that fructifies in the life of others, and (3) she is lovingly devoted to her son (as Arjuna to Krishna). Interspiritually, the implications between Krishna and Mary reinforce the self-emptying surrender of dying-in-every-moment—the "real destination" of spiritual practice.[46]

Impossible Union (*The Dry Salvages* V)

In each of the *Quartets*, the fifth movement shifts from a meditative landscape and associated temporal illumination, from spiritual disciplines and purgations, to moments of unitive immediacy, which reanimate redemptive intuitions previously explored. The fifth movements of *Burnt Norton* and *East Coker* opened with an attempt to make sense of the ever-present, ever-challenging gap between words and meaning. While this pattern will be followed again in *Little Gidding*, it is absent from the final movement of *The Dry Salvages*. Instead, the poet returns to the theme of time, especially to those who unravel the future.

At the outset of the fifth movement, the poet calls attention to erroneous and misleading ways in which people try to control the temporal process. The poet begins by mocking pseudomystical approaches to spirituality that "communicate with Mars, converse with spirits," or "report the behaviour of the sea monster," or "evoke / Biography from the wrinkles of the palm." All these attempts—whether those of the fortune-teller, theosophist, psychologist, or psychedelic mystic—"to explore the womb, or tomb, or dreams," to discover the secret of time in time's domain, the poet wryly contends, wind up clinging "to that dimension." Those who delve into the past to escape the boredom of the present are like those who would escape into the future to find clues to the present. Astrology, superstitious myths, séances, crystal-ball gazing, palm readings, tea-leaf speculation, card predictions (recalling Madame Sosostris in *The Waste Land*), pseudo-scientific explorations of dreams and genes—"all these are usual pastimes and drugs, and features of the press." Like his mentor Dante, who consigned fortune-tellers and diviners to a level in Hell below that of murderers, past clutchers and future gazers are here consigned to perpetual boundedness in time.

In contrast to these quasi-mystical distractions, and having recognized that we can no longer rely on the rose garden illumination—and rather than transcending the limitations of time—the poet now realizes more accurately that

> to apprehend
> The point of intersection of the timeless
> With time, is an occupation for the saint—
> No occupation either, but something given
> And taken, in a lifetime's death in love,
> Ardour and selflessness and self-surrender.

While Eliot was a communicant of a church that emphasized in its spiritual traditions the redemption of time through the Incarnation, in this passage such redemption appears available only to saints.[47] Rather than escaping from the horrors of time into timelessness, to be extricated here and now from the horror of present suffering one needs to be transfigured by "a lifetime's death in love / Ardour and selflessness and self-surrender." However, this act of acceptance, and of self-surrender, requires taking a risk that the personae in Eliot's earlier poems were not able to accomplish.

In the closing movement of *The Dry Salvages*, the poet returns to the spiritual approach of the fourth movement of *East Coker* by evoking God's personal presence, only here Incarnation is interspiritually situated. Without much difficulty, we can follow the rhythms of the poet's thoughts about apprehending "the point of intersection of the timeless / With time" as they move from: (1) apprehension being "an occasion for the saint," and thus (2) "For most of us there is only the unattended / Moment, the moment in and out of time," which (3) is then retrieved from "a shaft of sunlight." Therefore, there are only "hints and guesses." This sequence of realizations leads him to the necessity, "for most of us," of "the hint" that is Incarnation.

> For most of us, there is only the unattended
> Moment, the moment in and out of time,
> The distraction fit, lost in a shaft of sunlight,
> The wild thyme unseen, or the winter lightning
> Or the waterfall, or music heard so deeply
> That it is not heard at all, but you are the music
> While the music lasts. These are only hints and guesses,
> Hints followed by guesses; and the rest
> Is prayer, observance, discipline, thought and action.
> The hint half guessed, the gift half understood is Incarnation.

For most of us (and for Eliot), moments of timelessness necessarily inspire practical, day-to-day, spiritual disciplines: "prayer, observance, discipline, thought and action." Again, the poet returns to those images that glimpse moments of vital reciprocity, moments in which "There rises the hidden laughter / Of children in the foliage" (BN V) or when he hears in the third movement of *East Coker*, the

> Whisper of running streams, and winter lightning.
> The wild thyme unseen and the wild strawberry,
> The laughter in the garden, echoed ecstasy

Four Quartets, as we have seen, sets the limiting confines of chronological time into hints of a more encompassing sense of time. For this reason, the poem involves us in sympathetically reexperiencing the retrieval of these moments as the poet attempts to appropriate the illumination they offer into the present. To put it another way, directly experiencing timeless moments of genuine reciprocity with the world—moments infused with spiritually redemptive value—are lost or forgotten in the "enchainment of past and future" (BN II) yet are retained and re-presented in memory and then restored through a disciplined imagination.

Leonard Unger, examining this passage, correctly suggests that "the use of the second-person pronoun marks Eliot's characteristic evocation of an experience that is at once intimate and common—common in the sense of *human* rather than of commonplace."[48] At the end of this passage, the moment both "in and out of time," the hint only "half-guessed" and "half-understood" through the poem, now becomes explicitly "Incarnation." In fact, the term "Incarnation" (not *the* Incarnation) captures the movement of the entire poem toward grace. In the context of the third movement, the divine presence is embodied here as a contrapuntal balance between the incarnation of Krishna and that of Christ. Descriptive resonances between these seemingly incommensurate religious figures are suggested in "Choruses from *The Rock*," in which Eliot wrote:

> Then came, at a predetermined moment, a moment in time
>   and of time,

A moment not out of time, but in time, in what we call history:
    transecting, bisecting the world of time, a moment in time
    but not like a moment of time,
A moment in time but time was made through that moment:
    for without the meaning there is no time, and that moment
    of time gave the meaning. (CPP 107)

In unique ways, through graced reconciliations, each of these holy incarnations embodies and reconciles the way of transcendence and the way of immanence.[49]

The marked differences between Christ of the Gospels and Krishna of the *Gita* in their nature and context challenge attempts to find common ground between them. While Krishna is God, Christ is the son of God. While Krishna is finally a mythic figure, Christ is historic. While Krishna only teaches from the platform of the chariot, Christ both teaches and enters into daily village life; he interacts with friends and enemies alike. Yet in each case God speaks to humans through a person. And here, Krishna and Christ are closer to each other than to figures in other religious traditions.[50]

Having delineated a gap between the "saint" and the "rest of us," between apprehending "the point of intersection" directly and receiving only "hints and guesses," the poet once again ponders the dynamics between timelessness and time. "The intersection point" between timeless realization and time-bound spiritual practice—incarnation—overcomes the movement "driven by daemonic, chthonic / Powers," and through grace frees one from "past and future" alike.

Here the impossible union
Of spheres of existence is actual,
Here the past and future
Are conquered, and reconciled,
Where action were otherwise movement
Of that which is only moved

And has in it no source of movement—
Driven by daemonic, chthonic
Powers. And right action is freedom
From past and future also.

Suggestively, in earlier drafts of the poem, Eliot used the word "meeting" in place of "union," so that the "impossible meeting" of the timeless with time is "Incarnation."[51] Just as his use of the "one" at the end of *Little Gidding* will not be meant to imply the total collapse of the human into God, "union" here is not to be understood in the narrow sense. By "union" Eliot means genuine reciprocity between the two. But while the central mystery of incarnation, the meeting of heaven and earth, is "actual," here and now, it is yet "impossible" to conceive. St. John's self-denial and Krishna's *bhakti yoga*, the temporal and the nontemporal, the way forward and the way back, are included and transmuted through the "middle way" meeting between that which is present and that which is apprehended. Thus, incarnation is everywhere distinct, everywhere manifest.

The distinction between two kinds of people on a spiritual path, expressed earlier, reechoes at the end of *The Dry Salvages*.

For most of us, this is the aim
Never here to be realised;
Who are only undefeated
Because we have gone on trying;
We, content at the last
If our temporal reversion nourish
(Not too far from the yew-tree)
The life of significant soil.

The contrast Eliot makes between saints (who experience truth directly) and the rest of us (who at best receive hints and make guesses) might appear as serving to temper human resolve or to weaken human confidence, especially if the perception of timeless moments is only the "occupation" or prerogative of the holiest of humans. The observation of this distinction, which arose from Eliot's practical experience, suggests a difference not between saints and sinners but between those whose communion with the divine arises from austere practices mixed with divinely infused grace and those whose experience of the divine comes more primarily through devotional practices infused with grace.[52]

Eliot, who once indicated the need for "the most Latin kind of discipline," recognized the difficulty of such a spiritual path, writing to William Force Stead that "I do not expect myself to make great progress at present, only to 'keep my soul alive' by prayer and regular devotions."[53] Through incarnation, as Evelyn Underhill (whose theological writings deeply influenced Eliot) explains, "the imperfect and broken life of sense is mended and transformed into the perfect life of spirit."[54] However, Eliot knew that it was only by fully living the tensions (whether between time and the timeless, Krishna and Christ, or saints and the rest of us) without dismissing either that we find consolation in the "temporal reversion."[55] The return to chronological time after encountering the "unattended moment" of unexpected illumination outside of time continues to challenge and nourish the lives of saints and the lives of the rest of us as well.

4

Little Gidding

CHOOSING BETWEEN TWO WORLDS

Almost immediately after completing *The Dry Salvages* early in 1941, Eliot began working on the final quartet. Arguably, *Little Gidding* should have been the easiest of the four poems to write, since the form and themes of the collection had already been established; it proved however to be the most difficult. Eliot was still exhausted from the strain of the war, and he often contracted feverish colds while battling his ongoing bronchial trouble. Yet, for various reasons, including the incessant bombing raids conducted by Hitler's air force on London, he felt pressured to finish the poem. As he told his close friend John Hayward, however, he thought that his writing had become too forced and self-conscious. He wrote: "My suspicions about the poem are partly due to the fact that as it is written to complete a series, and not solely for itself, it may be too much from the head and may show signs of flagging."[1] Therefore, in July 1941, after completing a first draft, he abandoned the project until August of the following year. Before he was finished, he had produced five drafts of *Little Gidding* (more drafts than for any other quartet) and thirteen typescripts. *Little Gidding* was to be his last published poem.

Embodying the spirit of Nicholas Ferrar, who established the first lay community of the English church there in 1625, the small and obscure shrine of Little Gidding had (and has) become a place of spiritual pilgrimage. Originally, the Little Gidding community consisted of about thirty men, women, and children who adopted a common rule of disciplined prayer and daily work. While the community was not monastic (only Ferrar and two of his nieces chose to remain celibate), the members led lives of ritualized worship. Distrustful of both Anabaptist communities on the one hand and Catholic religious orders on the other, Ferrar had established a strict covenant at Little Gidding based around the *Book of Common Prayer*. Central to the community's covenant was the Little Gidding church, where, three times a day, members gathered for worship. The community's regimen—6:30 a.m. morning prayer, followed by breakfast; 10:00 a.m. litany, followed by lunch; 4:00 p.m. evening prayer, followed by supper—would have reminded Eliot of the contemplative rhythms he experienced at Kelham. Even before his visit to the quiet, underspoken chapel in May 1936, Little Gidding must have occupied a special place in Eliot's spiritual imagination, for here we encounter the most intensive reflections of his Anglo-Catholic sensibilities.

Little Gidding had a psychological and literary interest for Eliot in addition to a spiritual one. The earlier metaphysical poets Richard Crashaw, John Donne, and George Herbert, who Eliot rediscovered in the 1930s and in whom Eliot found the highest expression of the English mystical tradition, had all congregated around Ferrar's charisma and associated themselves with this developing spiritual community. For this reason, Ronald Schuchard has persuasively suggested that Herbert and the fourteenth-century English mystics are the "guiding spirits" of *Little Gidding* and that Herbert's spirit in particular "informs the poem." Schuchard writes that Eliot "saw Little Gidding as a distant paradigm of the contemplative life, founded as it was on a mystical devotional spirit which [Eliot] would embrace with increasing intensity."[2] It is no wonder that Eliot, finding Herbert to be a genuine and passionate devotional poet, said in a 1938 lecture: "What is relevant is all there, and we do not ask to know more of him [Herbert] than what is conveyed in his utterence of his meditations on the highest spiritual mysteries. Within his limits, therefore, he achieves the greatest universality in his art; he remains as the human soul contemplating on the divine."[3]

From its inception the Little Gidding community was thrust into intense liturgical conflicts. The high church position, maintained by the likes of Bishop Laud and King Charles, favored elaborate liturgies held in richly furnished churches. Puritans, on the other hand, to counter what they deemed the "papist idolatry" of the Church of England, preferred more austere forms of worship. While Ferrar preferred high-church sensibilities, he was perfectly willing to adopt forms of Puritan worship as he saw fit. Because he was able to strike a compromise between the primary warring factions in English Christianity, the community remained strong during Ferrar's life and lasted until 1647, and as a result of Oliver Cromwell's victory it was dispersed by the Puritan parliament toward the end of the Civil War. The poem *Little Gidding* thus takes as its backdrop two wars—the three hundredth anniversary of England's Civil War and the third year of World War II.

Eliot's 1936 visit to Little Gidding's restored medieval church (it was rebuilt in the nineteenth century after being ruined by fire) was likely motivated by the fact that sometime earlier George Every, himself a poet and playwright, whom Eliot had visited at the Society of the Sacred Mission at Kelham, had sent Eliot the draft of an unpublished verse play, *Stalemate: The King at Little Gidding*. Every's play focuses on Charles I's last visit to the cloister in May 1646, when he sought refuge after the battle of Naseby. In the play Ferrar converses with Richard Crashaw, who argues that, since King Charles's ecclesiastical cause has been defeated in the war and bloodshed of the Reformation era, the Ferrarites should escape over the channel, where "the monks chant their plainsong, while in England the forest fire burns." Ferrar responds: "Would you walk away or walk your way through the fire? . . . We do not know what is beyond the fire. / We can only know enough to see the fire."[4] Fire, as we will see, was to become the governing element of Eliot's last quartet.

Tongued with Fire (*Little Gidding* I)

The road to Little Gidding leads north of London through Cambridge and then west through Peterborough to the Hamlet of Great Gidding in the county of Huntingdonshire. Almost hidden in the sparsely populated countryside, situated behind a farm and next to a pigsty, the Little Gidding church, like Burnt Norton's manor, is not easy to find, even with a map and an experienced driver. At the time of Eliot's visit, other than the church only a farmhouse remained of the original manor where Ferrar's community had moved to escape the urban dampening of religious spirit. The remote countryside surrounding it is populated with a few farmhouses, cottages, and barns. Today, one approaches Little Gidding from the northeast by a narrow, rough lane, which leads to a farmhouse, an adjoining chapel, and more recently constructed residential dwellings.[5] Passing through the farmyard, visitors "turn behind the pig-sty to the dull facade / And the tombstone." Ferrar's tombstone sits in the middle of a narrow path leading to the church and must, therefore, be walked around on the way in. Over the entrance of the Little Gidding church, a stone memorial bears Ferrar's words: "This Is None Other But the House of God and the Gate of Heaven."

Not surprisingly, the poem *Little Gidding* follows the basic pattern established in the other quartets. Coming from the almost hidden rose garden of *Burnt Norton*, the quiet village of *East Coker*, and the powerful river and ocean of *The Dry Salvages*, Eliot concludes *Four Quartets* at a place of spiritual pilgrimage. The landscape meditation of the first movement (the prayer tongued with fire) and the related temporal illumination of the second movement (a dialogue with the compound ghost) lead to the spiritual discipline in the third movement (purifying the motive) and the associated purgatorial lyric of the fourth movement (pyre or pyre) that culminates in a unitive vision of the "complete consort dancing together." Having moved through the visionary, airy images of *Burnt Norton* and through the earthy

East Coker and watery *The Dry Salvages,* here in the final quartet we will encounter the pentecostal fire, which "stirs the dumb spirit" and quickens the soul.

In fact, on a notepad Eliot jotted his preliminary scheme for *Little Gidding,* indicating his intention, in the final poem, to juxtapose fires of the Inferno and Pentecost:

Winter scene. May.
Lyric. air earth water end &
demonic fire. The Inferno.
  They vanish, the individuals, and
our feeling for them sinks into the
flame which refines. They emerge
in another pattern & recreated & reconciled
redeemed, having their meaning together not apart, in a union
which is of beams from the central
fire. And the others with them
contemporaneous.

Invocation to the Holy Spirit[6]

Eliot's outline for *Little Gidding* reveals a trajectory of thought that remarkably parallels Martin Buber's understanding of Heracliltus's *logos.* Similarly, Eliot writes that when "individuals" (those who sink into the Inferno) become transformed (recreated, reconciled, and redeemed by the power of the Holy Spirit) they become "We," persons "having their meaning together" through communal speech-with-meaning.

The first movement of *Little Gidding,* one of the most powerful movements in the poem, is comprised of three stanzas: from a season "suspended in time," to a rough road in England in the "voluptuary sweetness" of May, to the Little Gidding church itself. Initially, we find ourselves in an ephemeral season of "midwinter spring" that recalls lines from the second movement of

Sequential Pattern					
	I	II	III	IV	V
BN: (Air)	Lotos Rose	Still Point	Descend Lower	Kingfisher's Wing	The Co- existence
EC: (Earth)	Open Field	Wisdom of Humility	Be Still	Wounded Surgeon	Union and Communion
DS: (Water)	River and Sea	Sudden Illumination	Fare Forward	Queen of Heaven	Impossible Union
LG: (Fire)	Tongued with Fire	Compound Ghost	Purify the Motive	Pyre or Pyre	Dancing Together

East Coker: "What is the late November doing / With the disturbance of the spring . . . ?" The Heraclitian elements of the first three quartets—air, earth, and water—are now completed by the element of pentecostal fire that "stirs the dumb spirit." In this "springtime / But not in time's covenant" apparent opposites—frost and fire, pole and tropic, melting and freezing, budding and fading—are held together, as a "glare that is blindness in the early afternoon" converts what is most darkened and most frozen into what is most alive. This winter season "between melting and freezing" is trans-seasonal: light is reflected from ice and suspended; fire is not consumed. The sky is clear. Whereas the poet in *Burnt Norton* appeared to feel a bit like a trespasser in the garden, in *Little Gidding* he has a more immediate relationship to the landscape: here, there are no pauses, no conditional phrases, no hesitations. Completely in tune with the thawing trees, "The soul's sap quivers." Death and rebirth coexist.

The dualities between winter and spring dissipate in the paradoxical season of "Midwinter spring," a season that is "not in the scheme of generation." With the question "Where is the summer, the unimaginable / Zero summer?" we recall how the poet responded to a timeless moment in the second movement of *Burnt Norton*: "I can only say, there we have been: but I cannot say where. / And I cannot say, how long, for that is to place it in time." Wedding the natural scene to a spiritual perception, the midwinter "zero summer" blazes with pentecostal fire into the natural sphere like sun reflecting off the frozen pond, evoking the heart's heat. Martin Buber's words, in another context, fittingly reflect and reinforce the spiritual clarity of this passage: "only now can his own being thrive, ripen and bring forth fruit, and the law by which seasons of greenness and seasons of withering succeed one another in the life of the living being, no longer holds for him—his sap circulates continually in undiminished freshness."[7]

The conversational verse paragraph that follows grounds this visionary landscape in May's "voluptuary sweetness" at a specific place of pilgrimage near Cambridge. The places from which one would likely have come to enter Little Gidding's church have already been imaged in the earlier quartets. We have emerged from *Burnt Norton*'s underground, where a light flickers upon the advertising boards that run from platform to ceiling and conversation is reduced to a dull, flat, voiceless chattering; from the chain of endless deaths and rebirths envisaged in *East Coker*; and from the wailing uncertainties of the fishermen's travail and their wives' fears of a futureless future in *The Dry Salvages*, where the ocean tosses up reminders of our past and where the tolling bell reminds us of a time older than we can measure. These are the places that entrap us between past and future, where servitude to history breeds fear of death.

Having come to *Little Gidding*'s sacred place, where the power of incarnate *logos* had shaped a believing community, Eliot discovers that what held that community together—valid prayer—is more than anything that is uttered by "the praying mind" itself. More than words, more than sounds, more than meanings, valid prayer is vital reciprocity between the one praying and the One who perfectly hears and perfectly responds in language, like the communication of the dead, "tongued with fire." Called deeper

The church at Little Gidding.

into the spring day's landscape, we are brought to enter the "dull façade." For

> . . . what you thought you came for
> Is only a shell, a husk of meaning
> From which the purpose breaks only when it is fulfilled
> If at all. Either you had no purpose
> Or the purpose is beyond the end you figured
> And is altered in fulfillment.

The poet is compelled by his placement in this situation to break loose from the restrictive implications of tradition-bound spiritual practices.

Here, at the end of the pilgrimage, the usual linear relationship between "purpose" and "fulfillment" is undone. The fulfillment, itself beyond his original purpose, alters that purpose from accomplishing a goal imagined in the past by placing him in the middle of a future possibility in which each accomplishment becomes a prelude to a new discovery. Ironically, this place, which had become a shrine attracting pilgrims, is bland on the outside, lacking any aesthetic quality, dull and situated behind a pigsty. Seemingly nothing in itself, this church nevertheless embodies the whole of spiritual substance. Inside, beyond the narrow benchseats that face one another across a narrow aisle, an altar stands at the front, behind which three brass tablets are engraved with the Lord's Prayer, the Ten Commandments, and the Apostle's Creed. Above these tablets, an arched stained glass window depicts Christ on the cross, flanked by his mother, Mary, and the beloved disciple.

Recalling those who came this way (the likes of Ferrar and Herbert), the poet continues:

> If you came this way,
> Taking any route, starting from anywhere,
> At any time or at any season,
> It would always be the same: you would have to put off

Sense and notion. You are not here to verify,
Instruct yourself, or inform curiosity
Or carry report. You are here to kneel
Where prayer has been valid. And prayer is more
Than an order of words, the conscious occupation
Of the praying mind, or the sound of the voice praying.
And what the dead had no speech for, when living,
They can tell you, being dead: the communication
Of the dead is tongued with fire beyond the language of the
    living.

Now we are placed where spirit has been embodied, where the sacrament of the Eucharist has been practiced, and, most significantly, where prayer has been valid. Now we see what Eliot was referring to in "Usk," a brief landscape poem written several years earlier, when he warned against putting faith in the "old enchantments" of fertility rituals or the grail legend; instead he sought the spirit "Where the gray light meets the green air / The hermit's chapel, the pilgrim's prayer" (CPP 94).

Once again, in this place of *Little Gidding* ("where prayer has been valid"), and at this moment in history, the poet recognizes that what he used to think (that prayer is "the conscious occupation / Of the praying mind") is no longer authentic. Rather, valid prayer is intimately connected with the speech of the dead. In light of the common *logos*, even the dead, with whom the poet once took part in dialogue (either in person or through what they handed on to posterity), join with him in prayer. Readers here are asked to exercise both physical imagination (in other words, to imagine walking into Little Gidding's church) and what William James called "ontological imagination," through which we sympathetically coexperience the spiritual sensibilities of a pilgrim's kneeling practice of prayer.

Commenting on the lines "You are here to kneel / Where prayer has been valid," Eliot once noted: "What I mean is that

Side view of church at Little Gidding.

for some of us, a sense of place is compelling. If it is a religious place, a place made special by the sacrifice of martyrdom, then it retains an aurora. We know that once before a man gave of himself *here* and was accepted *here*, and it was so important that the occasion continues to invest the place with its holiness."[8] If "you" were to come to this place, you too, like the pilgrim, Eliot is saying, would first have to empty yourself of the reasoning mind in order to kneel humbly in prayer beyond the confines of time. According to the poet, the nature of prayer—its essence—is entering the deepest reciprocity with God through submission and self-surrender. Indeed once, while visiting Virginia Woolf in her London home, Eliot was asked about what he experienced while praying. In response to this question, he "described the attempt to concentrate, to forget self, to attain union with God."[9] Recalling his study of Patanjali's *Yoga Sutras,* in which the practice of yoga begins with "controlling" or "stopping" physical distractions and calming the mind, the prayer into which we are invited demands yogic-like concentration. While the presumption of genuine prayer is the person's readiness to turn wholeheartedly and unreservedly toward God's presence, according to Buber, in a person's speaking to God "whatever else is asked, ultimately [a person] asks for the manifestation of the divine Presence, for this Presence's becoming dialogically perceivable."[10]

The stone set in the Poet's Corner of Westminster Abbey on January 4, 1967, to commemorate Eliot's life and death invokes the key lines from this section of *Little Gidding*:

Thomas
Stearns
Eliot
O.M.
Born 26 September 1888
Died 4 January 1965
"the communication
of the dead is tongued with fire beyond
the language of the living."

But who are "the dead"? And how do they communicate? Are they the voices of Ferrar and his community, or voices of all the saints and mystics throughout the history of the church whose experiences have inspired faith? Are they, as well, dead poets from whom the living poet continues to learn? In response to an inquiry about these lines, Eliot once said,

I had chiefly in mind that we cannot fully understand a person, grasp the totality of his being, until he is dead. Once he is dead, the acts of his life fall into their proper perspective and we can see what he was tending toward. Also with the living presence removed, it is easier to make an impartial judgment, free of the personality of the individual.[11]

A provocative double meaning is implied. On the one hand, "the dead" refer to those former teachers and influential poets (like Dante, Herbert, and Yeats [and Eliot as well]) and philosophers (like Augustine, Henri Bergson, and Francis Herbert Bradley) and spiritual teachers (like St. John, Ignatius, and Lancelot Andrewes) who, because they are no longer living, provide the living with access to the direction in which their lives were heading. On the other hand, "the dead" refer to those who, while yet living, completely surrender themselves into the deepest aspects of reality, which is necessary to make prayer valid. Eliot has already pointed to the necessary "agony / Of death and birth" (EC III), to the reality that "the time of death is every moment" (DS III), and to the suggestion that the "intersection of the timeless / With time" occurs "in a lifetime's death in love" (DS V).

What is discovered here is a kind of unity across persons and time: communication between the dead and the living requires the humility and courage of letting go, of surrendering oneself into the unknown, of dying to one's time-conditioned identity. When this happens, prayer's communication is "tongued with fire," that is, made possible by the same spirit present at Pentecost (to which he will return in the fourth movement). A dual grace is embodied in the pentecostal metaphor—collective and individual. According to the teachings of the church, the pentecostal spirit (tongues of fire) gave birth both to a new community (the church) and to a new consciousness (the rebirthed believer). This pentecostal spirit, thus, contains and gives rise to the inextricable connection between the body of redeemed humanity (the church) and the liberating effects of redeeming time (inner freedom from suffering and attachments).

This spiritual sensitivity resonates with the way Ferrar described his community in a letter to Arthur Woodnoth: "All day they laboured and in the night they found time for long prayer; and while they laboured, they ceased not from contemplation. They spent all their time with profit; every hour seemed short for waiting upon God."[12] Putting away categories, suspending desires, not attempting to prove, judge, learn, or describe anything, the poet aligns his will with the divine will through prayer beyond words. Indeed, it was this spirit of contemplative prayer that Eliot drew from the seventeenth-century Church of England bishop Lancelot Andrewes, whose work he was introduced to by fellow American William Force Stead shortly after they met in 1923. Andrewes was the first great preacher of the English Catholic church because he was, as Eliot once noted, born spiritual. Eliot saturated himself with Andrewes's devotional prose and sermons, arguing that Andrewes's devotional writings were superior to those of John Donne because Donne was primarily a personality, whereas Andrewes spoke with the authority of the church. Eliot was most deeply influenced by a slim volume called *Private Prayers*. Printed after Andrewes's death, these prayers, like his sermons, harmonized intellect and sensibility and took a place, for Eliot, beside the *Exercises of Saint Ignatius* and the works of St. Francis de Sales. Andrewes's ability to constantly find objects adequate to his feelings and to be wholly absorbed in the emotions of the object led Eliot to remark that "Andrewes' emotion is purely contemplative; it is not personal, it is wholly evoked by the object of contemplation, to which it is adequate; his emotions wholly contained in and explained by its object."[13]

Two cryptic lines bring the opening meditation in *Little Gidding* to a close: "Here, the intersection of the timeless moment / Is England and nowhere. Never and always." We have passed through a season beyond the natural order, to a specific road leading to the historic church, to enter it and to kneel in prayer. This movement from physical to metaphysical awareness now repeats itself in these two lines. For the poet, the timeless present occurs simultaneously on two planes: on the plane of the "here and now" (which, in this instance, is England's restored church at Little Gidding) and on the plane of "nowhere" (which, in this instance, points to everywhere). If the place of deepest prayer were limited and bound to the physical and temporal plane, communion with God would be culturally and temporally limited, and

Interior of the church at Little Gidding.

offer little redemptive possibility for the larger human community. Genuine prayer is only possible because of this intersection between "here and now" and "never and always"—"never," because it does not come into existence and then disappear, and because it only manifests itself occasionally, at the right moment, and "always," since the "one end" is continuously present. This theme, struck throughout the *Quartets*, finds an objective correlative at Little Gidding, where the pilgrim comes from the bondage of endless birth, death, and time to rest in the fiery grace of God's redeeming presence.

Compound Ghost (*Little Gidding* II)

The associated second movement of *Little Gidding* begins, following the established pattern of the *Quartets*, with a formal lyric that leads to a longer-lined temporal illumination. Recapitulating Heraclitus, the poet offers a powerful rehearsal of death and decay, gathering together symbolisms that run throughout the *Quartets*. In three brief songs, three faces of death—psychological death (the temporary and reversible termination of cognitive, emotive, and spiritual vitality), physical death (the irreversible cessation of bodily functions), and spiritual death (the transformational termination of inauthenticity through death and rebirth of the self)—appear consecutively. To put it somewhat differently, Eliot was aware that the variety of the world's sacred religious traditions have encouraged both the de-repression of death anxieties (dread and fear in the face of dying) and the cultivation of methods for overcoming these anxieties. In that sense, dying spiritually before dying physically fosters fearlessness (at least in the moment of rebirth) in the face of death.[14]

Recalling the "twittering world" of the London Underground of *Burnt Norton* III—a "place of disaffection" where wind blows "in and out of unwholesome lungs," and where the "strained time-ridden faces" of "unhealthy souls" are "whirled by the cold wind"—death's psychological face comes into focus. The poet now alludes to the German aerial bombings over London, when the accumulated debris and dust after a bombing raid was suspended in the air for hours before slowly descending to cover one's clothing. The fragrant beauty of *Burnt Norton's* roses have now become "Ash on an old man's sleeve;" and the houses of *East Coker* have now crumbled into dust. Especially in light of

Eliot's earlier poetry, this dust, "the death of hope and despair," suggests cognitive impotence, emotional dissonance, volitional habitude, and intuitive paralysis. It was to this debilitated state of human consciousness that Eliot referred in *The Waste Land* when he wrote, "A crowd flowed over London Bridge, so many, / I had not thought death had undone so many" (CPP 39). In the first stanza a life story ends, yet the storyteller still lives (albeit emotionally numbed). In the second stanza, however, not only is there no one left to despair, now even the water and the sand are "parched" and "eviscerate[d]," drained of all life. Physical death here—"Dead water and dead sand / Contending for the upper hand"—recalls the open field of the first movement of *East Coker*, where "Bone of man and beast, cornstalk and leaf" both "live and die"—"This is the death of earth."

The most intriguing of the three faces of death is the third, a spiritual death, which points toward a transformation of consciousness rather than to a cessation of faith. Spiritual dying— "the death of water and fire"—is neither a subjective activity nor an objective forgetfulness. Rather, it is a death/rebirth through which attachments to the self-reflexive, isolated ego again and again naturally and spontaneously dissolve through contemplative practice. He writes:

> Water and fire succeed
> The town, the pasture and the weed.
> Water and fire deride
> The sacrifice that we denied.
> Water and fire shall rot
> The marred foundations we forgot,
> Of sanctuary and choir.
> This is the death of water and fire.

Commenting on these lines, A. David Moody rightly notes that "the natural elements [of water and fire] may assume religious overtones," suggesting "the waters of baptism and purgation, and the fire of purification and the Holy Spirit." If this is the case, he continues, "The water would be the living not the dead water, and so the answer to the dust and the death of the earth; and the final word would not look back to 'Ash,' but toward the refining fire and descent of the dove."[15] Notably, the fire in Eliot's cosmology is not just literal fire but an internal and purgative fire as well, descending from above and ascending from within—namely, a graced process of purgation from sin. Significantly, in an earlier draft Eliot concluded this stanza with three extra lines that underscore his intention to develop the theme of spiritual death and rebirth:

Fire without and fire within
Shall purge the unidentified sin.
This is the place where we begin.[16]

What follows the beginning lyric of the second movement of the previous three quartets is a discursive reflection on time and timelessness. Here, instead, we next overhear an intense dialogue between the poet and a composite figure of several former teachers. The closing passage of the second movement of *Little Gidding* stands out from the rest of the poem both in terms of style and content. For Eliot, they were among the most difficult lines in the poem to write because they were written to carefully approximate Dante's three-line *terza rima* verse form (an Italian rhyme scheme: aba, bcb, cdc). In "What Dante Means to Me," Eliot wrote that this section of *Four Quartets* was "intended to be the nearest equivalent to a canto of the *Inferno* or the *Purgatorio*, in style as well as content, that I could achieve."[17] It is also the only passage in the entire poem in which the poet encounters another speaker.

The main scene that closes the second movement of *Little Gidding* occurs "In the uncertain hour before the morning / Near the ending of interminable night" filled with the horrific sight of diving, dark-dove bombers with flickering tongues that serve as an ironic counterpart to the flaming tongues of the dead and to the pentecostal tongues of fire. The hellacious night ends with the "all clear" signal, after which no sound can be heard other than the rattling of dead leaves. Smoke rises "between three districts" (suggesting, perhaps, Dante's Hell, Purgatory, and Heaven). Fulfilling his responsibilities as an air raid warden, while on his dawn round, Eliot meets, through the smoke, "one walking, loitering and hurried," a stranger who at first has the appearance of a half-recalled dead master whose eyes remind him of several former teachers.

> I caught the sudden look of some dead master
> Whom I had known, forgotten, half recalled
> Both one and many; in the brown baked features
> The eyes of a familiar compound ghost
> Both intimate and unidentifiable.

These, and the remaining lines of this movement, are among the most powerful in the entire quartet.

Many interpreters of these remarkable lines attempt to identify the "compound ghost" with either some individual or a combination of traits: William Butler Yeats;[18] a Yeatsian current and a Dantean current;[19] a combination of Brunetto Latini (Dante's beloved master whom he meets in the *Inferno* XV) and Yeats;[20] a kind of Yeats "towards a greater generality";[21] Dante, Shakespeare, or Tourneur;[22] Jonathan Swift;[23] Irving Babbitt.[24] Cleo McNelly Kearns, meanwhile, writes that the "compound ghost" is part other, part deep self, "a less tangible figure, one that has aspects of the etheric or astral double of the occultists, or even the double as deep self or witness, the *atman*."[25] A. Walton Litz suggests that the compound ghost "is both the masters of the past and Eliot's complex Anglo-American other self."[26] As if in response to these suggestions, Derek Traversi reminds readers that "it is essential to understand, however, if we are to respond to the full scope of the poet's intention, that we are here dealing with an intimate self-confrontation."[27]

> So I assumed a double part, and cried
> And heard another's voice cry: 'What! are *you* here?'
> Although we were not. I was still the same,
> Knowing myself yet being someone other—
> And he a face still forming; yet the words sufficed
> To compel the recognition they preceded.
> And so, compliant to the common wind,
> Too strange to each other for misunderstanding,
> In concord at this intersection time
> Of meeting nowhere, no before and after,
> We trod the pavement in a dead patrol.

Almost immediately, like Brunetto Latini, whom Dante was astonished to meet in Hell, the ghost is humorously aghast to meet the poet. The "What! are *you* here?" question is delightfully ambivalent—it addresses poet, stranger, and reader alike. It asks, which "you" is really present before these words? What questions, needs, and concerns do "you" bring to the text? At the same time, it would be textually inaccurate to assume that both voices are Eliot's own because the poet *sees* the stranger's eyes and the poet *hears* "another voice" addressing him as "you." But who speaks when the spirit of the dead master encountered on the London streets "speaks"? To what extent the ghost's voice is mostly the poet's own voice or achieves a life of its own remains an open question. While Eliot intimated in the first movement of *Burnt Norton* "My words echo / Thus, in your mind," here the poet sympathetically co-experiences (i.e., assumes a double part) another's shifting voice while retaining his own.

The dynamics of this exchange are hinted at in an earlier draft of this section, where Eliot wrote:

> Although we were not. I was always dead
> Always revived, and always something other,
> And he a face changing.[28]

The "meeting" with the "compound ghost" occurs in a time that seems outside of time, fixed identity, and life or death.[29] In response to the poet's request for the stranger to speak, the ghost is, at first, "not eager to rehearse / My thought and theory which you have forgotten." The confrontation between the poet and his envisioned double produces deliberate renunciations of "last season's" creative efforts: "For last year's words belong to last year's language / And next year's words await another voice." This only serves as a reminder of the poet's need to confront himself, and to seek some estimate of a lifetime's creativity. Since there is no obstacle between himself and

> . . . the spirit unappeased and peregrine [foreign]
>> Between two worlds become much like each other
> So I find words I never thought to speak.

What is clear is that the presence of death enters the dialogue from each side,[30] and the dialogue is not directed to some other whom Eliot wished to place in Hell.

Provocatively, the poet's pentecostal perspective is located "between two worlds," not only between life and death, but also between a timeless moment and time. The interlocutor, like Brunetto Latini in the *Divine Comedy*, in response to being asked to "speak," now offers counsel grounded in hindsight by disclosing what death has helped him to realize.

> '. . . Since our concern was speech, and speech impelled us
>> To purify the dialect of the tribe
>> And urge the mind to aftersight and foresight,
> Let me disclose the gifts reserved for age
>> To set a crown upon your lifetime's effort.
>> First, the cold friction of expiring sense
> Without enchantment, offering no promise
>> But bitter tastelessness of shadow fruit
>> As body and soul begin to fall asunder.

> Second, the conscious impotence of rage
>> At human folly, and the laceration
>> Of laughter at what ceases to amuse.
> And last, the rending pain of re-enactment
>> Of all that you have done, and been; the shame
>> Of motives late revealed, and the awareness
> Of things ill done and done to others' harm
>> Which once you took for exercise of virtue.
>> Then fools' approval stings, and honour stains. . . .'

Many commentators, at this point, focus on the intersection between poetic vocation and the vicissitudes of daily life. Yet, more significantly, this passage embodies revealing words spoken by a former mentor, which reminds the poet of their common concern with speech (evident in the final movement of three of the four *Quartets*), a concern that bonded them in a mutual vitality "to purify the dialect of the tribe. . . ." As the fragment from Heraclitus, quoted in the first epigraph of the poem, reminds us, the process of this purification can no longer be limited to the eloquence of one poet's craft. Rather, purifying language now manifests more fully in the common *logos*, a communal speaking and listening in the service of meaning.

Accordingly, in the communal speaking between the stranger and the poet, they "genuinely think with one another because they genuinely talk to one another," a common speaking and thinking that existentially effects a "communal guarding of meaning" and shapes "a single common world whose unity and community they work on in all real waking existence."[31] His challenge to refine language and revitalize speech—to appropriate the right words from tradition and society, which, when properly aligned, as perfectly as possible, articulate and evoke their purpose—always coincidental to the poet's spiritual process, urges "the mind to aftersight and foresight." That is, the former (aftersight from the perspective of death) generates the latter (foresight from life's vantage point).

Reenacting past motives that cut throughout his life with honesty and sincerity, the poet's self-centered, capricious, and virtueless acts evoke a "rending pain" that stings and stains the soul.

The stranger now gives voice to the ironic disclosure that advancing age bestows three gifts upon the writer: diminished senses, lacerated consciousness, and shameful memories. Moreover, as "body and soul begin to fall asunder," the stranger indicates that an ever-narrowing creativity will be experienced. After directing the poet to an agonizing self-assessment upon the effort of a lifetime through the eyes of old age, the ghost ends:

> '. . . From wrong to wrong the exasperated spirit
> Proceeds, unless restored by that refining fire
> Where you must move in measure, like a dancer.'

The poet's "exasperated spirit" rages at "human folly" and at "the shame / Of motives late revealed," continuing to move back and forth "unless" (the key word in this passage) restored through a purging fire. If there is to be a remedy, it will come via a "refining fire" of deprivation and endless humility in which one moves "like a dancer" in partnership with the divine. This image of the dance echoes the second movement of *Burnt Norton* ("at the still point, there the dance is"), the first movement of *East Coker* ("Keeping the rhythm in their dancing"), and the third movement of *East Coker* ("So the darkness shall be the light, and the stillness the dancing"). This necessary renewal of spirit occurs, for the poet, at the intersection of his life and his art, where the one enriches the other. About this redeeming turning point, Derek Traversi writes: "It may, therefore, be an appropriate occasion for us, as readers, to ask ourselves certain questions. What, we may fairly ask, does all that we have read in following this series of poems add up to in terms of actual, definitive achievement?"[32] Or, to put it more practically, how do these poems influence and shape our lives in specific ways?

I will return to this question in the conclusion, but it is important here to recall that, while the main redeeming reciprocity in *Burnt Norton* occurs between poet and rose garden, in *East Coker* between poet and sacramental ritual, and in *The Dry Salvages* between poet and sacred text, here, for the first time, it occurs between poet and the "other." When reciprocity is genuine, one enters a timeless domain, since self-reflective awareness is temporarily suspended, replaced by, as Martin Buber wrote, "a memorable, common fruitfulness which is to be found nowhere else," that is "the dynamic of an elemental togetherness," that emancipates individualistically oriented attachments to temporal existence.[33] By stepping into a direct relationship with this "brown baked stranger," the poet comes to discover that entering reciprocal relationship involves both being chosen and choosing, both acting and surrendering. Nothing foreknown, no agenda, no distraction intervenes between them. The poet *recognizes*, in his meeting with the ghost, that the renewing spirit arises again and again through relational space (the oscillating sphere between himself and what meets him) when dialogical partners are able to express themselves in truth by mutually and unreservedly turning toward one another, listening attentively and responding responsively. In this interaction, what would otherwise remain hidden can unfold in a way that transforms each person.

For this reason, according to Buber, if not Eliot as well, the words spoken by the stranger become "tongued with fire" in that the poet glimpses the divine presence in their interaction. If God is the nearest One, the always ready, supreme partner in dialogue, if God addresses us by standing with us directly, nearly, and lastingly as the eternal partner who is always ready to become dialogically present, we might then wonder what type of mutuality can exist between human beings and God. Doesn't dialogue require each partner to speak? In describing God as "absolute Person," Buber was signifying the empowerment of interhuman relationships by suggesting the dynamics of how God communicates with humans.[34] As a "Person," God enters into direct relationship with us in creative, revealing, and redeeming acts, making it possible for us in turn to enter into direct relationships with God and with others. Not a person in any finite way, God becomes personal in order to speak to us through the language of everyday interhuman exchanges. God speaks to the whole person, in contrast to the individual (neither the starting point nor the goal of human existence), who turns body and soul—honestly, attentively, withholding nothing—to another. In this section, God's speaking penetrates through their genuine relationship, especially when the words of the stranger stand out for the poet (penetrate into his innermost being) as "instruction, message, demand."[35]

Purify the Motive (*Little Gidding* III)

The third and centering movement in each quartet shifts from the apprehended wisdom of a temporal illumination of the second movement to a spiritual practice moving toward the redemption of time. While the third movements of *Burnt Norton* and *East Coker* adapt St. John of the Cross, and *The Dry Salvages* primarily appropriates insights from the *Bhagavad Gita*, *Little Gidding* combines Lord Krishna's emphasis on detachment with the teachings of the devotional mystic Dame Julian of Norwich. Having experienced the fiery presence of the "zero summer" and having entered into a dialogue with the "familiar compound ghost" (who both is not and is himself), the poet begins by recalling Krishna's teaching of the "three conditions which often look alike"—attachment, detachment, and indifference. Of the three, "indifference" (psychological death) is most to be avoided. "Attachment to self and to things and to persons" corresponds to desire ("movement / Not in itself desirable") in *Burnt Norton*, while "detachment / From self and from things and from persons" corresponds to "abstention from movement" and to "waiting without thought."

Both attachment and detachment play a necessary role in

spiritual life. "Growing between / Them, indifference," however, is unliberating.[36] These three conditions parallel Krishna's advice to Arjuna in the *Bhagavad Gita*:

> One must understand the nature of prescribed action,
> And must understand the nature of prohibited action,
> And one must understand the nature of inaction:
> The way of action is mysterious. (IV:17)[37]

From Krishna's point of view, "prescribed," or detached, action is not attached to desired outcomes, while prohibited action spawns indifference. Disciplined action, which liberates one from being trapped in karma-bound temporality, inaction in action, is detachment from everything, including himself or herself, that distracts a person from being fully present in the moment. Eliot's sense of the complex and subtly layered relationships between attachment and detachment is expressed in a brief summary for the third movement, written in the process of composing these lines:

> The use of memory.to.detach oneself
> ones own
> From the past.—they vanish & return
> in a different action.a new relation-
> ship. If it is here, then, why regret it? . . .
> Detachment
> & attachment
> only a hair's width
> apart.[38]

Neither by attachment nor detachment alone is redemption attained, Krishna teaches, nor by inaction, for no one can be freed of action for even a moment (III:5). For Krishna, as for Eliot, the key to actionless action lies in throwing off the delusion of an imaginary ego, of an "I" who acts or does not act (III:27). But how, if the goal is not to be self-conscious, is this to be attained?

Pondering what Krishna meant by the "three conditions" of attachment, detachment, and indifference, the poet evokes an interplay between self-transcendence and self-consciousness by reintroducing the power of memory. Memory, here, means more than a mere repetition of past ideas or events. Rather, through the "grace of sense," when linked with a disciplined imagination, reanimated moments of timelessness point the way toward redeeming time:

> . . . This is the use of memory:
> For liberation—not less of love but expanding
> Of love beyond desire, and so liberation
> From the future as well as the past. Thus, love of a country
> Begins as attachment to our own field of action
> And comes to find that action of little importance
> Though never indifferent. History may be servitude,
> History may be freedom. See, now they vanish,
> The faces and places, with the self which, as it could, loved
> them,
> To become renewed, transfigured, in another pattern.

Echoing the English mystics and St. John, for whom purifying the memory is a necessary ingredient of mystical union, Eliot suggests that the emancipating practice of remembering one's actions in a way that brings freedom requires detachment from desires, from intellectual constructs, and from the power of one's own insights. Memory, we discover—as a primary faculty of the soul when engaged without desires for a predicted outcome but as a pointer toward what has yet to be realized—exists for liberation. Eliot uses the term "memory" here not simply to refer to the pastness of the past but in the sense suggested by the Greek word *anamnesis*, which refers to the immediate presence of the past evoked through its detailed re-presentation. Through non-attached memory, the power of grace expands human love beyond worldly desires and attachments; in the meditative process love becomes renewed, "transfigured in another pattern." The poet deliberately uses the word "expanding" to indicate a process that surpasses the ordinary frontiers of the mind.[39] This new perspective—"memory / For liberation"—both points *from* past-oriented compulsions and leads *to* a condition "not less of love but expanding / Of love beyond desire."

At this point in the poem, another voice is recalled: that of Dame Julian of Norwich (1343–1416), a contemporary of Geoffrey Chaucer, an anchoress (a solitary person living in a cell) who devoted her life to prayer and meditation. Often in the depths of prayer this English visionary was given a vision from a "courteous" God who is concerned with human well-being and desirous of human love. Exemplifying the liberational dynamics of detached memory, the poet's words, here, integrate lines from Julian's mystical treatise *Showings*, or *Revelations of Divine Love*:

> Sin is Behovely, but
> All shall be well, and
> All manner of thing shall be well.[40]

Just as in *The Dry Salvages*, in which Krishna's teaching and Mary's selfless actions were juxtaposed, here Krishna's teaching of detachment is counterpoised with Julian's teaching of purification. Yet as Julian notes, the sins of believers (by "behovely," Julian means a necessary and unavoidable aspect of human behavior) shall be transformed into joy and glory. Though it would seem at first that Julian's *Showings* has little in common with the *Gita*, this is not the case for the poet. An inner dialectic comes to life between Christian sin and the Indic description of ignorance (*avidya*). In Hindu and Buddhist teachings the Sanskrit term *avidya* (beginningless ignorance) suggests *maya* (illusion, or false appearance) and *karma* (action-reaction). Like sin, *avidya* undermines attempts at human liberation. At the same time, just as *avidya* can be overcome by yogic practice, the effects of sin can be overcome through entering into the presence of God by devotion, prayer, and sacrifice.

Realizing the impossibility of translating with "a painstaking exactitude the Hindu and Buddhist philosophy and experience into his own original Christian vision,"[41] Eliot shifts our attention to an instance of Christian spiritual practice, recalling, once again, the historical visitors to Little Gidding. The poet reflects back over three hundred years to the English Civil War with a detached mind, and in the process he becomes aware that "History may be servitude, / History may be freedom." In the light of the poet's contemplation of the *Gita* and Julian's *Showings*, "the faces" and "the places" now "become renewed, transfigured, in another pattern," as contemplation of history gives way to "the inner freedom from the practical desire, / The release from action and suffering" (BN II).

Even while remembering and detaching from the history of the Reformation, the poet imaginatively reanimates the Little Gidding community ("If I think again of this place") and the people associated with it: "All touched by a common genius, / United in the strife which divided them." A straightforward definition of memory as sentimental attachment to the past comes into play here, but only insofar as it is contrasted with the deeper meditation suggested by the presence of the compound ghost that memory creates. Recalled in this spirit is the "peculiar genius" of the Church of England poet George Herbert and the "common genius" of Ferrar along with Charles the First (who visited the chapel at nightfall), Crashaw (who befriended Nicholas at Cambridge and also visited the Little Gidding community), and Milton ("who died blind"). The poet, however, even while remembering the compound ghost, wonders "Why should we celebrate / These dead men more than the dying?" As long as we merely escape into the past, refusing to face present inadequacies, we only "ring the bell backward," or "summon the spectre of a Rose," or "follow an antique drum." These historic figures on both sides of the civil war are now seen to be united by Ferrar's "common genius" and by the silence of death—"folded in a single party." While they cannot be revived, they leave behind what is to be celebrated—"A symbol perfected in death"—a sacrifice of one's attachments to body and spirit.

As his mind slips back and forth among memories of these earlier writers, the poet again recalls Julian, this time adding two more lines from different revelations in her *Showings*:

> And all shall be well and
> All manner of thing shall be well
> By the purification of the motive
> In the ground of our beseeching.

The term "beseeching" (referring to the soul's longing for the will of God) is here used to reinforce the notion of journeying, of not possessing, of enduring till the end—a devotion. Julian writes: "Beseeching is a true and gracious enduring will of the soul, united and joined to our Lord's will by the sweet, secret operation of the Holy Spirit."[42] In Julian's words, "Our Lord brought all this suddenly to my mind, and revealed these words and said: I am the ground of your beseeching."[43] Beseeching is closely related, for Julian, with real prayer. She writes that one needs to pray wholeheartedly, even though one may feel nothing; for in dryness and in barrenness, in sickness and in weakness, then is your prayer most pleasing to God, though you think it almost tasteless to you. In other words, "all shall be well," insofar as our motives are inspired by faith and rooted in prayer that invites divine grace into the foundation of our action.

Here, then, the goal and direction of historical awareness are linked with ascetic practice of contemplative prayer already spoken of in the first movement. As a result, the history of Little Gidding becomes transformed through purified or graced motives in the ground of nonattached beseeching. Having been perfected beyond indifference, the lives of Ferrar, Herbert, Charles, Laud, Strafford, Crashaw, and Milton all participate in catapulting this transformative recomposition of the poet's imagination into his life. These figures embodied, or sought to embody, divine will in the midst of their daily activity. As "symbols perfected in death," they exemplify Eliot's recontextualizing of Krishna's teaching in *The Dry Salvages*—that "the time of death is every moment."

Pyre or Pyre (*Little Gidding* IV)

As we have seen, the associated lyrical fourth movements of *Four Quartets* not only recapitulate, in a more intense manner, major thematic motifs running throughout the sequence but also provide progressive glimpses into redemptive moments. In *Burnt Norton* IV an unearthly light glistened off the kingfisher's wing; in *East Coker* IV the wounded surgeon plied the steel; in *The Dry Salvages* IV the Lady was petitioned to intercede for those in need. Moving from the divine light of *Burnt Norton* to the paschal sacrifice of Jesus to the selfless service of Mary, we arrive at *Little Gidding*, in which each of these sensibilities is celebrated and affirmed by the purifying fire of the Holy Spirit. Now,

> The dove descending breaks the air
> With flame of incandescent terror
> Of which the tongues declare
> The one discharge from sins and error.
> The only hope, or else despair
>   Lies in the choice of pyre or pyre—
>   To be redeemed from fire by fire.

It has been suggested that this stanza offers the most challenging moment of *Little Gidding* for the reader because it "asks our participation and assent, demands not just elucidation and appreciation but communion in prayer."[44] While the insistence of this statement somewhat limits its challenge, it can be said that this passage draws us into a close encounter with the poet who asks us to reflect on our own spiritual sensibilities in light of *Little*

Gidding's affirmation of hope. In light of the "tongued with fire" prayer in the first movement, the "incandescent terror" leads to one last freedom and obligation: the freedom, and the obligation, to decide between the flame of senseless death and destruction and the eternal flame of redemptive love.

While one cannot finally understand whether, or the extent to which, we are consumed by fire, we can (indeed, must) decide *which* fire we are seeking: the consuming, torturous flame of Dante's *Inferno* ("each wrapped in what is burning him" [XXVI:48]), or the refining, redeeming fire of the *Purgatorio* (in whose midst "you would not lose one hair" [XXVII:27]). This choice between two opposing fires also suggests a choice between worlds of two opposing wills—the will to earthly power (leading straight to the fire of the *Inferno*) or the will to God (perfected in the fire of *Purgatorio*). Indeed, like Dante's *Divine Comedy*, the *Bhagavad Gita* speaks of two kinds of fire: an insatiable fire of desire, passion, and anger (III:37, 39), and the fire of wisdom that transforms works of desire to ashes (IV:37). Further, like Dante's purgatorial fire, wisdom's fire in the *Gita* has "the power to cleanse and purify" (IV:38).[45]

In the Anglo-Catholic counterpoint to this background of Eliot's poetry, the Apostles' experience at Pentecost recalls the divine fire pouring forth from heaven. Fifty days after Passover, followers of the crucified Jesus were gathered together, tradition records, in the upper room where the Last Supper had transpired. Without warning, a powerful wind filled the entire house: "Divided tongues, as of fire, appeared among them, and a tongue rested on each of them. All of them were filled with the Holy Spirit and began to speak in other languages, as the Spirit gave them ability" (Acts 2:3-4). Yet, these "tongues" were understood by those present as if spoken in each other's own language. As in Dante's *Purgatorio* and the Buddha's sermon, fire here paradoxically brings liberation from suffering. Through purgatorial love, spiritual death/rebirth brings with it the realization of renewed life. Through the power of the Spirit descending on the disciples, as Bede Griffiths wrote: "a new consciousness dawned, a consciousness beyond the ordinary rational consciousness, which set the apostles free from the limitations of our present mode of existence and consciousness and opened them to the new world of the Resurrection."[46] As a result of this dawning consciousness, the Spirit begins drawing those who are encountered by it into the mystery of a redemptive relationship to life and, in the process, to the Divine.

By juxtaposing the sacred stories and associated rituals of Indic and Anglo-Catholic spiritual traditions, the poem intensifies and deepens its contemplative attentiveness. Had Eliot not evoked multiplicitous fires, the question that follows in the poem would not have the impact it now wields:

> Who then devised the torment? Love.
> Love is the unfamiliar Name
> Behind the hands that wove
> The intolerable shirt of flame
> Which human power cannot remove.
> We only live, only suspire
> Consumed by either fire or fire.

Though the word "love" has not been absent from *Four Quartets*, we may reasonably be caught off guard by the poet's assertion that love is the generative force behind both "incandescent terror" and purgative awakening. Here, the necessity of detachment and renunciation (developed in the first three quartets) is now given its proper name.

In both a destructive sense and a divine sense (in the purgative discipline that burns away the passion of self-love), love either weaves the "intolerable shirt of flame" (Hercules was consumed by the poisoned shirt of Nessus as a result of his human passions) or authors pentecostal tongues that no human power can apprehend. Eliot seems to be preparing to draw the *Quartets* together by affirming the purifying force of suffering and that which lies behind suffering—namely, love's fire, which both torments and liberates. To the extent that this is the case, then the course of our lives is determined according to which fire consumes us: Dante's infernal "flame" that destroys the soul or St. John's eternal "living flame of love" that purifies the soul. In a profoundly subtle manner, *Little Gidding* presents its readers a demanding choice, not just between two worlds (old and new), but between two fires (redeeming love or aversion and desire): "We only live, only suspire / Consumed by either fire or fire."

While "love" makes a somewhat surprising appearance in a poem that brought us through several literal and figurative purgations and hells, if we look back at each fourth movement, it is possible to discern the trace of the poet's interrelated intuitions that support this assertion of needing to make a choice. In *Burnt Norton* he apprehends a natural epiphany, an illumination of light reflected off the kingfisher's wing, at the "still point of the turning world." *East Coker* shifts to an image of the "wounded surgeon" who practices the "sharp compassion of the healer's art," as readers are invited to participate in Good Friday's "frigid purgatorial fires." *The Dry Salvages* then focuses on the selfless action of the "Lady" whose shrine stands on the promontory and who is both "Queen of Heaven" and "daughter of her Son." In *Little Gidding* these are drawn together in a redemptive, purifying fire. That fire—the compound illuminating fire of Mary, Krishna, Christ—burns at the still point of compassionate love.

Dancing Together (*Little Gidding* V)

The last movement of *Little Gidding* contains two conclusions: the conclusion to *Little Gidding* itself and the conclusion to *Four Quartets* as a whole. In this movement, we encounter a final gathering together of motifs and a final celebration of timeless possibilities within temporal inevitability. The unitive spirit of contemplative concentration appears—for instance, in *Burnt*

Norton V—as "the co-existence" of words and silence, of beginning and end, of movement and stillness. In *East Coker* V it appears in the call for "a further union, a deeper communion" brought about through being "still and still moving." In *The Dry Salvages* V contemplative attention leads to the apprehension of an "impossible union" between spheres of transcendence and the historic. From the perspective of "timeless moments" penetrating chronological time, these primal opposites are *included* in reciprocal fruitful communion with each other and *transmuted* into the discernment of a higher viewpoint.

The last movement starts:

What we call the beginning is often the end
And to make an end is to make a beginning.
The end is where we start from. And every phrase
And sentence that is right (where every word is at home,
Taking its place to support the others,
The word neither diffident nor ostentatious,
An easy commerce of the old and the new,
The common word exact without vulgarity,
The formal word precise but not pedantic,
The complete consort dancing together)
Every phrase and every sentence is an end and a beginning,
Every poem an epitaph. And any action
Is a step to the block, to the fire, down the sea's throat
Or to an illegible stone: and that is where we start.

Echoing the opening phrase of *East Coker*, the poet retrieves the recognition that any accomplishment, resulting from his exploration, cannot be affirmed as final, or completed. Doing so would remove him from the temporal process. At the same time, he recognizes that if the beginning of poetry is silence, its end is wisdom. Where every word is at home with every other word, where none are brash or ostentatious, where each provides an easy footpath from old ideas to new ones, and where each voice is exact, precise, formal, but never pedantic, the distinction between poetry and philosophy is rendered insignificant. The poet's idiosyncratic connections between words continue:

> We die with the dying:
> See, they depart, and we go with them.
> We are born with the dead:
> See, they return, and bring us with them.

"We die with the dying" to the extent that we share in and empathize with their sufferings; at the same time, "we are born with the dead" in that we are continually renewed by the genius and compassion of previous generations. The interplay between death and rebirth, central to these memorable lines, recalls the "new and shocking / Valuation of all we have been" in *East Coker* II.

The confluence of eternity and time is thus a pattern of history, a cycle of births and deaths, in which we all play a part. In terms of Eliot's poetry itself, the confluence of eternity and time is implicit in the endless interactions between lines that have "died" in earlier quartets and then are continuously reborn as the series progresses, every word depending on what has passed on before. Along these lines, it is instructive to note that prior to the completion of *Little Gidding*, Eliot wrote a preface for an anthology of mystics, poets, philosophers, and saints from all traditions. In it the anthologist included a passage from Maurice Maeterlinck, which provides us with a valuable interpretive lens that can be utilized to clarify this stanza: "The dead and the living alike are but moments, hardly dissimilar, of a single and infinite existence," and then continues that "they live in us even as we die in them."[47]

Approaching the hour of winter dusk, we are reminded that

> The moment of the rose and the moment of the yew-tree
> Are of equal duration. A people without history
> Is not redeemed from time, for history is a pattern

Of timeless moments. So, while the light fails
On a winter's afternoon, in a secluded chapel
History is now and England.

Just as in *The Dry Salvages*, in which we were exhorted to consider the rose and the yew tree with an equal mind, symbolically this equation gives new meaning to history. The pattern of history is crucial, for if time is to be redeemable, pivotal experiences need to be brought back into the present and then fulfilled in light of one's current circumstances. This double movement—retrieval and renewal—of timeless moments brings a new fullness to life, a new meaning to the present in light of the sacramental immediacy of existence itself—not because it is "eternally present," but because it is eternal *and* present. The rose and the yew underscore this insight by evoking temporal and eternal life simultaneously. On the one hand, a rose lives only a few days, the yew tree for centuries, but seen through the vision of time redeemed by grace, their duration is equal. Of course, this equality includes their difference: they are not tree and rose conflated. That is, they are not a kind of hybrid "eternal presence"; from a contemplative perspective in which human history is restored as "a pattern / Of timeless moments," they do not become only "the same."

In the transition to the concluding passage of *Little Gidding* the poet calls on the anonymous English author of *The Cloud of Unknowing*, a fourteenth-century treatise on contemplative prayer, to reiterate the point that redemption is an act of mutual love: "With the drawing of this Love and the voice of this / Calling." Typographically suspended on the page, forming a hinge between what came before and the final summing-up, these lines bring us near the conclusion of *Little Gidding* and *Four Quartets* as a whole. *The Cloud of Unknowing's* author writes, "A weary and wretched heart, indeed, is one fast asleep in sloth, which is not awakened by the drawing power of his love and the voice of his calling!"[48] This short exhortation, in its context, is addressed to those whose hearts, in the stirring impulse of one's own consent, are to be awakened by the power of God's unending love for humans. Similar to Julian's *Showings*, the *Cloud* reveals a loving God who desires to enter into union with those who turn wholeheartedly toward the divine. Yet, whereas Julian speaks from the heart of personal experience, the author of the *Cloud*, as a teacher, invites his pupils to study the experience of deeply loving God from the outside in order to bring that endless love into their lives.

By introducing *The Cloud of Unknowing* at this point, Eliot reiterates the purifying necessity of "prayer, observance, discipline, thought and action" (DS V). Writing for those who were unsatisfied with more standard practices of Christian piety, the author of *The Cloud of Unknowing* proposes pursuing relentlessly the double cloud of unknowing and of "forgetting" the self and, paradoxically, becoming more aware of the self. For Julian of Norwich as well, forgetting is letting go, leaving oneself "naked" (i.e., profoundly forgetful of self) and prepared for the calling of grace-infused love. *This* "Love" and *this* "calling" emerge, as the poet continues to discover not by virtue of his own actions only, but through a graced enactment of endless humility.

The pivotal significance of this "calling"—the "devout impulse of love that is continually worked in the will, not by the soul itself but by the hand of almighty God, which is always ready to perform this work in every soul that is disposed for it"[49]—arises from ever-new responses to inspired texts on the one hand and the natural world on the other. From this perspective, we can now more fully appreciate the poet's contemplative vision of love that appears especially in each fifth movement: "Love is itself unmoving, / Only the cause and end of movement, / Timeless, and undesiring / Except in the aspect of time" (BN V); "Love is most nearly itself / When here and now cease to matter" (EC V); "a lifetime's death in love, / Ardour and selflessness and self-surrender" (DS V); and "With the drawing of this Love and the voice of this / Calling" (LG V). When read together, this spectrum of images affirms the compassionate heart of the poem, which beats just beneath its lyrical surface yet continues to animate the suite of poems. The transforming power and redeeming grace of love—beyond (though not without) human passion and desire—clarify the poet's *recognition* that the "one end" of life depends upon the radiance of unconditional love. We come to see that human life is redeemable when unconditional love, implicitly present from the beginning, renews the face of the world by in-dwelling the poet's *relationship* to the world.

Weaving together key symbols and metaphors from preceding movements, the last stanza is one of the most musical stanzas of *Four Quartets*. The poet reiterates that unending exploration is inherent in his spiritual journey.

> We shall not cease from exploration
> And the end of all our exploring
> Will be to arrive where we started
> And know the place for the first time.

This imperative challenges both readers *and* poet alike. At the end (being present here and now) of our exploration, "we" (poet and reader in dialogue) are brought back to our "beginning"(always right here, right now)—now, however, recognizing the necessity of unending exploration. These four lines are reinforced and energized by echoes from the beginning of this stanza:

> What we call the beginning is often the end
> And to make an end is to make a beginning.
> The end is where we start from.

Considered in consort, these two passages activate complementary insights: (1) we arrive ceaselessly "where we started" only now ready to make a new, more aware start; (2) the end of our exploring is not to conclude the journey, but to reenter the world, ever-differently, with a "beginner's mind." Indeed, the momentum of these lines reemphasizes one of the most important themes running through *Four Quartets*: the redemptive significance of timeless moments, rather than something known, is a new way of knowing, a "new innocence."[50] In contrast to ending with an enclosed, logocentric view of the world, the poet "arrives," each time as if for the first time, in the midst of choosing to be chosen by the world and of surrendering into relationship with what meets him in the moment.

As he has in each of the quartets, the poet recalls several such moments:

> Through the unknown, remembered gate
> When the last of earth left to discover
> Is that which was the beginning;
> At the source of the longest river
> The voice of the hidden waterfall
> And the children in the apple-tree
> Not known, because not looked for
> But heard, half-heard, in the stillness
> Between two waves of the sea.
> Quick now, here, now, always—
> A condition of complete simplicity
> (Costing not less than everything).

The gate through which poet and reader entered *Burnt Norton* is both "unknown" ("the door we never opened / Into the rose-garden") and "remembered" ("the first gate / Into our first world"). *Burnt Norton*'s gate, the "last earth" of *East Coker,* the source of the "longest river" of *The Dry Salvages,* and the voice of the "hidden waterfall" and the original innocence of "children in the apple-tree" of *Little Gidding* are all "half-heard, in the stillness" of contemplation. The inner silence of soul evoked in *East Coker* ("be still, and let the dark come upon you") here becomes analogous to "the stillness / Between two waves of the sea." In this stillness we hear again: "the hidden laughter / Of children in the foliage" (BN V), the "whisper of running streams, and winter lightning" (EC III), and the "music heard so deeply / That it is not heard at all" (DS V).

The words "Quick now, here, now, always" are identical to a line in the last movement of *Burnt Norton*. Whereas in *Burnt Norton*, as William Spanos rightly remarks, these words evoke the presence of an "abiding *logos*—the still point in the turning world," in *Little Gidding* they come to mean "something quite *different* to Eliot and the reader."[51] However, this difference is not just another experience, or awareness, or even, as Spanos suggests, "a new kind of music of poetry," but rather a new attitude, the poet's willingness to turn back into the world, toward the vital reciprocity arising between himself and what comes to meet him. A deeper difference is evoked, I believe, by the poet's retrieval of "beginnings" in the "end." More than an inner experience, or realization, he turns toward the realm of mutuality, a relational space that ever-and-again reconstitutes his meetings with the world such that a liberating freedom arises. Emerging from a "new innocence," his perception of what otherwise remains hidden within earth-bound time now becomes a "condition of complete simplicity." In this purification of his motives, the urgency of the dance ("Quick now, here, now, always") and the quiet of the still point in-fold into one another.

Recalling Dante's ending to the *Paradiso*, the last five lines of *Four Quartets* conclude in a final orchestration of the whole, which reemphasizes Eliot's spiritually charged one end–one way convergences:

And all shall be well and
All manner of thing shall be well
When the tongues of flame are in-folded
Into the crowned knot of fire
And the fire and the rose are one.

In the end, being still yet "faring forward" costs not less than authentic and humble self-surrender. Indeed, as Julian indicated, "beseeching" is the soul's will "united and joined" to divine will. It is the fiery "crowned knot" or convergence of earthly rose and heavenly fire that lights his path, and its power magnifies when "we die with the dying" who "return, and bring us with them."[52]

Notably, in an earlier draft of *Little Gidding*, Eliot gave the poem a slightly different final line, "And the fire and the rose are the same." When he showed this version to John Hayward, Hayward responded by putting "as one" in place of "the same." Eliot further modified the suggested change and replied in a letter, "Very well then, And the fire and the rose are one."[53] To fully appreciate the subtle difference between "the same" and "one," we should keep in mind that, for Eliot, oneness is not the monistic oneness of Brahmanic practice as it is reflected in the *Upanishads* but rather a union-with-difference "oneness" of the Mahayan Buddhist tradition. "Fire" and "rose," while one, do not conflate. Rather, their differences include and transmute each other. Eliot's "oneness" reflects the co-inherence (not merger) of diversity and unity, of timelessness and time, of self and letting go of self, of contemplation and action. The relational oneness of "fire" and "rose" is impossible to comprehend or apply unless received traditions and teachings are included and transmuted by a new consciousness. Rather than resolving or covering over the immediate differences between "fire" and "rose," Eliot's end re-reconciles them in moments of "new innocence," only to return again into the world of difference.[54]

Four Quartets begins and ends recognizing that the immediate reciprocity of timeless events, when retrieved by an interplay of revivifying memory and disciplined imagination, opens fresh possibilities for redeeming time. Unlike Dante, who began his journey confused and lost, and unlike Arjuna, who began his adventure on the battlefield confused and dejected, in a very real sense the poem begins at its end ("What we call the beginning is often the end") and ends where it began ("The end is where we start from").[55] Indeed, the closing affirmation of *Little Gidding*—"And the fire and the rose are one"—returns us exactly to the place the poet's contemplative framework suggests it must. Just as we have entered *Little Gidding* through "the unknown, remembered gate," we entered *Burnt Norton*, and therefore the entire poem, through the first gate, into "our first world," into the "heart of light." Illuminated by the flames of human purgation, self-denial, and suffering, *and* by graced moments of self-less love, we return to our places in the world, our places in time, only to remember "where we started / And know the place for the first time."

Conclusion

INTERSPIRITUAL PRACTICES

My purpose in this book has been to use interpretative clues from a variety of writings to highlight and explore the spiritual substance of *Four Quartets*—namely, T. S. Eliot's attempts to explain "his intenser human feelings in terms of the divine goal."[1] Throughout this journey, we have been afforded an unusual apprehension of time, in which redeeming reciprocities—deeply binding mutual contact between poet and world—break through his habits of thought and disclose the unified wholeness of *this* garden (BN I), of *this* sacrament (EC I), of *this* text (DS III), of *this* person (LG II). As a result, directly experienced interrelationships with the world, infused with redemptive spiritual value, are lost or forgotten in the "enchainment of past and future / Woven in the weakness of the changing body" (BN II), yet are then recollected and retrieved through detached memory "in a different form," which enables the poet to be at home in the universe by releasing him from attachments to desires and suffering. Now that we have explored the poem's meditative landscapes, can anything more be said about the significance of Eliot's intenser feelings that would bring them into clearer light?

While I agree with John Cooper that *Four Quartets* suggest "new modalities of Being," especially in the building of "a new life of the spirit," I would not associate this new life with a "new subjectivity" through which, as Cooper suggests, the *Quartets* were read during and after the war as offering an "aesthetic refuge" to artists and intellectuals.[2] In this book I have suggested that the spiritual substance of the *Quartets* comes into focus through a new intersubjectivity—a common *logos*, a communal speaking with meaning—in which true subjectivity (interhuman personhood) arises from the midst of a genuine reciprocity between poet and what meets him in his life. This new attitude of choosing to be chosen, of being willing to surrender one's individuality into ever-deepening reciprocal relationship with the world, gives rise—in self-less and thereby time-less moments—to a liberating freedom that releases him, temporarily at least, from self-imposed limitations.

Martin Buber's discussion of the term "spirit" provides a perspective through which the phrase "new life of the spirit" can be appropriately applied to the *Quartets*. Since spirit, according to Buber, is "a thoroughly natural and formless phenomenon which demands of us that we give it form," it is to be understood as emerging from the relationship between persons and who or what is encountered. In other words, spirit does not dwell in us; we dwell in it. Accordingly, spirit arises on the way to becoming wholly human, between the ever-new point of starting out to grasp and what is shaped into aesthetic thinking and thereby grasped.[3] For this reason, Buber wrote, spirit "is not like the blood that circulates in you, but like the air in which you breathe."[4] Analogously, the spirit of Eliot's "intertemporal epiphanies," rather than occurring in an object or in his experience, happen *between* poet and particularities in the world and *between* timeless moments and their recovery in detached memory. Redeeming time in the *Quartets*, therefore, generates a new life—both the "inner freedom" from suffering and desires along with a renewed relationship to the natural world.

In keeping with the poet's highlighting four spiritual paths of contemplative action, at the end of our inquiry a question remains. What do these interspiritual wisdoms and practices tell us about our relationship to the Absolute? If redeeming time initially involves awakening from the deadening routinization of mass culture, what else must occur to facilitate this new "condition of complete simplicity" (LG V)? The texture of Eliot's response to this vital question is not solely a reflection of his experience of what he once called "the highest spiritual mysteries." Of equal importance to Eliot, and of even greater significance for those deeply engaged by the poem, is the way in which his words bring us, as philosophical language cannot, directly to the doorway of spiritual reciprocity. We cannot, in that light, comprehend the fuller significance of *Four Quartets* without addressing the poet's specific interspiritual practices for both surrendering one's self in acts of endless humility and transforming one's will into detached action.

Four Quartets, in light of this question, embodies a meditative alternative to being swallowed up in a race to save time, or spend time, or slow time, or find time. Rather than trying to escape the habit-inducing flux of time's enchantments, or locate its secrets from those who predict the future, the poet, borrowing from the great classical mystics, accentuates four interspiritual practices through which time-bound routinization may be, temporarily at least, overcome. Four seemingly different yet mutually transformative paths have been described individually as *Burnt Norton's* way of darkness, *East Coker's* way of stillness, *The Dry Salvages'* way of yogic action, and *Little Gidding's* way of purification. Using *Four Quartets* as a guide, those who are pursuing a spiritual path—however imperfect that pursuit feels—will move through a series of stages, some of which, in small ways, are analogous to those experienced by the greatest contemplatives on their journey toward the Absolute. When the spiritual consciousness is awakened, a sense of solidarity with the contemplatives quoted in *Four Quartets* arises, a kindred spirit that impels one, in a compatible fashion, to endure dark moments of not knowing and spurs one to a deeper participation in the purgative process.

In-Dwelling Practices

I have referred to the poet's aspiration to retrieve timeless moments of deep reciprocity with the world that have been suppressed or forgotten in the temporal flux. But what exactly is involved in regaining access to these moments in a transfigured way that would lead to a more direct, more enlivening encounter with the fullness of life? One answer, for Eliot, can be located in a unitive perspective developed over the course of his life, one in which spiritual practices in seemingly dissimilar traditions come to be experienced as mutually in-dwelling and therefore mutually enriching. This co-implicating perspective, which came to deeply influence Eliot's own spiritual life, was grounded in spirit-awakening contemplative silence and expressed a sense of interspiritual communion.

Eliot's conversion (as noted in the introduction to this volume) was informed by and nurtured through the practice of contemplative meditation and inner silence. In a conversation with Raymond Preston, Eliot once mentioned "that it was for each of us to discover that degree of contemplative 'withdrawal' which he needed in order to give the 'maximum potency to his action'; and that each withdrawal was not escape."[5] That is, periods of monastic retreat, inspired by the relational unity that he found in religious traditions, served as a necessary requisite for Eliot's ever-renewed spiritual energy in living and writing. While from Eliot's viewpoint it is necessary to withdraw temporarily from the daily go-round of activity in order to gain a deeper, meditative grounding in life, he indicated that withdrawal into mindfulness is not the ultimate goal of a spiritual life but rather a preparation for entering back into the world with more energy, vitality, and compassion. Contemplative withdrawal, therefore, is not to be confused with escaping from one's duties, responsibilities, or work.

Consistent with his contemplative predilections, Eliot was attracted to the many ways in which the Absolute found expression in Western and Indic cultures, and he was fascinated by how their differences were significant for one another. Since Eliot did not write much expository prose about the importance of non-Christian religions, perhaps the fullest statement of his attitude toward them is found in the preface he wrote to *Thoughts for Meditation*, an anthology of texts from the world's classical religious traditions. Recognizing the wide variety of approaches that one can take to different religions, he noted that while some readers, especially Christians, may regard Asian scriptures as occult and therefore untrue, it is crucial to learn "how frequently contemplatives of religions and civilizations remote from each other are saying the same thing."[6] "The same thing," it is significant to observe, refers not to doctrinal or theological constructs but to what Eliot saw as the true spirit of religious life: the mature contemplative attitude, which beats at the heart of all major forms of spirituality. Without this shared value, religious practice devolves into sectarian disagreements over inflexible dogmatic beliefs.

A careful reading of Eliot's biographical materials, especially of events leading to his conversion, and on a dialogic reading of *Four Quartets*, suggest that what most interested Eliot was not so much the unity of religious teachings but rather the value of encountering and utilizing spiritual practices from various contemplative traditions that share a common spirit. This is not to suggest, however, that Eliot was a universalist, believing that all the world's religions lead to the same spiritual truth. In spite of his recognition that the major religions of the world share common ground, Eliot concluded his preface with a cautionary note about disregarding the differences between religious traditions. No one, he wrote,

> has ever climbed to the higher stages of the spiritual life, who has not been a believer in a particular religion or at least a particular philosophy. It was only in relation to his own religion that the insights of any one of these men had its significance to him, and what they say can only reveal its meaning to the reader who has his own religion of dogma and doctrine in which he believes.[7]

Eliot came to understand that the notion of only one identical truth is another philosophical viewpoint influenced and conditioned by the limitations of individual experience,[8] and he believed that the spiritual values through which one attempts to find liberation from self-centered actions are rooted in the same basic practices in all traditions. By choosing, intellectually and spiritually, one particular practice—but not to the exclusion of others—Eliot sensitized himself to compatibilities between Hindu and Christian spiritualities, which clarify and enrich each other.

Indeed, as Eliot had written earlier, it is possible to practice more than one point of view at the same time without evaluating, comparing, judging, or analyzing one against the other. In his dissertation on the philosophy of F. H. Bradley, for example, Eliot described a method for contemplating the discordant viewpoints of his contact with the unique particulars of life. In his reflection, he provides a verbal image of how one can practice self-transcendence through "occupying more than one point of view at the same time": "The life of a soul does not consist in the contemplation of one consistent world but in the painful task of unifying (to a greater or lesser extent) jarring and incompatible ones, and passing, when possible, from two or more discordant viewpoints to a higher which shall somehow include and transmute them."[9] Sympathetically holding opposing views in tension, while at the same time imaging fruitful interchanges and implications between them, challenges faith and liberates spiritual attentiveness. Attaining the interior illumination of the higher viewpoint, or mindfulness, opens up a unitive state of awareness in which oppositions are not fused but joined in a "deeper communion." The poet's mind, when concentrated upon this higher union, remains undistracted by his own anxieties. A new certitude about life results, a new innocence that emancipates one, if only briefly, from former entanglements.

Because *Four Quartets* appropriates me as I appropriate the poem, my attention continues to be drawn to the divergent interspiritual practices of its centering third movements: in the first two quartets these are "descend lower" and "be still," and in the second two "fare forward" and "purify the motive." When the centering insights of the third movement of each quartet are juxtaposed, it becomes increasingly clear that spiritual practice in *Four Quartets* includes and transmutes two streams of energy flowing into each other from opposite directions, a downward movement and a counter energy moving upward. The seemingly opposed yet interrelated practices of stillness and activity, abandoning control and transforming will, withdrawal and engagement, relate to one another as oxygen to the bloodstream. Embedded traces of each practice are continually discovered in the other. The way of darkness arises from the way of yogic action and vice versa, just as the way of purification arises from the way of stillness and vice versa. That is, descending practices indwell and give rise to ascending practices, each of which would be incomplete and less productive without the other. Of course, as the poet realizes again and again, the inevitability of being "distracted from distraction by distraction" (BN III) reminds him of the need to act with endless humility.[10]

The Way of Darkness

The first two paths elaborate what Heraclitus called the "way down." *Burnt Norton's* "descend lower" comes on the heels of a passage in which the poet describes *this* place in time as "a place of disaffection," where the revelatory still point is barely, if at all, recalled. In the third and centering movement of *Burnt Norton*, the poet recognizes the need to sink into spiritual darkness. Calling on the aid of canonical spiritual writers like Pseudo-Dionysius the Areopagite, Thomas Aquinas, and especially St. John of the Cross, he tailors their advice for those pursuing a spiritual path to fit his situation. To practice the way of darkness, he discerns, requires a radical shift of consciousness, a suspension of one's normal patterns of thought. One must willingly enter the dark night of sense (the purgative, negative way of letting go, of subordinating reflexive will) in order to become open to receive the liberating empowerment of divine grace.

After his rose-garden awakening to a timeless dimension in

the temporal cycle, it becomes necessary, if retrieving that experience is to bear fruit in his life, for the contemplative poet to

> Descend lower, descend only
> Into the world of perpetual solitude,
> World not world, but that which is not world,
> Internal darkness, deprivation
> And destitution of all property,
> Desiccation of the world of sense,
> Evacuation of the world of fancy,
> Inoperancy of the world of spirit (BN III)

Surprisingly, the poet does not retreat from the "disaffection" of his life but insists on diving more deeply into it. But into what? Into a world of spiritual darkness. Despite the distractions of sensual fantasies "empty of meaning" and "tumid apathy with no concentration," the initial period of the spiritual life for the poet necessitates "darkness to purify the soul." To the extent that Eliot followed Evelyn Underhill's analysis of the Dark Night or Mystic Death—directed toward utter self-surrender, the death of selfhood—he would have elaborated upon it from two points of view: psychological and spiritual. Psychologically considered, the Dark Night is often triggered by fatigue, stress, or loss and is exemplified by deeply felt awareness of absence, aridity, and privations. Yet the Dark Night not only exhausts all possible value and meaning but also involves moving toward a renewed purification of will. Spiritually considered, the soul dwells in the Dark Night in as much as it remains blinded—blinded by the light of divine wisdom greater than it can bear and blinded to the uncreated light of divine love.

According to St. John of the Cross, who is the classic authority on this stage of the journey, to enter the Dark Night and dwell there our spiritual nature must be on fire with noble passion and deep courage. The Dark Night of the soul, for St. John, is a "passive purification" in which the self does nothing to resist the sufferings and confusions and distractions of life. One of the most bitter sufferings of the Dark Night, according to St. John, is consciousness of a profound emptiness of the natural, temporal, and spiritual worlds. Indeed, the soul is plunged into deeply felt anguish by the conviction that God has abandoned it. St. John writes that "since these imperfections are deeply rooted in the substance of the soul, it usually suffers besides this poverty and this natural and spiritual emptiness an oppressive undoing and an inner torment."[11] Only when a person learns to cease thinking of himself or herself at all—no matter how negatively—can the soul gain access to higher levels of spiritual awakening.

Abandoning one's control, deliberately choosing "deprivation" and "internal darkness," becomes the first spiritual path for combating the time-dominated condition of life. Whether it involves a direction of movement (i.e., an intentional "desiccation," "evacuation," and "inoperancy" of sense, fancy, and spirit) or an "abstention from movement," the way of darkness necessarily precedes illumination. That is, to become infused with God's grace one needs to become empty of self-reflective will, for the sensual part is purified in emptiness. This descending path, it is suggested, will gradually break down in the face of advancing liberation from the succession of "time past and time future." By quieting one's time-dominated mind, which is forever distracted, the soul is prepared to be redeemed through ordinary events that otherwise often seem empty of significance.

The Way of Stillness

Analogous to the first, the second interspiritual practice, explored in the third and centering movement of *East Coker*, involves a further quieting of the soul and a willingness to wait in the "darkness of God." In each quartet, as Ronald Schuchard has noted, "the eternal stillness of a divine pattern of reality is set against the endless movement of a temporal pattern, a pattern characterized by action and appetency, desire and knowledge, hope and despair."[12] Here, rather than resting within a moment of illumination and seeking to duplicate its effect, "I said to my soul, be still, and let the dark come upon you / Which shall be the darkness of God" (EC III). The images in *Burnt Norton*, "a world of perpetual solitude" and "internal darkness," echo in these lines. While the first step on a spiritual path necessarily involves renouncing private wisdoms, this emptying out of self-reflective concerns cannot finally be achieved by one's own efforts. Rather, the grace of unconditional Love infuses the practitioner with true emptiness, in which the incessant chatter of will is silenced, the recurring fanciful images of imagination are stilled. This graced negation of thought, by which one passes beyond I-hood and slips into complete stillness, becomes a sacrament of the whole spiritual quest.

Then, deepening his resolve, the poet continues: "I said to my soul, be still, and wait without hope / For hope would be hope for the wrong thing" (EC III). While difficult if not impossible to understand intellectually—"Wait without thought, for you are not ready for thought"—this sought-for stillness suspends ordinary consciousness, even though consciousness of the person naturally remains. There are, at the same time, two dimensions of this profound stillness and silence: the dimension of a gradual emptying of ordinary consciousness and the dimension of a gradual acquisition of humility and receptivity of what cannot be known for "the faith and the love and the hope are all in the waiting." The soul, in other words, remains still and still waiting, not knowing for what. Hoping for nothing, loving nothing, his silence opens a place for God to speak.

Fittingly, the prayer that concludes Eliot's 1930 poem *Ash-Wednesday*—"Teach us to care and not to care / Teach us to sit still" (CPP 67)—amounts to an instructive preview of how being still embodies and expresses indwelling acts of caring and not caring. We have recognized that, for Eliot, not caring (e.g., a detached recognition of the impermanence of life) does not cancel out the energizing dynamic of caring (e.g., recognizing one's moral responsibilities and compassionate acts in life). Rather, the behavioral metaphor of "sitting still" reconciles the seemingly opposite behaviors of "not caring" and "caring" in mutually transforming ways.

To advance spiritually, according to the *Quartets*, we must sink ever more deeply into silence and, in a way, become as if nothing. This direct and unequivocal advice to his soul—"be still!"—is grounded, of course, in the faith that redeeming time, no matter how briefly, is possible if one is willing to wait "without thought" and "without hope," which, in a time-manacled frame of mind, is easily misdirected. Along with the obvious influence of St. John of the Cross, Eliot's debt to Patanjali's *Yoga-Sutras* (second century BCE) is also evident here, especially his withdrawal of the senses, which leads to mind-absorbed meditation. The spiritual explorer is not yet ready for thought, is not yet able to hope. Temporally conditioned thought, even the desire to transcend thought, only leads to more distractions; to overcome temporal illusions, it is necessary to enter into the dark night of not knowing. By thus renewing the depths of the soul, one becomes ready to genuinely engage and be engaged by the all-revealing radiance of uncreated light.

The Way of Yogic Action

Having been incorporated by the downward way of darkness and stillness (in BN III and EC III), the third and fourth quartets exemplify what Heraclitus called the "way up" in the second aphorism quoted at the beginning of the poem. That is, the poet's response to the enchainments of time is not just to sink ever more deeply into darkness, not just to cultivate interior stillness, but then to move ahead in a way that does not breed attachment to either the movement itself or to the one who moves. The balance to be struck in these interspiritual practices can only be adequately expressed, Eliot discovered, through paradox. The true condition of stillness, according to St. John, is at once receptive and active, self-emptying and self-giving. While a pure surrender is essential to spiritual maturation, it does not abandon the energy of renewed compassion. The third and fourth practices, accordingly, give expression to the active component.

In the midst of the poet's surrender to ever-deepening stillness, therefore, in the third movements of *The Dry Salvages* and *Little Gidding* a dynamic and purposive reversal of stillness occurs. In *The Dry Salvages* this element is presented as the way of yogic action, especially when the poet engages and is engaged by Krishna's advice to Arjuna:

> At the moment which is not of action or inaction
> You can receive this: 'on whatever sphere of being
> The mind of a man may be intent
> At the time of death'—that is the one action
> (And the time of death is every moment)
> Which shall fructify in the lives of others:
> And do not think of the fruit of action.
> Fare forward. (DS III)

In the "Holy Dialogue," Krishna urges Arjuna to "fare forward" into battle—not as a means to an end, but spontaneously—by pointing to the futility of worrying about the future. Like a modern-day Arjuna, the reader of *The Dry Salvages* too, is urged to "fare forward," not by trying to escape from time, not trying to overcome the numbing effects of the temporal flux through goal-directed activity, but by letting go of attachments to individualistic identity. This movement forward is thus not to be equated with action as usual. Instead, Krishna's advice is rooted in *karma yoga*: action that, when grace-infused, is nonaction. In other words, to "fare forward" yogically one surrenders attachments to self-deluded sensibilities. "Faring forward" thus emerges from and embodies the way of negation and the way of stillness.

In light of the poet's advice in the third movement of *East Coker* ("be still"), Eliot's "fare forward" brings to the fore an apparent contradiction between stillness and action. Calling upon Krishna's yoga of surrendering attachments serves, however, to resolve this contradiction between movement and stillness. The word "forward" here implies moving not just in a spatial direction but in a spiritual direction—namely, implementing an equanimity of purpose. For this reason, Eliot added "and the time of death is every moment" to Krishna's teaching that one should be "intent" (concentrated, equal-minded) at the moment of dying. When practicing equal-minded intent in life, balancing intellectual and emotional intensities that pull in opposing directions, one's actionless actions bear fruit in the lives of others. By reiterating Krishna's emphasis on an active spiritual discipline, one that integrates *karma yoga* (the renunciation of the fruits of action) and *bhakti yoga* (surrender and self-less devotion), the words "fare forward" can include and transmute the spiritual darkness of *Burnt Norton*'s third movement and the interior stillness of *East Coker*'s third movement.

The way of yogic action accordingly involves remaining still within action and being active within stillness. The interrelational identity of these seeming opposites is embodied by the traveler who is not the same person "who left that station / Or who will arrive at any terminus" (DS III). Both genuine action and genuine stillness lead the traveler to full participation in the real destination of *this* moment. Krishna's teaching therefore suggests deep humility equal to the recognition that at the end of the journey (indeed, at any point along the way) the traveler (no longer the same person who began the journey) simply responds to the task at hand honestly, attentively, responsibly, without withholding anything. Together with the other practices, yogic action combines mindful awareness and cleansing one's self of self-absorption.

The Way of Purification

While *Burnt Norton* and *East Coker* adapted St. John of the Cross, and *The Dry Salvages* primarily appropriated insights from the

Bhagavad Gita, the third movement of *Little Gidding* integrates the wisdoms of Lord Krishna and Julian of Norwich. The poet begins the centering movement of *Little Gidding* by exploring "three conditions which often look alike." In the *Bhagavad Gita,* Krishna names them as attachment, detachment, and indifference. "Attachment" (to persons, places, and things) corresponds to desire ("movement / Not in itself desirable") in *Burnt Norton.* "Detachment" (from persons, places, and things) corresponds to "abstention from movement" and to "waiting without thought." Both attachment and detachment play a necessary role in spiritual life—the former to be acknowledged and deconstructed, the latter to be realized and integrated. However, indifference (psychological death) is most to be avoided.

Against this background the fourth interspiritual path—the way of purification, of cleansing the powers of perception—is then introduced.

> And all shall be well and
> All manner of thing shall be well
> By the purification of the motive
> In the ground of our beseeching. (LG III)

Just as the poet realized that perfecting humility is an endless activity, purification becomes a perpetual process of stripping away the tangled motives of self-love and foolish interests and cleansing, renewing, and elevating the remaining elements of personality to a purer state. The poet turns to the fourteenth-century mystical visionary Julian of Norwich, who affirmed the necessity of purifying the motives behind our actions, of becoming purged of everything that stands between the self and the boundless grace of divine presence. The term "beseeching" refers, for Julian, to the soul's longing to encounter the will of God; it is used by Eliot to reinforce the notion of *journeying toward* rather than of possessing anything. Accordingly, beseeching is closely related, for Julian, with the spiritual power of genuine prayer. She writes that one needs to pray wholeheartedly even though one may feel nothing, for it is the prayers that arise in dryness, in barrenness, and in weakness that are the most pleasing to God.

For this reason, Julian's purification brings us back to the heart of prayer, about which the poet spoke in the first movement of *Little Gidding*: "You are here to kneel / Where prayer has been valid." What makes prayer valid—purified—is not verifying God's will or seeking instruction or satisfying one's curiosity or even the "conscious occupation / Of the praying mind." Rather, for Julian, the essence of prayer involves entering into life with humble self-surrender and trust in the presence of God. Consequently, prayer becomes valid when a self-renewing mutuality occurs between the one who prays and the One to whom prayer is addressed. By grounding one's motives in an ever-deepening prayer to divine love, one is able to choose the purgative fires over the fires of passion and self-will—that is, "to be redeemed from fire by fire" (LG IV).

For Eliot, juxtaposing Krishna's teaching of yogic action with Julian's teaching of purifying our motives both clarifies what each was pointing toward and enriches the spiritual benefits to be gained by this practice. A fruitful inner dialectic occurs for Eliot, and in the process he is enlivened by resonances between purifying motives and actionless action, between real prayer and equal-mindedness. The more powerful our surrender to downward movements of silence and stillness, the more effective our movements upward and forward become. Just as equal-minded activity is made possible by Krishna's compassion, so purifying one's motives is finally made possible by the grace of God's unconditional love. And just as actionless action depends upon intense dedication to studying the scriptures and practicing its yogas, so purifying one's motives requires turning away from ignorance or sin and taking on humility and devotion.

Reanimating a communion of opposites, the final image of *Little Gidding* affirms that "tongues of flame" are "in-folded / Into the crowned knot of fire." Just as caring and not caring mutually challenge and support one another, "the tongues [teachings] of fire [practices]" of one tradition in-dwell and fructify in another tradition's teachings and practices. As a consequence of practicing mutually in-dwelling, interspiritual paths, old understandings of static, logocentric teachings are de-habituated. The temptation to forget that spirit does not only exist in a person is replaced by an openness to enter enriching relationships with the *logos* common to all. The ripening of interspiritual practice—yoking "faring forward" with "stillness" and concentrating the direction of one's movements—will interrupt recurring temptations to reduce the otherness of the world into the content of one's own experience, or, as Buber writes, to "psychologize the world."[13] In contrast, the interplay of stillness in movement, of the way down and the way up, helps distinguish genuine from disingenuous caring and promotes surrendering into new connections with the world by choosing them. Rather than settling into "private wisdoms" with habitual ease, practicing the structure of these methods opens up fresh possibilities for engaging and being engaged by the inner rhythms of *this* moment. When encountered with "beginner's mind," these mutually transforming practices provide "maximum potency" for a new life *in* the spirit.

Pulling back from Eliot's *Quartets,* even after such a lengthy engagement, in no way completes my wrestling with the music of his words and the value of his meanings. At the same time, I hope that what this reading glimpses will evoke "a new and shocking / Valuation of all we have been" (EC II). Although it was a temptation in response to earlier readings, I do not wish to conclude by speculating on future possibilities of interspiritual practice. Instead, my hope is that readers, especially ones seeking a renewed spiritual path, can recognize that appropriating seemingly dissimilar practices moves one toward becoming reconciled with the world in ever-new ways.

Eliot, for this reason, wrote that without history (especially a history of deeply reciprocal relationships) we are "not redeemed from time" (LG V). Yet in graced moments, when action and nonaction complement and fulfill each other, along with the poet we are able temporarily to relinquish our private wisdoms. These moments embody a sacramental integration of spirit and sense. Redeeming time, in the *Quartets*, thus "does not take place merely once at the end but also at every moment throughout the whole of time."[14] We come, then, to recognize that the reciprocal immediacies between poet and rose garden, poet and dancers, poet and sacred text, and poet and stranger are equally timeless. By bringing our voice into dialogue with Eliot's *Quartets*, the common *logos* of which Heraclitus wrote, the communal speaking that shapes and is shaped by our common world unfolds. From this engaging mutuality, unexpectedly, a "deeper communion" between the sacred presence and the world, which would otherwise remain hidden, creates a fresh universe, a new intelligence.

Notes

Preface

1. T. S. Eliot, Letter to William Force Stead, August 9, 1930, Beinecke Rare Book and Manuscript Library, Yale University.

2. Kenneth Paul Kramer, "A New Kind of Intellectual: Eliot's Contemplative Withdrawal," *Religion and Literature* 31, no. 3 (Autumn 1999): 43–75.

3. In *The Art of T. S. Eliot* (London: Faber & Faber, 1949) Helen Gardner writes:

> *Burnt Norton* is a poem about air, on which whispers are borne. . . . *East Coker* is a poem about earth, the dust of which we are made and into which we shall return. . . . *The Dry Salvages* is a poem about water, which some Greek thinkers thought was the primitive material out of which the world arose. . . . *Little Gidding* is a poem about fire, the purest of the elements . . . which consumes and purifies. (44–45)

4. Redemption (liberation from displacement and suffering), it will be seen throughout *Four Quartets*, does not simply depend upon God. Each person helps to bring about and to renew the unity of God and the world through genuine relationship. From the midst of the experience of division, an impulse emerges that enables a person to reenter the world. Redemption from the human side, both personal and historical, involves an ever-renewed willingness, or openness, to risk one's individuality by coming into the presence of authentic reciprocity with what one encounters.

5. In these graced moments of authentic engagement between poet and who or what encounters him, according to the philosophical anthropology of Martin Buber, the "indwelling of the Present Being [Divine Presence] is between them" (Martin Buber, *Between Man and Man*, trans. Ronald Gregor Smith [New York: Macmillan, 1948], 30). Buber expands this understanding when he indicates that "the eternal rises in the Between, the seemingly empty space: that true place of realization is community, and true community is that relationship in which the Divine comes to its realization between man and man" (Buber, *On Judaism*, ed. Nahum N. Glatzer [New York: Schocken Books, 1967], 110). Moreover, the presence of God

(the divine Shekinah, the immanent glory of God) can be glimpsed, according to Buber, in and through every real relationship between persons (and between persons and nature, and persons and spirit) in which one turns wholeheartedly toward the other by choosing to enter into reciprocal exchanges. Only when time is bound up in redeeming reciprocity, according to Buber, does the world become "house and home, a dwelling for man in the universe" (*I and Thou*, trans. Ronald Gregor Smith [New York: Scribner, 1958], 115). All references to *I and Thou* are taken from Smith's translation unless otherwise noted.

Introduction: Theme-Word Design

1. T. S. Eliot, "The Metaphysical Poets," *Selected Essays*, new ed. (New York: Harcourt, Brace, 1950), 247.

2. T. S. Eliot, Letter to William Force Stead, August 9, 1930, Beinecke Rare Book and Manuscript Library, Yale University. Biographer Lyndall Gordon, quoting Eliot's remarks about Ben Jonson—that there is a "transfusion of the personality or, in a deeper sense, the life of the author" into his writing—suggests that at each stage of Eliot's career there existed in his poetry "a persistent self-portraiture," and that when he reached the *Quartets* his feet were "firmly planted on an Anglican platform" (*Eliot's Early Years* [Oxford: Oxford University Press, 1977], 137–38).

3. William Force Stead, "Mr. Stead Presents an Old Friend," *Alumnae Journal of Trinity College* 38, no. 2 (Winter 1965): 6, Beinecke Rare Book and Manuscript Library, Yale University. A more complete version of the material in this section, "Eliot's Conversion," and the next, "A New Type of Intellectual," can by found in my article "A New Kind of Intellectual: Eliot's Contemplative Withdrawal," *Religion and Literature* 31, no. 3, (Fall 1999): 43–56.

4. Quoted in Donald Gallup, "T. S. Eliot and Ezra Pound: Collaborators in Letters," *Atlantic Monthly* 225 (January 1970): 62. After joining the Church of England in 1927, Eliot became an almost daily communicant at Mass, deepening and clarifying his Trinitarian sacramentality. Seldom, if ever, did Vivienne accompany her husband to St. Cyprian's (or later, St. Stephen's), deriding his church affections as "monastic." Nevertheless, in the early years after his conversion (1927–1935), a period of reflection and realignment, he plunged wholeheartedly into minute details of the Anglo-Catholic tradition and liturgy. One might say that, at precisely the point where his life began finding its way down, he began searching for the practical philosophy that would show him the way back up again.

5. T. S. Eliot, Letter to Paul Elmer More, August 3, 1929, Princeton University Library. More, also a friend of Irving Babbit, was one of Eliot's clos-

est confidants until he died in 1937. Like Eliot, More had approached the Indic tradition with great fascination. He had turned to the *Upanishads*, the *Bhagavad Gita*, and the *Dhammapada* and, like Eliot, had rejected Babbitt's humanism. When Eliot read More's account of his Christian conversion, he was deeply touched and wrote to his friend that his "spiritual biography . . . is oddly, even grotesquely, more like my own . . . than that of any human being I have known." When Eliot read More's article, "An Absolute and Authoritative Church," which Eliot published in *The Criterion* (July 1929), and which was reprinted in More's book *The Catholic Faith*, Eliot said that More had come "by somewhat the same route, to almost the same conclusions" as his own. See Paul Elmer More, *The Catholic Faith* (Princeton: Princeton University Press, 1931), 75, and letter from Eliot to More, June 2, 1930, Princeton University Library.

Eliot read More's *The Catholic Faith* with great enthusiasm, and approved of the fact that it opened with a chapter on "Buddhism and Christianity." More, like Eliot, recognized the parallels between Buddhist and Christian moral teachings and historical developments. And, like Eliot, he perceived an unbridgeable theological difference between Christianity and the Indic traditions: "Buddha based his practice of religion on a denial of God and the human soul, whereas Christ carried the belief in both of these to their highest development." More finally rejects the Upanishadic insistence that "I am Brahma" as inconsistent with the Christian command to "Love the Lord thy God," and viewed Buddhism "as a preface to the Gospel." Responding to criticism of his own work, in a 1930 letter Eliot indicated that his own position was close to More's.

For commentary on Eliot's Unitarian background, see Herbert Howarth's *Notes on Some Figures Behind T. S. Eliot* (New York: Houghton Mifflin, 1964).

6. T. S. Eliot, "The 'Pensées' of Pascal," in *Selected Essays*, 363. Eliot was attracted to Christian conversion stories, especially that of Pascal, a prominent mathematician who was converted in 1654. In his introduction to Pascal's *Pensées*, Eliot notes that even more than St. John of the Cross and Francis de Sales, Pascal had "the mind to conceive, and the sensibility to feel the disorder, the futility, the meaninglessness, the mystery of life and suffering, and [he] can only find peace through a satisfaction of the whole being" (Introduction in Pascal's *Pensées*, trans. W. F. Trotter [New York: Dutton, 1958], xix). What appealed to Eliot was Pascal's emotional fervor and religious passion that integrated skepticism into faith, his willingness to subordinate, not abandon, his scientific and philosophical investigations to his pursuit of mystical experience. Eliot calls to the reader's attention the note Pascal wrote dated November 3, 1664, which was found after his

death, sewn into the lining of his coat. It read: "From about half-past ten in the evening until half-past twelve, midnight, fire. God of Abraham, God of Isaac, God of Jacob, not of the philosophers, not of the wise. Assurance, joy, assurance" (cited and translated by R. M. D. Bucke in *Cosmic Consciousness: A Study in the Evolution of the Human Mind*, Library of the Mystic Arts [New Hyde Park, NY: University Books, 1961], 226–27).

7. T. S. Eliot in *The Listener*, January 9, 1947. In his review of Bertrand Russell's *What I Believe* (1927) Eliot wrote: "I am amazed at Mr. Russell's capacity for believing... within limits.... I cannot subscribe with what conviction to any belief" ("The Preacher as Artist," *Athenaeum* [November 28, 1919]: 1252).

It is worth pausing, at this point, to highlight the central method—"rejection and elimination"—by which Eliot proceeded. As Jeffrey M. Perl writes: "Eliot was a Christian skeptic," but "the Christianity in which Eliot believed was consonant with his skepticism" (*Skepticism and Modern Enmity: Before and After Eliot* [Baltimore: Johns Hopkins University Press, 1989], 110). Eliot's skeptical attitude was founded not only in the philosophy of Bradley but also, as Perl notes, in his study of Indic philosophy, from which "Eliot had learned that skepticism implies not simply the incredibility of all beliefs, but also their equivalent conventional validity" (92). And in an essay written on Bradley (in the year of Eliot's "conversion"), Eliot noted that "wisdom consists largely of skepticism and uncynical disillusion," and that "skepticism and disillusion are a useful equipment for religious understanding" ("Francis Herbert Bradley," in *Selected Essays*, 399).

8. Lyndall Gordon, *T. S. Eliot: An Imperfect Life* (New York: Norton, 1998), 23, 24. Grover Smith, however, disagrees with Gordon's assessment, as stated in a letter he wrote to me (March 25, 2000):

> I think Gordon is entirely wrong about youthful religious aspirations or ambitions in Eliot, and about early mystical dizzy spells. The hunger was there, but William James's "sick soul" identifies its nature, surely. And Eliot's religious sensibility, his emotional orientation, had been defined for him by church-going and family feelings—whatever snubs the Anglo-Catholic convert administered to his religious upbringing.

9. T. S. Eliot, *Inventions of the March Hare: Poems 1909–1917*, ed. Christopher Ricks (London: Faber & Faber, 1996), 18. In the same year that he wrote "Silence," Eliot published a short poem in *The Harvard Advocate* 38, no. 8 (January 12, 1910), titled "Spleen." In it he depicted a middle-aged gentleman, "languid, fastidious, and bland," who "waits, hat and gloves in hand," impatiently "on the doorstep of the Absolute." It is also valuable to

consider two other poems of early youth written late in 1914 to early 1915. Critics have linked "The Death of St. Narcissus" with "The Love Song of Saint Sebastian." Each poem articulates Eliot's resistance to polluted forms of spirituality (T. S. Eliot, *Poems Written in Early Youth* [London: Faber & Faber, 1967], 32, 34).

10. Gordon, *Eliot's Early Years*, 123. In Michael Hastings's 1984 play *Tom and Viv*, and the film of the same title made a decade later, their marital dynamics are presented as doubly tragic. From Eliot's side, he was not informed at all by Viv's family about her ongoing mental and physical problems that flared with such excesses that he was constantly guarded and protective toward her. His love for her, modeled as it was after his own parents' relationship, cautiously expressed and maintained a Unitarian, Calvinistic, British propriety. From Viv's side, she was trapped by internal demons, biophysical imbalances, and the affliction of various drug addictions. Anything but normal, she was histrionic, erratic, vivacious, witty, intelligent, self-destructive, and especially literate. And she knew how to create "scenes." Her love for Tom was made more desperate by her condition. In *Painted Shadow: A Life of Vivien, First Wife of T. S. Eliot, and the Long-Suppressed Truth about Her Influence on His Genius* (London: Constable, 2001), Carole Seymour-Jones amasses a plethora of Vivien's diaries, unpublished prose fiction, and letters, to tell the story of their marriage from Vivien's side. She argues that each of them were victims in the marriage and further suggests that Tom destroyed potentially compromising personal papers to protect his reputation.

11. The word "interspiritual" here suggests the possibility and actuality of mutual enrichment, through the dialogic interaction, between two (or more) different religious beliefs or practices. Eliot came to understand that the notion of only one identifiable truth is another philosophical viewpoint influenced by, and conditioned by, the limitations of individual experience, and that the spiritual values through which one attempts to find liberation from self-centered actions are rooted in the same basic practices in all traditions. By not choosing, intellectually or spiritually, one practice to the exclusion of another, Eliot sensitized himself to compatibilities between Hindu and Christian spiritualities, which clarified and enriched each other. For a discussion of the term "interspiritual" along with a description of its ethos, see Wayne Teasdale, "The Interspiritual Age: Practical Mysticism for the Third Millennium," *Journal of Ecumenical Studies*, 34, no. 1 (Winter 1997): 74–91.

12. Eliot, Letter to More, August 3, 1929.

13. T. S. Eliot, *The Varieties of Metaphysical Poetry*, ed. Ronald Schuchard (London: Faber & Faber, 1993), 103.

14. Wallace Fowlie, *Journal of Rehearsals* (Durham, NC: Duke University Press, 1977), 138.

15. George Every in a recorded conversation with the author at Oscott College, Sutton Coldfield, England, May 27, 1989. When I asked Every why Eliot decided to become Anglican instead of Roman Catholic, he replied:

> I would say that his real choice was between being an Englishman and still being an American. Once he got clear of America, he wanted to discover something that couldn't be found in America. Buddhism and Christianity were still hypothetical possibilities. They are universal religions. At the time of *The Waste Land*, they [Buddhism and Christianity] were on par. But when decisions have to be made under really intense spiritual pressure, they have to be made in the here and now. He joined the Church of England because the meaning of its ritual was flexible. It was something he could accept. I don't really think that to become a Roman Catholic in England, in 1927, was for him really an option.

16. Thomas Merton distinguishes two ways in which the word "contemplative" is used: (1) juridical (synonymous with "clustered life"), and (2) mystical (individual, interior realization and practice). Merton writes that contemplation simply cannot be institutionalized. See *Contemplation in a World of Action* (New York: Doubleday, 1971), 207. Along these lines, interreligious dialogian Raimundo Panikkar suggests that "monkhood (i.e., the archetype of which the monk is an expression) corresponds to one-dimension of the *humanum*, so that every human being has potentially the possibility of realizing this dimension" (see *Blessed Simplicity: The Monk as Universal Archetype* [New York: Seabury, 1982], 5–25). According to Eliot's long-time personal friend George Every, who first met Eliot at the Society of the Sacred Mission in Kelham (an Anglican religious community of which Every was a member), Eliot's decision to join the church was influenced by his living situation. Eliot became a Christian in London, not in Rome. Had he settled in France, he might have been a Roman Catholic. According to Every (whom Eliot called "one of the ablest young men in the Church"), Eliot found himself in a situation that could not be explained through psychiatry. He told Every that once he got clear of America, his decision not to return was made in a fairly rebellious mood, for all the wrong reasons.

17. T. S. Eliot, Letter to William Force Stead, March 15, 1928, Beinecke Rare Book and Manuscript Library, Yale University. For further treat-

ment of Eliot's conversion, see my "A New Type of Intellectual," especially 43–57.

18. Ronald Schuchard, *Eliot's Dark Angel: Intersections of Life and Art* (New York: Oxford University Press, 1999), 21. Schuchard writes that "the tension in his personal life was further complicated by the austere religious commitments—including the vow of celibacy—made in the aftermath of his conversion," and that "Eliot found a way of working out the conflict between personal and religious emotion in a new mode of contemplative poetry—*Four Quartets*" (176).

19. Peter Ackroyd, *T. S. Eliot: A Life* (New York: Simon & Schuster, 1984), 70 (italics mine). A pattern can be a specimen, a sample, or an exemplar designed to be imitated (as a dressmaker follows a pattern to make a dress). A pattern, too, can be a finished configuration, a standard measure, or a diagram against which another configuration is measured. Eliot found the first two meanings of "pattern" most useful to his work. For Eliot, the detail of the pattern is dynamic, ever changing; whereas the exemplar, the fixed pattern, needlessly limits and thereby falsifies.

See also Gordon, *T. S. Eliot: An Imperfect Life*. This work and her two-volume set, *Eliot's Early Years* and *Eliot's New Life*, are indispensable for placing the *Quartets* in a biographical context. One discovers, as Eliot discovered in Dante, the insatiable drive of the poet to fulfill his "obligation to explore, to find words for the inarticulate, to capture those feelings which people can hardly even feel, because they even have not words for them." This is "a reminder that the explorer beyond the frontiers of ordinary consciousness will only be able to return and report to his fellow citizens, if he has all the time a firm grasp upon the realities with which they are already acquainted" (T. S. Eliot, "What Dante Means to Me," in *To Criticize the Critic* [New York: Farrar, Straus & Giroux, 1965], 134).

20. T. S. Eliot, "Poetry and Drama," in *On Poetry and Poets* (London: Faber & Faber, 1957), 76. Accordingly, Nancy K. Gish (*Time in the Poetry of T. S. Eliot: A Study in Structure and Theme* [Totowa, NJ: Barnes & Noble, 1981], 96) writes:

> The *Quartets* as a whole must be regarded as developing through a series of explorations towards greater understanding of the initial experience. "We had the experience but missed the meaning" perhaps best defines its structure. Although the timeless moment is the idea behind the entire work, its structure is determined by movement towards the meaning of that moment. If the timeless moment is recurrently evoked, the discursive passages consider its meaning for temporal life.)

21. T. S. Eliot, *The Use of Poetry and the Use of Criticism* (London: Faber & Faber, 1933), 19. Depending on one's temperament, philosophical training, and religious grounding, *Four Quartets* evokes a wide range of responses. Eliot's language, to some, will appear as a devotional stepping stone, as spiritual inspiration, as an avenue for coming to grips with elements of Christian theology or practice that, prior to reading this poem, were obscure, distasteful, incomplete, or insubstantial. Others will reject Eliot's vision as pious romanticism, unsubstantiated rhetoric, mystical obfuscation, or paradoxical double-talk.

In *Four Quartets Rehearsed* (London: Sheed & Ward, 1946), Raymond Preston offers a helpful reminder in this regard:

> No reading of poems so inexhaustible is perfect either: and what
> is needed to correct the deficiencies of one's personal reading
> is not an exchange of critical gun-fire, but quiet co-operative
> discussion of detail. Such co-operative reading requires patience,
> and a willingness to submit to a discipline of trial-and-error in
> the effort to reach the purest contemplation of what the poetry
> offers for contemplation. (64)

22. Martin Scofield, along these lines, has emphasized the "danger of *imposing* a pattern which will distort the true nature of experience (for instance, by over-valuing one side of life at the expense of another) and precluding a proper and vital response to further experience." For this reason, he concludes, "the evolution of [a] pattern also involves the re-examination and re-creation of earlier feelings with a new perspective" (*T. S. Eliot: The Poems* [Cambridge: Cambridge University Press, 1998], 173–74).

For a further discussion of "pattern" in Eliot's poetry see Leonard Unger, *T. S. Eliot: Movements and Patterns* (Minneapolis: University of Minnesota Press, 1966); and Peter Reinan, *Recurring Patterns in T. S. Eliot's Prose and Poetry: A Stylistic Analysis* (Bern: A. Francke, 1978).

23. Elizabeth Drew, *T. S. Eliot: The Design of His Poetry* (New York: Scribners, 1949), xi.

24. Eliot, Letter to William Force Stead, August 9, 1930.

25. Cited in Kristian Smidt, *The Importance of Recognition: Six Chapters on T. S. Eliot* (Tromsø: Norbye, 1973), 34.

26. Paul Murray, *T. S. Eliot and Mysticism: The Secret History of Four Quartets* (New York: Macmillan, 1991), 7. In "On the Metaphysical Poetry of the Seventeenth Century," given as the 1926 Clark Lectures at Trinity College, Cambridge, Eliot presented a comparative study of Dante, Donne, and the French symbolists. He distinguished between seventeenth-century Spanish mysticism, characterized by its emotive sensitivities, and the mys-

ticism of the thirteenth-century writers, characterized by the intellectual spirit. Genuine mysticism, in Eliot's view, emphasized at least two constants: a path of negation and a path of affirmation. See T. S. Eliot, *The Varieties of Metaphysical Poetry,* ed. Ronald Schuchard (London: Faber & Faber, 1993).

While it might be too ambitious to imply that *Four Quartets* is solely "a search that culminates in the mysticism of the middle way" (Donald J. Childs, *T. S. Eliot: Mystic, Son and Lover* [London: Athlone, 1997], 203), it would not require a stretch of the critical imagination to suggest that a subtle and rich interplay of "middle way" immediacies from various spiritual traditions flourish throughout the poem, such as in the Indic and Christian allusions that Eliot called upon frequently. These religious tropes serve to dramatize Eliot's middle-way co-inherence of "one end" and "one way," timelessness and time. Traces of the unitive formulation of the poem's religious imagery and contemplative rhetorical strategy are present, for instance in *Burnt Norton's* visionary silence in the rose garden, in *East Coker's* meditative waiting through the "darkness of God," in *The Dry Salvages'* invocation of Mary and Krishna, and in *Little Gidding's* world-bridging Pentecostal flames.

27. See Evelyn Underhill, *Mysticism: A Study in the Nature and Development of Man's Spiritual Consciousness* (New York: Dutton, 1911), especially part 2, chapters 6 and 7. To grasp the meditative ingredients of Eliot's taste for mysticism, it is helpful to recall that, when he first began studying Western monasticism at Harvard (1911–1912), he came under the influence of this book, from which he took extensive notes. In *Mysticism* Underhill examined mystical consciousness as a gradual process of maturing toward an apprehending of God. Eliot later came to know Underhill personally, and, in response to her death in June 1941, he wrote that "her studies of the great mystics had . . . a consciousness of the great need of the contemplative element in the modern world" (Murray, *Eliot and Mysticism,* 85.). Underhill's *Mysticism* contributed to Eliot's disciplined imagination a structure of meditational practice that, in Underhill's analysis, takes place in three stages: *recollection,* which is deep concentration or reverie upon one aspect of reality; *quietude,* which is the stilling of both will and imagination; and *contemplation,* which is illumined, nonecstatic, unitive awareness.

Underhill's co-implicating stages of meditation, like the traditional methods of meditation they reflect, provided Eliot not only, as his biography suggests, with personal spiritual disciplines, but with an inner structure for his poetry—namely, the three-part framework for each of the four quartets.

28. Louis Martz, *The Poetry of Meditation* (New Haven: Yale University

Press, 1954), 330. For Martz, a precursor to Schuchard, *Four Quartets* is a meditative poem. In *The Poetry of Meditation, The Meditative Poem* (1963), and *The Poem of the Mind* (1966), Martz has described the meditative genre of poetry existing alongside pastoral, epic, and lyric verse. Martz suggests that Eliot's *Quartets* (along with poems by Wallace Stevens, Theodore Roethke, and William Carlos Williams) bears striking resemblances to seventeenth-century English poets like John Donne and George Herbert. For these poets, the practice of meditation led to devotion, and at times to a state of mystical contemplation. That is, as an essential preparation for higher stages of mystical experience, the process of mediation cultivated lower levels of spiritual life. According to Martz, a meditative poem

> is a work that creates an interior drama of mind; this dramatic ac-
> tion is usually (though not always) created by some form of self-
> address, in which the mind grasps firmly a problem or situation
> deliberately evoked by the memory, brings it forward toward the
> full light of consciousness, and concludes with a moment of il-
> lumination, where the poet's self has, for a time, found an answer
> to its conflicts. (*The Poetry of Meditation*, 34–35)

Along with John Donne, George Herbert (and other "metaphysical" poets), Walt Whitman, Emily Dickinson, Theodore Roethke, and Wallace Stevens, Martz designates Eliot (especially in *Four Quartets*) as a meditative poet. The essential process of meditative poetry, according to Martz, depends on an interaction between a "projected, dramatized part of the self" (e.g., introspective self-examination) and the whole mind of the mediator (e.g., an illumined self-knowing). Martz suggests that this threefold process relates to Augustine's division of the soul into memory, understanding, and will. A meditative poem, for Martz, represents the convergence of two arts—one religious, the other poetic—upon a single subject. It may be said that meditative poetry is one possible concrete expression of meditative thinking, a lyrical actualization of that process. If meditative thinking is the process of being attentively open, then meditative poetry is one expression of that openness. The irreducible, untranslatable poetic fabric of metaphor, symbol, and paradox offers containers for ecstatic thinking, even if these are ultimately inadequate.

29. A. David Moody, "*Four Quartets*: Music, Word, Meaning and Value," in *The Cambridge Companion to T. S. Eliot* (Cambridge: Cambridge University Press, 1994), 143–45, and *Thomas Stearns Eliot: Poet*, 2nd ed. (Cambridge: Cambridge University Press, 1994), 197–200, 238–42. To Moody, voices might be thought of as "modes of mind" in which "the mind of the poem operates as it works out its themes" (144). To resist any suggestion

that the poet's voice is static, one can speak of *modulations* of mind. Moody writes that Eliot's voice is "a musical organization of the mind's resources," a form that "is genuinely not like any other in English literature" (156). He distinguishes four voices in the *Quartets*: (1) "natural experience"; (2) critical thought (about inexperience); (3) the contemplative's ascending thought; and (4) spiritual apprehension (148–49). In a conversation at York University in England (June 1994), Moody distinguished these four voices in a somewhat different fashion: (1) natural experience, (2) thinking about it, (3) meditating upon it, (4) and integrative contemplation.

In a lecture presented to the National Book League in 1953, Eliot addressed the problem of poetic communication by distinguishing three voices: (1) "the poet talking to himself—or to nobody" (e.g., meditative verse); (2) "the poet addressing an audience" (e.g., dramatic monologue); and (3) the poet speaking through "one imaginary character addressing another imaginary character" (e.g., dramatic verse) ("The Three Voices of Poetry," in *On Poetry and Poets* [New York: Farrar, Straus, and Cudahy, 1957], 96).

30. D. W. Harding, "Little Gidding," in *T. S. Eliot: A Collection of Critical Essays*, ed. Hugh Kenner (Englewood Cliffs, NJ: Prentice-Hall, 1962), 126.

31. Hugh Kenner, *The Invisible Poet: T. S. Eliot* (New York: Harcourt, Brace, 1959), 193.

32. T. S. Eliot, "English Letter Writers," cited in F. O. Matthiessen, *The Achievement of T. S. Eliot* (New York: Oxford University Press, 1959), 90 (italics in original). Matthiessen notes: "These remarks were included in an unpublished lecture on 'English Letter Writers'—primarily on Keats and Lawrence—which was delivered in New Haven, Conn. during the winter of 1933" (96).

33. T. S. Eliot, Letter to John Hayward, September 3, 1942, cited in Helen Gardner, *The Composition of Four Quartets* (London: Faber & Faber, 1978), 26. A string quartet, composed of three, four, or five movements, can represent stages in a journey, each depicting separate experiences and each reaching fulfillment in its final movement.

34. Eliot, *On Poetry and Poets*, 32. While Hugh Kenner, among others, associates the *Quartets* with Bartok's string quartets numbers 2–6, a preponderance of critics suggest that the *Quartets* are more nearly influenced by Beethoven's last string quartets. See "Eliot's Four Quartets and Beethoven's Last Quartets," by John Holloway in *The Fire and the Rose: New Essays on T. S. Eliot*, ed. Vinod Sena and Verma Rajiva (Delhi: Oxford University Press, 1992), 145–59.

35. According to J. W. N. Sullivan (whom Eliot knew personally) in his book (familiar to Eliot) *Beethoven: His Spiritual Development* (New York: Vintage, 1927), Beethoven's later quartets (especially the C-Minor Opus

132), each movement is generated by a central illumination already present from the beginning. Sullivan writes: "This is characteristic of the mystic
vision, to which everything in the world appears unified in the light of one
fundamental experience" (154).

36. Eliot met Buber only once, in London in 1951. They were brought
together, along with J. H. Oldham and Melville Chaning-Pearce, by the
original translator of Buber's *I and Thou* (1937), Ronald Gregor Smith. The
main topic of conversation, based on a book that Buber had just finished
(*Two Types of Faith*), was about the Jewishness of Jesus and the inacces-
sibility of understanding Jesus in simple, third-person statements (Ronald
Gregor Smith, *Martin Buber* [Richmond, VA: John Knox Press, 1967], 39).
It is worth noting that for Eliot, Buber's *I and Thou*, which Eliot read in
English, had a profound effect on modern religious thought (William Levy
and Victor Scherle, *Affectionately, T. S. Eliot* [New York: Lippincott, 1969],
39). Although Eliot was very shy, he was nevertheless directly frank, which,
Maurice Friedman notes, "Buber did not usually find with persons when
they first met him." Of his meeting with Buber, Eliot wrote to Friedman: "I
once had a conversation with Dr. Buber . . . and I got the strong impression
that I was in the company of a great man. There are only a very few men of
those whom I have met in my lifetime, whose presence has given me that
feeling." (After Buber died in June 1965, an editor of *Newsweek* took Eliot's
quotation from Friedman—"In the Presence of Greatness"—and used it as
the title of a story on Buber.) When Buber told Friedman about his meeting with Eliot, five days after it took place, Friedman asked Buber: "Don't
you find that your opinions and those of T. S. Eliot differ in important
respects?" "When I meet a man," Buber responded, "I am not concerned
with his opinions but with the man." In 1962, several years before Buber
died, Eliot joined other prominent signatories in supporting the nomina-
tion of Martin Buber for a Nobel Prize in literature. See Maurice Friedman,
Encounter on the Narrow Ridge: A Life of Martin Buber (New York: Paragon
House, 1991), 19, 334, 419.

37. Buber, *I and Thou*, 40. Buber's dialogical philosophy provides a lens
through which the spiritual substance of Eliot's *Four Quartets* becomes
more vivid and takes on deeper meaning. The unifying alignment of this
Buberian perspective, along with its significance for understanding the poem,
can be traced throughout this book in the following notes—preface: n. 5;
introduction: nn. 36, 37, 39, 40, 41, 43; chapter 1: nn. 4, 29, 31; chapter 2: nn.
17, 18, 19; chapter 3: nn. 15, 16, 18, 26; chapter 4: nn. 7, 10, 31, 33, 34, 35; conclusion: nn. 3, 4, 13, 14.

38. Mikhail Bakhtin, *Speech Genres and Other Late Essays*, trans. Vern
McGee (Austin: University of Texas Press, 1986), 170. Bakhtin continues:

"At any moment in the development of the dialogue there are immense, boundless masses of forgotten contextual meanings, but at certain moments of the dialogue's subsequent development along the way they are recalled and invigorated in renewed form (in a new context). Nothing is absolutely dead: every meaning will have its homecoming festival" (170).

39. Buber's interpretive method has been summarized in four steps: (1) treating the text as a Thou (a person) with the attitude of receptive waiting, which quickly moves to a more active give-and-take dialogue; (2) allowing the otherness of the text to bring to consciousness the interpreter's own individual and cultural presuppositions; (3) exercising critical distance and employing methods of explanation to analyze the structure and rhetoric of the text; and (4) reflecting on the author, who serves as a reminder to reconnect the text to life (Steven Kepnes, *The Text as Thou: Martin Buber's Dialogical Hermeneutics and Narrative Theology* [Indianapolis: Indiana University Press, 1992], 78). To enter into a meaningful dialogue with a text, therefore, Buber proposes making the words immediately present, as if hearing the voice of the speaker, and turning with one's whole being toward that voice. Accordingly, my reading of *Four Quartets* is situated in a dialogical hermeneutic in which the reader remains faithful to the text by discerning the text's relation to "the reality which was once perceived and is now expressed, . . . to the person addressed, whom the poet means as such, . . . [and] to its poet, that is, to his factual existence in all its hidden structure" (Martin Buber, *The Knowledge of Man: A Philosophy of the Interhuman*, trans. Maurice Friedman and Ronald Gregor Smith [New York: Harper & Row, 1965], 120).

40. Buber, *The Knowledge of Man*, 118. Poetry, Buber writes, "does not originate from one of the senses' standing over against the world, but from the primal structure of man as man, his primal structure founded upon sense experience and overarched by the spirit's power of symbols, from language. . . . But poetry is not obedient to anything other than language, whether it calls and praises, narrates, or allows the happening between men to unfold in dialogue" (162). Buber's dialogic hermeneutic first and foremost preserved the oral origin of the written text. The reader's ability to hear the author's voice, that is to hear the text speaking, according to Buber, is the gateway through which understanding occurs. For an extended discussion of Buber's dialogical textual hermeneutic, especially in comparison to the dialogical hermeneutic of the Russian literary critic Mikhail Bakhtin, see Kepnes, *The Text as Thou*, 61–78. See also Maurice Friedman, *The Affirming Flame: A Poetics of Meaning* (New York: Prometheus Books, 1999), 209–31. In his "Hermeneutical Appendix: Toward a Poetics of Dialogue," Friedman writes that a nonabsolutist, nonrelativist

hermeneutic embodies "the dialogue between a reader whose self is constituted in dialogue and a text which is not limited either to author's intention or reader's interpolation, but stands open to the ever new life and the ever new literary event of the moment" (230–31).

41. Martin Buber and Franz Rosenzweig, *Scripture and Translation*, trans. Lawrence Rosenwald (Bloomington: Indiana University Press, 1994), 76. Buber adds: "But its unfamiliarity is itself necessary, is indeed the one necessity, if, with all our false expertise about the Bible, all our condescending solidarity with it, a translation is to produce an *encounter* between the Bible and people today" (italics mine).

42. Eliot, *On Poetry and Poets*, 25.

43. For the theme word (*Leitwort*) approach to interpretation, I am primarily indebted to Martin Buber. While Buber's *Leitwort* technique focuses more on repeated verb stems and uncommon words, here the guiding word technique focuses on interconnected themes and voices. When applied to reading sacred texts, for example, Buber wrote: "By *Leitwort* I understand a word or word root that is meaningfully repeated within a text or sequence of texts or complex of texts; those who attend to these repetitions will find a meaning of the text revealed or clarified, or at any rate made more emphatic." And "interpretation by *Leitwort* style can only be interpretation *toward*, demonstration can only be demonstration *toward*—toward something that is to be perceived in its actuality, but not paraphrased in language or thought." See Buber and Rosenzweig, *Scripture and Translation*, 114, 116. See also Dan Avnon, *Martin Buber: The Hidden Dialogue*, Twentieth-Century Political Thinkers (Lanham, MD: Rowman & Littlefield, 1998), 49.

44. Harry Blamires, *Word Unheard: A Guide through Eliot's Four Quartets* (London: Methuen, 1969), 3. Emerging from the poetry, the leading theme words embody and reflect contemplative, interreligious sensibilities and provide readers with a cross-referential matrix.

45. According to Helen Gardner (in "*Four Quartets*: A Commentary," in *T. S. Eliot: A Study of His Writings by Several Hands*, ed. B. Rajan [London: Dennis Dobson, 1947], [italics mine]):

The publication of *Quartets* in one volume has made their interpretation easier in one way but more difficult in another. Read *consecutively* each illuminates the others, and the symbols employed become richer and more solid with repetition; but the *cross-references* between the poems are now seen to be so various, subtle and complex that formal interpretation seems more than ever clumsy and impertinent, and may even mislead readers, by appearing to impose a logical scheme on poems which continually escape from the logic of discourse into something nearer to the conditions of musical thought. (57)

Without a doubt, the most valuable secondary source for any serious reader of the *Quartets* is Gardner's *Composition of* Four Quartets. This indispensable book provides materials (Eliot's notes, letters, comments, proposed outlines, edits, and cancellations) that lie behind the final text and that allow readers to trace it origins and growth.

46. T. S. Eliot, "Tradition and the Individual Talent," in *Selected Essays*, 5. As he became more comfortable with English society, Eliot endorsed at least two interrelated sets of English tradition, the Anglo-Catholic church and English literary history. In his seminal essay, "Tradition and the Individual Talent," he insisted that all writers recognize something outside themselves to which they owed "allegiance" and "devotion." The something outside to which one sacrifices the idiosyncrasies of personality he described as "tradition." Tradition is an "historical sense" that involves "a perception, not only of the pastness of the past, but of its presence." "Tradition," for Eliot, was not just an "indiscriminate bolus" that is handed on by prior generations; nor is it merely an unquestioning imitation of "one preferred period." Rather, it is a conscious effort to acquire a sense of "the timeless and of the temporal together" that "makes a writer traditional." Tradition was neither fixed nor static, because every new work of art modifies or alters it; nor does it demand the extinction of individuality, for "novelty is better than repetition." Like Babbitt before him, Eliot perceived "tradition" and "creative talent" interdependently: tradition provided aesthetic principles, and new works of art necessarily altered those principles.

47. T. S. Eliot, Preface in *Thoughts for Meditation: A Way to Recovery from Within*, ed. Nagendranath Gangulee (London: Faber & Faber, 1951), 12. "We must abandon some of our usual motives for reading," he insists.

We must surrender the Love of Power—whether over others, or over ourselves, or over the material world. We must abandon even the Love of Knowledge. We must not be distracted by interests in the personality of particular authors, or by delight in the phrases in which they have expressed their thoughts. What these writers aim at . . . in whatever language or in the terms of whatever religion, is the Love of God. (12–13)

48. What Eliot is suggesting here bears a strong similarity to the Christian monastic practice of *lectio divina*, or "sacred reading," the contemplative, prayerful recitation of scriptural passages. In *lectio divina*, one: listens

to the text deeply, with an open mind, especially to that "still small voice" of God; meditates upon a word, or group of words, with an open heart; takes these words into a prayerful dialogue with God; and rests in the eternal presence of unconditional love. In this practice, the contemplative is called, through words, to go beyond words and to encounter God's presence in the silence and stillness of the soul.

1. *Burnt Norton*: Entering Our First World

1. T. S. Eliot, *New York Times Book Review*, November 29, 1953. During his stay in America, he delivered the Page-Barbour lectures (later published as *After Strange Gods*), and took up the Charles Eliot Norton professorship of poetry at Harvard for a year.

2. See Derek Traversi, *T. S. Eliot: The Longer Poems* (New York: Harcourt Brace, Jovanovich, 1976), 91. Note the similarity of the words "common" in the first fragment, and "same" in the second fragment. The translation used here follows closely Traversi:

> Although the law of reason the Logos is common, the majority of people live as though they had an understanding [or wisdom] of their own.

The way up and the way down are one and the same.

Eliot's interest in Heraclitus began early, when, as a student, he read the pre-Socratic philosophers, and this interest continued with his conversion, when his intellectual quest was joined with his ongoing personal and spiritual searching. It is no accident that Eliot turned to the pre-Socratic Greek philosopher Heraclitus of Ephesus (circa 500 BCE) to frame the poem. His sayings about universal change, the newness of everything, the harmony of opposites, and the common *logos* together point to the way of authentic existence.

Philip Wheelwright, in his excellent work, *Heraclitus* (New York: Athenaeum, 1969), notes that if one translates *logos* more literally as "word," then the question becomes, whose words? Is the *logos* primarily "a transcendental and universal Other who speaks" or primarily the "utterance that Heraclitus is making?" (21). For Wheelwright, "the strongest likelihood is that Heraclitus regarded the Logos as the Truth in its objective and trans-human character, and yet also regarded himself as being especially qualified and privileged to reveal the nature of that truth" (23). See Merrell D. Clubb, "The Heraclitean Element in Eliot's *Four Quartets*," *Philosophical Quarterly* 40, no. 1 (January 1961): 19–33.

The second epigraph—"The way up and the way down are one and the same" (Fragment 108)—rests on Heraclitus's theory of cosmic change and flux. For Heraclitus, all matter is in a process of constant change—the movement downward (fire into water into earth) being balanced by a corresponding movement in the opposite direction. For an extended commentary on the epigraphs, see Clubb, "The Heraclitan Element."

3. William Spanos, "Hermeneutics and Memory: Destroying T. S. Eliot's *Four Quartets*," *Genre* 11, no. 4 (Winter 1978): 530, 533. Spanos argues against the privileged position of these modernist logocentric interpreters who attempt to resolve tensions between conflicting realms of existence and insist on presence rather than absence. He argues instead that there is absence at the still point of the poem. Eliot, however, avoided being trapped by an either/or worldview, especially grounded, as he was, in the Indic tradition in which nothingness is true presence and in which true presence is empty of substance. While I agree with much of what Spanos suggests with regard to the limits of a modernist perspective, it seems to me that by arguing for absence rather than presence at the heart of the poem, he simply replaces one side of the duality with another. Elsewhere, Spanos suggests that "the postmodern Eliot [is] constantly at war with his modernist self who seeks in art 'a way of ordering, of giving a shape and a significance to the immense panorama of futility and anarchy which is contemporary history.'" (*Repetitions: The Postmodern Occasion in Literature and Culture* [Baton Rouge: Louisiana State University Press, 1987], 47). Spanos quotes from T. S. Eliot, "Ulysses, Order, and Myth," in *The Dial*, November, 1923, 123.

4. Martin Buber, *The Knowledge of Man: A Philosophy of the Interhuman*, trans. Maurice Friedman and Ronald Gregor Smith (New York: Harper & Row, 1965), 107 (italics mine). In light of Heidegger's suggestion that the *logos* of Heraclitus does not designate an unchanging center but rather the gathering of being in emergence, Buber further indicates:

- "when Heraclitus says of the logos, the meaning of being that dwells in the substance of the word, that it is common, he thereby asserts that all men in the eternal originality of their genuine spoken intercourse with one another have a share in the consummation of this indwelling" (90);

- "we may understand the logos by understanding one another [become a "genuine We"] in our truth, through whose voice the logos speaks" (91);

- therefore, the logos is "human speech-with-meaning . . ." through which "the cosmos is preserved amid the changes of the world images" (107).

Living by our own private wisdoms, when personal lives become feeling-oriented, when emotions dominate us to the point of determining our life-attitudes, it becomes difficult to realize that personal feelings by themselves yield no interhuman life. Missing from a life of mere feelings is what Buber calls the "essential we." By referring to the "living word," the "common *logos*," "communal speaking," and the "genuine We," Buber directs the process of textual interpretation away from forms of subjectivity and toward interhuman discourse. Poetry, Buber writes, "does not originate from one of the senses' standing over against the world, but from the primal structure of man as man, his primal structure founded upon sense experience and overarched by the spirit's power of symbols, from language.... But poetry is not obedient to anything other than language, whether it calls and praises, narrates, or allows the happening between men to unfold in dialogue" (162).

5. The road to the Burnt Norton manor is northeast of London, between Birmingham and Oxford, ten miles south of Stratford on Avon, one and a quarter miles north of Chipping Campden on B4081. To reach the house and garden, which stand on the edge of the Cotswolds, one must traverse a long private road, over a cattle grid, and past the caretaker's house. Walking to the right of the manor, one passes through a gate to a rose garden and then down two levels of steps that lead to the center of the garden in which there is a large, drained pool. The original title of *Four Quartets*, in fact, was the *Kensington Quartets*.

6. Helen Gardner, in *The Composition of Four Quartets* (London: Faber & Faber, 1978), notes that in the 1740s Sire William Keyte abandoned his wife and family for his wife's maid. Moving to the current site, he built a grand mansion with lavish gardens but dissipated his fortune by indulging in a reckless lifestyle accompanied by heavy drinking. When his attentions turned to a young dairy maiden, his mistress left him. After a week's frenzy, his new mistress left him as well. Abandoned and desperate, he set fire to the mansion and was burnt alive in it. Some ten years later, the estate and its original farmhouse came to be owned by the Earl of Harrowby (36).

7. While writing *Burnt Norton* between 1934 and 1935, Eliot wrote a series of five minor landscape poems. In these lyrical "Landscapes" Eliot shifted his attention from urban settings to rural ones like "Virginia," "Rannoch, by Glencoe," and "Cape Ann." In the first landscape poem, "New Hampshire," an autobiographical poem that Eliot felt influenced the opening of *Burnt Norton*, the poet recalls "children's voices in the orchard / Between the blossom and the fruit-time." Suddenly the "black wing" of death's presence intrudes into the pastoral presence of golden and crimson heads. "Twenty years," he wrote, "and the spring is over." Now adults, the children

of the poem grieve, for both today and tomorrow (CPP 93). See also Donald Childs, "Risking Enchantment: The Middle Way Between Mysticism and Pragmatism in *Four Quartets*," in *Words in Time: New Essays on Eliot's Four Quartets*, ed. Edward Lobb (Ann Arbor: University of Michigan Press, 1993), 123.

8. About Eliot's landscape poems, Alan Weinblatt (*T. S. Eliot and the Myth of Adequation* [Ann Arbor: UMI Research, 1984]) writes:

> These I call poems of incantation, for they resemble language used to enchant or produce a magical effect through word and sound. In the poetry of incantation—a designation inclusive of those poems gathered, in *Collected Poems*, under the rubric *Landscapes*, as well as a number of other passages that dot Eliot's work—the sound is made to elicit feelings of ecstasy before the reader's mind can grasp the sense of failing conveyed by the words. While sound delays the mind from grasping sense, the reader's mind seems to tremble or hover on the brink of meaning. (125)

9. Marshall McLuhan, "Symbolic Landscape," in *T. S. Eliot: Four Quartets*, ed. Bernard Bergonzi (New York: Macmillan, 1969), 239, 240. Unfortunately, there is no way that I can include in this text the multimedia slide presentation (first prepared as part of my Ph.D. oral defense) in which I synchronized Eliot's voice reading the first movement of each *Quartet* with selections from Beethoven's String Quartets (Opus 132) in the background and with slides taken at the four locations (intermixed with the interpretative graphics) projected back and forth from two slide projectors with a dissolve control. I find that it is the best way to introduce students to the structure of the poems, the voice of the poet, and interpretative keys all at once.

10. Nancy Duval Hargrove, *Landscape as Symbol in the Poetry of T. S. Eliot* (Jackson: University of Mississippi Press, 1978), 15. While Hargrove notes that Eliot's landscapes are rich and specific, Steve Ellis, in *The English Eliot: Design, Language, and Landscape in Four Quartets* (New York: Routledge, 1991), argues that they are "extremely reductive" (79) on the one hand and "both constructive and destructive" (91) on the other. According to Ellis, *Four Quartets* presents a "depopulated England" (110) "inhabited solely by ghosts and spirits" (112), a "homocentric landscape with humans radically decentered" (122). This criticism misses the immediacy of Eliot's meditative landscapes, which are not, as Ellis suggests, simply "preliminary to a vision of reality 'without frontiers,' the 'England and nowhere' formulation" (140), but necessarily rooted in sunflowers and yew trees, in rose bushes and sea spray.

While *Four Quartets* differs from Eliot's earlier poetry, one cannot therefore say, as John Lynen has in an otherwise insightful essay, that the poet who emerges is T. S. Eliot himself. Lynen half-correctly writes: "Eliot can appear as himself in *Four Quartets* because he now enjoys a higher consciousness than that of this personae in his earlier poems and perhaps that which the flesh and blood poet of 1910–23 could feel justified in claiming." It is true that there is a higher state of awareness and concentrated consciousness achieved in the *Quartets,* but to infer that this voice merely reflects Eliot is to neglect the meditative and lyrical-reflective nuances in the *Quartets.* They are polysymphonous but in a more unifying way than in *The Waste Land.* See John Lynen, *The Design of the Present: Essays on Time and Form in American Literature* (New Haven: Yale University Press, 1969), 431; see also 409, 416, 426.

11. *Burnt Norton* came into being partially because the producer of *Murder in the Cathedral*, Martin Browne, convinced Eliot to delete fragments of an overly poetic section from the dramatic play. After *Murder in the Cathedral* was written, and before it was performed, Browne suggested that Eliot could intensify the play's emotional impact by including the second priest's reaction to the tempters' speeches. In response, Eliot wrote a thirteen-line meditation on time, on "what might have been and what has been." During the production of the play, Browne encouraged him to remove the lines because they impeded the action of the play. Those lines—beginning with "Time present and time past / Are both perhaps present in time future"—would eventually become the opening meditations of *Burnt Norton.* Eliot explained that "when I saw it produced, I thought there were certain obvious faults of construction and I wanted to sit down and write immediately another play free from those faults. Well, the war came and I had other duties and things to do, and I was here and there, so I turned to writing the other three quartets, and they occupied the war years very well. I was able in the conditions in which I was living to write poems of that type and length. When the war was over, I wanted to turn again to write the play which I had planned to write in 1939" ("A Conversation, Recorded in 1958 between T. S. Eliot and Leslie Paul," *Listener*, September 11, 1969, 335).

12. Nancy K. Gish, in *Time in the Poetry of T. S. Eliot: A Study in Structure and Theme* (Totowa, NJ: Barnes & Noble, 1981), argues that Eliot's poetic form and content depend largely on philosophical concepts of time and timelessness. R. L. Brett, in *Reason and Imagination: A Study of Form and Meaning in Four Poems* (London: Oxford University Press for the University of Hull, 1960), contends that the "main preoccupation for the *Four Quartets* is the Christian doctrine of time and eternity." He maintains that

Eliot finds in the Christian position of the intersection of time and eternity a way of transcending the notion that time is an endless process with no direction and the notion that time is an illusion (120). Morris Weitz persuasively argues that Eliot's understanding of time is neither Heraclitan nor Bergsonian but Neoplatonic ("T. S. Eliot: Time as a Mode of Salvation," *The Sewanee Review* 60 [1952]: 48–64). H. Reid MacCallum is even more explicit about designating time as the organizing thematic pattern. He characterizes the five sections of each *Quartet* accordingly: (1) time as succession, (2) time at a "given" moment, (3) "meantime"—in the interval, (4) invocation, (5) the timeless through time ("Time Lost and Regained," in *Imitation and Design and Other Essays*, ed. William Blisset [Toronto: University of Toronto Press, 1963], 137).

13. Toward the conclusion of *Little Gidding*, Eliot writes: "This is the use of memory: / For liberation." As does *Little Gidding*, *Burnt Norton* begins with a remembered personal experience and then invites the reader to pursue the contours of the remembered journey.

14. Stephen Sicari, "In Dante's Wake: T. S. Eliot's Art of Memory," *Cross Currents* (Winter 1988–89): 414. Furthermore, Sicari suggests that Dante taught Eliot "to assign meaning to a past experience from the perspective of final causes, to interpret the past based on an attraction to God." He writes that the *Quartets* are a "dialectically arranged meditation on 'the use of memory' as the faculty of the human mind that can liberate us from attachment to the world and bring us ever nearer to a revelation of the divine" (413).

Indeed, as Søren Kierkegaard has insisted, there are two modes of memory: "repetition and recollection are the same movement, only in opposite directions; for what is recollected has been, is repeated backwards, whereas repetition properly so called, is repeated forwards" (*Repetition: An Essay in Experimental Psychology*, trans. Walter Lowrie [New York: Harper Torch, 1964], 33).

15. H. Z. Maccoby, in his "Commentary on 'Burnt Norton,' I," *Notes and Queries* 15 (February 1968), argues that the "we" is addressed to the reader and includes all shared experience among the poet, his person, and the reader at large (53).

16. After a hiatus of thirteen years, Emily had approached him for advice about which writers to include in her literature classes at Milwaukee Downer College. For extended treatment of Emily Hale, see Lyndall Gordon's *Eliot's New Life* (New York: Farrar, Straus, Giroux, 1988), especially chapter 4, "Lady of Silences," 146–90: "Through the six years from 1928 to 1934, Eliot's celibate course was challenged by the alternative that Emily

presented, the possibility that grace could come through natural love, and as she awaited a sign, he had to balance the evanescent charms of this way against the solider fains of renewed asceticism" (136).

17. By 1933, Eliot was legally separated from his wife, Vivienne Haigh-Wood (1888–1947), a frail and lovely woman whose liveliness and poetic sensibility awakened Eliot's nascent sensuality. A picture of Tom and Viv show them strolling at the edge of the city, casually but formally dressed, looking at each other with some enjoyment. Those who knew Viv described her as vivacious, sensitive, romantic, self-conscious, and sharp-witted. Almost from the start, however, the marriage headed toward disintegration. In a way they were torn in opposite directions, for they had entered into marriage with opposite goals and values. Eliot wanted to enter more deeply into the fabric of English culture, and Vivienne wanted to escape it.

18. They both had a penchant for letter writing. The personal letter allowed Emily to be warm and playful. Her words demonstrated a mix of affection, honesty, and restraint. Eliot's letters, on the other hand, were confessional and reserved, subtle and witty, sarcastic and ironic. After his sudden, rash marriage, Eliot wrote more than a thousand letters to her (an average of one every week or two) for over thirty years (Gordon, *Eliot's New Life*, 153). It is tempting to speculate on the intimacies of their relationship. Born in the exclusive Boston suburb of Chestnut Hill (October 27, 1891), Emily was raised with Bostonian propriety that appealed to Eliot. According to Emily's wishes and promise to him, the letters are formally sealed (until October 12, 2019) in the University Library at Princeton.

19. T. S. Matthews, *Great Tom: Notes towards the Definition of T. S. Eliot* (New York: Harper & Row, 1974), 149.

20. See Eric Thompson, *T. S. Eliot: The Metaphysical Perspective*, Crosscurrents: Modern Critiques (Carbondale: Southern Illinois University Press, 1963), 95. Gardner speculated that "the 'dignified, invisible' presences are the grown-ups, who create for happy children a world of security and love in which they play." Could they not be the children themselves? She cites a letter from Eliot to John Hayward in which he writes "the children in the apple tree tie up New Hampshire and Burnt Norton" (29). See Gardner, *Composition*, 83. Ronald Bush suggests that "one cannot specify who 'they' are," and that "they are capable of assuming different emotional valences" (*T. S. Eliot: A Study in Character and Style* [Oxford: Oxford University Press, 1984], 190). That Eliot encountered these presences Bush demonstrates by quoting *The Family Reunion*, in which Eliot writes, "The eyes stared at me," and "they were always there" (232).

21. John Cooper, *T. S. Eliot and the Ideology of* Four Quartets (Cam-

bridge: Cambridge University Press, 1995), 153. Aside from *Ash-Wednesday,* where the rose is explicitly religious, suggesting Dante's *"rosa sempiterna"* in *Paradiso,* multiple sources have been suggested for Eliot's rose garden. Louis Martz, for example, cites the influence of *Alice in Wonderland:* "Alice opened the door and found that it led into a small passage, not much larger than a rat-hole: she knelt down and looked along the passage into the loveliest garden you ever saw. How she longed to get out of that dark hall, and wander about among those beds of bright flowers and those cool fountains, but she could not even get her head through the doorway" (Lewis Carroll, *Alice in Wonderland,* ed. D. H. Gray [New York: Norton, 1971], 9–10).

A more biographical influence obtains between the *Burnt Norton* garden and Eliot's "Landscape" poems. The first of the series, "New Hampshire," evoked the "fruit-time" of a "golden headed" youth.

> Children's voices in the orchard
> Between the blossom- and the fruit-time:
> Golden head, crimson head,
> Between the green tip and root.
> Black wing, brown wing, hover over;
> Twenty years and the spring is over;
> To-day grieves, to-morrow grieves,
> Cover me over, light-in-leaves;
> Golden head, black wing,
> Cling, swing,
> Spring, sing,
> Swing up into the apple-tree. (CPP 93)

See Hargrove, *Landscape as Symbol,* 137; Leonard Unger, *Eliot's Compound Ghost: Influence and Confluence* (University Park: Pennsylvania State University Press, 1981), and *T. S. Eliot: Moments and Patterns* (Minneapolis: University of Minnesota Press, 1956). In *Eliot's Compound Ghost,* Unger writes that the rose garden has been "a basic and persistent theme in Eliot's poetry throughout the course of his career" (69). Unger points to the garden in *The Waste Land,* "Portrait of a Lady," *Ash-Wednesday,* and *The Family Reunion.* From Unger's point of view, "in the whole body of the poetry, the theme of the experience in the rose-garden is of central significance" (1).

22. See P. S. Sri, *T. S. Eliot: Vedanta and Buddhism* (Vancouver: University of British Columbia Press, 1985). He writes that the *Quartets* "as a whole may be seen to be a *mandala,* leading the poet and the reader toward a progressively greater awareness of unity in diversity" (105). The meaning of the Sanskrit word *mandala* is "circle," a form that encompasses the entire metaphysical diagram symbolizing wholeness. Usually the inner geometric

images include several concentric circles, which in turn enclose a square, or intersecting triangles, cut through by traverse lines. Whether mandalas are found in the East (in Indic and Chinese traditions) or the West (in Kabbalah and Hermetic traditions), the schematic unity is represented by the quaternary of the four cardinal points. But no matter how it is formed, one's attention is drawn finally to the center of the diagram, the minuscule circle, the doorway into spiritual awareness. Standing in the rose garden, another suggestion arises. The garden is at a lower level than the point of entry and as such is situated in a bowl-like amphitheater, as if the garden itself is the stage. Recalling the proximity of Burnt Norton to Stratford-on-Avon, one thinks first of Shakespeare, then of Greek theater.

23. Martin Scofield, *T. S. Eliot: The Poems* (London: Cambridge University Press, 1988), 204–5. One recalls that in *The Waste Land*, the protagonist returned from "the hyacinth garden" desolately inarticulate—

> . . . I could not
> Speak, and my eyes failed, I was neither
> Living nor dead, and I knew nothing,
> Looking into the heart of light, the silence. (CPP 38)

While sunlight represents the source of life (divine illumination), the imagery of the water is equally strong. Water is seen as the element that solidifies the earth and all in/on it in *The Chandogya Upanishad* (7.10.1). The image of the lotus rising up out of the water from the divine waters is even stronger: the water is the earthly source of the rising lotus/true self. The sunlight (divine source) gives forth divine waters, which nourish the temporal as well as spiritual self. This circular image also evokes the correlation to the Buddhist wheel of life.

24. The poet has always been, according to George Steiner, God's rival, wielding the power to evoke that which is beyond words. Even so, language has its necessary "frontiers" insofar as it borders on three other modes of statement—light, music, and silence—that give proof of a transcendent presence in the fabric of this world. Light is a limitation on poetry because the poet can only progress to a certain depth of sight before surrendering to the mystery of invisible light. See George Steiner, *Language and Silence: Essays on Language, Literature and the Inhuman* (New York: Athenaeum, 1967), 39.

25. *The Bhagavad Gita* XI:15, in *Hindu Scriptures*, trans. R. C. Zaehner (London: Dutton, 1966), 295. In ancient Hindu cosmology, the worship of Brahma (Creator) predates the worship of Vishnu (Preserver) and Shiva (Destroyer). Brahma's role was well defined. The world is created (during the day of Brahma) and is dissolved (during the night of Brahma) over mil-

lions of years in a repeated cycle. During the day of Brahma, the universe emanates from divine substance. During the night of Brahma, the divine remains in dreamless sleep. During this night, Vishnu lies unconscious. At dawn's arrival, a lotus blooms from Vishnu's navel out of which Brahma springs.

As Eliot knew, according to the Hindu *Vedas*, a thousand-petaled, pure gold, cosmic lotus emerges from the primordial waters as the mouth or womb of the universe. From this cosmic lotus (called "the Goddess Moisture" or "the Goddess Earth"), the creator (Brahma) issues forth, the *Atman* (true self). Just as the lotus grows in the mud and yet blossoms on the water's surface, the true self, growing within illusion and ignorance, transcends the limits of the corporeal body.

26. Eliot wrote, "All these are imperfect. In contrast the lotos alone is perfect because it has many flowers and many fruits at once. The flowers and the fruit are simultaneous. The real entity represented in the fruit, its manifestations in the flower—mutual relation of fruit reality and manifestations" (Eliot's notes from Masaharu Anesaki's course at Houghton Library, Harvard University, November 7, 1913).

27. See Dante Alighieri, *The Paradiso: A Verse Rendering for the Modern Reader*, trans. John Ciardi (New York: Mentor, 1961), 331. Dante is granted a graced vision of the blessed as they will be after Judgment Day circling on the eternal rose. Though the light gathered in the rose was greater than an inflaming sun, he did not lose his vision—even his eyelashes drank it in.

28. T. S. Eliot to Bonamy Dobrée, cited in Gardner, *Composition*, 137.

The first rose blooms in the opening movement of *Burnt Norton*, where we are taken from a world of speculation through a gate into a sensuous garden of radiantly red roses ("our first world") in which the air is "vibrant" and "unheard music" is "hidden in the shrubbery." Roses border the alleyway and grow abundantly in the formal English garden. The sun's flames bleach the clustered petals and crimson folds. But the sensuous roses are destined to become dried petals in a dust-covered bowl.

In *The Dry Salvages*, Eliot wrote of the second Rose: "the future is a faded song, a Royal Rose or a lavender spray," which is "pressed between yellow leaves of a book that has never been opened." The Royal Rose (associated with the War of the Roses) operates as a symbol of the future, which like the past is charged with "wistful regret for those who are not yet here to regret." Now pressed between pages of a book, this Rose will remind us of what Krishna meant in the *Bhagavad Gita*: to place one's hope in a future event is to forget, or to ignore, the reality that "you are not the same people who left that station or who will arrive at any terminus" (LG III).

The third rose, the spiritual rose, coexists with the first two and enfolds into "the crowned knot of fire." In the last movement of *Little Gidding*, Eliot echoes the final Canto of *Paradiso*. There, Dante's multifoliate rose unties the "swarthings of the universe" in love's knot. And in *East Coker*, the poet speaks of the necessity of quaking in "frigid purgatorial fires / Of which the flame is roses, and the smoke is briars." Each of those images is paradoxical. To be purified, to receive the "warmth" of fire, it is necessary to "freeze" in "frigid" fires whose flames become the rose of eternal life. The narrative of the *Quartets* moves through the sensuous sights and smells of garden roses (now faded and dried in a bowl), through recollection of the Royal Rose (now pressed between yellow pages), to the spiritual rose enfolded in the "crowned knot of fire."

29. Buber, *The Knowledge of Man*, 107. Not fully described until after *I and Thou*, the realm of "the between" is yet absolutely essential to all of Buber's dialogical philosophy. The interhuman (*das Zwischenmenschliche*) is generated by the immediate presence that binds together a conscious "self" with a conscious "other." In this mutual presence, yet reaching out beyond either person, the innermost self of each person arises simultaneously. "The between" then occurs when one turns to the other and enters into an undivided relationship. This interhuman sphere is significant because it refers to shared relationships—whether between single persons or persons in community whose spirit opens to transcendence.

A genuine relationship with nature, according to Buber, in which one is un-self-consciously wrapped up in the environment, is direct, exclusive, and reciprocal. Buber exemplifies the process of entering into a deeply reciprocal relationship to nature by referring to an ancient linden tree that, after he passed it many times without giving it special attention, seized him. He writes that the tree "had waited for me in order to become once again the blooming and fragrant linden of my sense world." In the same sense nature waits "for living beings to arise through whose meeting perception the green, the soft, the warm—all the qualities conditioned by the senses—should come into the world" (157–58).

30. See Eliot's discussion of "Immediate Experience" in his *Knowledge and Experience in the Philosophy of F. H. Bradley* (New York: Farrar, Straus, 1964), especially chapter 1. Eliot's dissertation on Bradley was influenced in two directions—both by what Eliot did not accept from its idealist presuppositions and by what he did. Clearly, Eliot rejected Bradley's doctrine of Absolute as a void that "dissolves at a touch into its constituents" (*Knowledge and Experience,* 200). At the same time, Eliot was attracted to Bradley's notion of the "finite centre" that represented the point of intersection between the individual and the Absolute. As one critic has observed, "it is

possible that the garden scene, representing a small experience of Eliot's own, is a symbolic enactment of a 'revelation' which Eliot himself had experienced. A 'revelation' is a term with a special meaning in mystical theology. It is a form of extraordinary mystical phenomena, with which God gives a person immediately, supernaturally, an understanding of some religious truth" (Michael Spenser, "Mysticism in T. S. Eliot's *Four Quartets*," *Studies in Spirituality* 9 [1999]: 260).

31. Although nature (e.g., a tree, a rose) lacks verbal expression, when our relationship with nature is genuine, according to Buber, "something lights up and approaches us from the course of [its] being." Buber, in *I and Thou* (trans. Ronald Gregor Smith [New York: Scribner, 1958]), writes that a genuine relationship, though unique to each person, can be expressed as "a reciprocity of the being itself, a reciprocity which is nothing but being in its course (*Seiend*)" (126). What Buber means by this phrase, "being in its course," is the full presence (its living *uniqueness* and living *wholeness*) of, for example, a rose that discloses itself only to the person who is fully present. When the relationship between the rose and a person is mutual (existing from both sides) and reciprocal (giving from both sides), whatever belongs to the rose (its form and color and chemistry and texture) discloses itself. What acts on us, according to Buber, is the effect of the ongoing relationship. For Buber, this reciprocity finally depends on relational grace to which a person must remain open and which cannot be generated by an act of consciousness alone. To paraphrase the final line of the 1923 edition of *I and Thou*: the reciprocal event that from the human side depends upon turning (spiritual practice) from God's side is called redemption (liberation of the whole person through genuine reciprocity with nature/persons/spirit). For further discussion of Buber's dialogical philosophy see my *Martin Buber's I and Thou: Practicing Living Dialogue* (New York: Paulist, 2003), especially chapters 1–2.

32. Charles Taylor, *Sources of the Self: The Making of the Modern Identity* (Cambridge: Harvard University Press, 1989), 479. Taylor argues that modern poetry rejects the unitary conception of the self embraced by the Romantics. Further, he suggests, modernists also affirmed, and profoundly so, a turn inward toward the experience of subjectivity that located a self beyond the self. Central to this discussion is the decentering of subjectivity achieved by interweaving the subjective and the transcendent. Taylor names the poet's "immediate experience" in the garden with his phrase "intertemporal epiphany" in order to account for the necessity of its recurrence in memory.

33. See T. S. Eliot, *The Varieties of Metaphysical Poetry*, ed. Ronald Schuchard (London: Faber & Faber, 1993).

34. Louis Martz, *The Meditative Poem: An Anthology of Seventeenth-Century Verse* (New York: New York University Press, 1963), 330.

35. In the light of the later quartets, Elizabeth Drew suggested that "bedded" and "tree" may refer to "manger" and "cross." She writes: "The only inanimate thing is the 'bedded axle-tree,' maybe a relic of some chariot or gun carriage in a 'forgotten war,' but reminding us of the symbol of the wheel" (*T. S. Eliot: The Design of His Poetry* [New York: Scribners, 1949], 135).

36. In (*T. S. Eliot: An Introduction* [New York: Barnes & Noble, 1963]) Frye writes:

> The top and bottom of the vertical line represent the goals of the way up and the way down, though we cannot show that they are the same point in two dimensions. The top and bottom halves of the larger circle are the visions of plenitude and of vacancy respectively; the top and bottom halves of the smaller circle are the world of the rose-garden and (not unnaturally for the inner circle) of the subway, innocence and experience. What lies below experience is ascesis or dark night. There is thus no hell in *Four Quartets*, which belong entirely to the purgatorial vision. (77)

According to Martz (Martz, *The Poem of the Mind: Essays on Poetry, English and American* [New York: Oxford University Press, 1966]),

> The stillness is not the static fixity about which Prufrock bitterly complained—"When I am formulated, sprawling on a pin"—but dynamic, like the eye of the hurricane. The still point gathers everything in time to itself and becomes a point of reference like Wallace Stevens' "Jar" in Tennessee. The still point is beyond mere rest or movement—it is where, as in Yeats' "Among School Children," the dancer and dance cannot be separated.
> The poet accuses himself; he talks to God within the self; he approaches the love of God through memory, understanding, and will; he sees, hears, smells, tastes, touches by imagination the scenes of Christ's life as they are represented on an inward, mental stage. (108)

37. To contemplate Eliot's image of the still point more deeply, it may be helpful to consider a musical analogy found in a solo violoncello piece by Ralf Yusuf Gawlick, Boston College, "At the Still Point of the Turning World" (2001–2002). In the "Program Note," Gawlick writes that, in coming to associate circularity (around the still point), he set each of the eight words in the title, one per stand, in an octagonal arrangement, and that he realized that any word could be the beginning or the end of the perfor-

mance. Surrounded by the eight stands, the performer navigates around/ towards still point(s), himself becoming the music's visual still point temporarily, as long as he does not change positions. Gawlick also writes that Eliot's speculation on time and existence "through the movement towards/ around/away from the still point . . . is a perceived moment in time, an echo of choice, the one end that is itself timeless."

38. T. S. Eliot, "I," in Gustaf Aulén et al., *Revelation*, ed. John Baillie and Hugh Martin (London: Faber & Faber, 1937), 31–32.

39. John Senior, *The Way Down and Out: The Occult in Symbolist Literature* (New York: Cornell University Press, 1959), 189. Although Senior overemphasizes the downward path, I agree with his simile: Eliot does pull the poem inside out by taking us from the manor house to the bowels of London's subway, from epiphany to the self's process toward epiphany.

40. "The Ascent of Mount Carmel" I:1, 3, in *The Collected Works of St. John of the Cross*, trans. Kieran Kavanaugh and Otilio Rodriguez (Washington, DC: KS Publications, 1979), 73. In this context, commentators have suggested that the first way is positive (*via affirmativa*), while the other (*via negativa*) is the negative way. As Cleo McNelly Kearns indicates: "Eliot's relation to St. John of the Cross was a complex one" in that he once differentiated what St. John meant by the "dark night" and what Eliot meant by it. Yet, by 1952, Eliot lauded St. John as one whose "emotion is so directly a consequence of the idea that the personality of the author is somehow annihilated." From these remarks, it can be inferred that Eliot did not simply accept St. John's views uncritically or uncreatively.

To understand these two ways as sequentially distinct is needlessly dualistic and chronologically bound (Cleo McNelly Kearns, *T. S. Eliot and Indic Traditions: A Study in Poetry and Belief* [Cambridge: Cambridge University Press, 1987], 238). The Eliot quotation is from a typescript in Hayward Collection, King's College.

To put it positively: emptiness results in the transparency of the self to what the self is not. Commenting on Nagarjuna's view of *shunyata*, Eliot noted in one of Anesaki's lectures: "Suppose it is not mere illusion but what appears actually, what is caused to appear, what appears and disappears according to necessary conditions" (see Eliot's notes on Anesaki's lecture of November 7, 1913, Houghton Library, Harvard University). It would be overstating the case, though, to ascribe Eliot's use of the word "emptiness" to some latent Buddhist faith in him.

In the Norton Lectures at Harvard (later published as *The Use of Poetry and the Use of Criticism* [London: Faber & Faber, 1933]) Eliot said, "I am not a Buddhist, but some of the early Buddhist scriptures affect me as parts of the Old Testament do" (91).

41. Eloise Knapp Hay indicates that St. John described two dark nights. In *The Ascent of Mount Carmel*, the first, the dark night of sense, is for beginners; the second, the dark night of the soul, he adds for those already proficient in the former. Rather than subordinating one night of purgation to the other, we can read the poem as including both equally (see Eloise Knapp Hay, *T. S. Eliot's Negative Way* [Cambridge: Harvard University Press, 1982], 155).

Paul Murray, in *T. S. Eliot and Mysticism: The Secret History of* Four Quartets (London: Macmillan, 1991), writes: "The night of the senses and the night of the spirit have both, he [St. John] tells us, a two-fold aspect: active and passive." Murray continues: St. John "makes it clear that his dark sayings are applicable both to the dark night of the senses and to the dark night of the soul of the spirit" (94). This descent also may have recalled for the poet Krishna's words to Arjuna in the *Bhagavad Gita* and Arjuna's question to Krishna:

> Renounce all works [action] thou recommendst.
> And then again thou sayest,
> Perform them!
> Which is better of these two? (V:1)

Without hesitation, Krishna answered: "Renouncing works, performing [yoga], / Both lead to the highest good." Even though Krishna indicated that of the two it is more excellent to engage in work, he exclaimed:

> By surmounting all dualities
> How easily
> You will release from bondage. (V:2, 3)

42. About these lines, Denis Donoghue writes: "The whole passage, one of Eliot's consummate achievements, is at once impersonal, as if the words were uttering themselves in a ritual to make sense of man's presence in the natural world, and irresistibly personal in the turns and trillings of the phrases" (*Words Alone: The Poet T. S. Eliot* [New Haven: Yale University Press, 2000], 265). See also Denis Donoghue, "On 'Burnt Norton,'" in Lobb, ed., *Words in Time*, 14.

43. Ronald Moore, *Metaphysical Symbolism in T. S. Eliot's Four Quartets*, Stanford Honors Essays in Humanities 9 (Stanford, CA: Stanford University, 1965), 34. According to Gardner, when asked about the mystical meanings of the sunflower and kingfisher, Eliot's reply was: "there was a kingfisher." According to George Every, while Eliot was staying at Kelham in the summer of 1935, he saw a kingfisher on a stream running into the Trent by Averham Church over the field from Kelham (see Gardner, *Composition*, 38–39).

44. Spenser, "Mysticism in T. S. Eliot's *Four Quartets*," 243, 244.

45. Spanos, "Hermeneutics and Memory," 541.

46. In "Choruses from *The Rock*," completed in 1934 about the same time Eliot was working on *Burnt Norton,* he wrote:

> Our gaze is submarine, our eyes upward
> And see the light that fractures through unquiet water.
> We see the light but see not whence it comes.
> O Light Invisible, we glorify Thee! (CPP 113)

47. Steiner, *Language and Silence,* 39. Steiner has spoken provocatively about poetry's ability to reach toward its own linguistic frontiers, suggesting that the poet has always been God's rival, for the poet more than others, has the power to evoke that which is beyond words.

48. T. S. Eliot, "English Letter Writers," cited in F. O. Matthiessen, *The Achievement of T. S. Eliot* (New York: Oxford University Press, 1959), 90.

49. The entire ladder image is taken from St. John's "Dark Night of the Soul" (Book II, chapter 19). Eight of the ten steps correspond to theological virtues. The final two have no correspondence to the virtues, since the virtues themselves must be purged in the dark night. See *The Complete Works of Saint John of the Cross,* trans. and ed. E. Allison Peers, 3rd ed. (Westminster, MD: Newman, 1953), 1:441.

50. Ibid.

51. The laughing children hidden in the garden recalls many analogous associations: the children's voices in the "New Hampshire" landscape poem; the children who appear to those who have lost their own children in Rudyard Kipling's story *They*; Alice's passage into "the loveliest garden you ever saw" in *Alice in Wonderland*; and Mary Lennox's discovery of a hidden, overgrown garden that is transformed into an Edenic paradise in Frances Hodgson Burnett's *The Secret Garden.*

2. *East Coker*: Adopting the Old World

1. Gregory Jay, *T. S. Eliot and the Poetics of Literary History* (Baton Rouge: Louisiana State University Press, 1983), 216. By 1936, Eliot had become a member of the Archbishop's committee, charged with preparing for a conference on the church to be held at Oxford on the impending wartime topic of "community, church and state," where Eliot delivered "The Ecumenical Nature of the Church and Its Responsibility toward the World." Not restricted to the monastery, Eliot incorporated devotional and contemplative practices into his daily life. Eliot's political and social attitudes were influenced by and had a good deal in common with his religious views. In

The Idea of a Christian Society (1939) and *Notes Towards the Definition of Culture* (1948), Eliot provides an illustration of the way he applied Anglo-Catholicism to the social order. It is clear in each that Eliot had little faith or hope in modern civilization, and the one choice available, from Eliot's viewpoint, was the Christian one.

Gathered at the Oxford Conference were delegates for forty countries and hundreds of denominations ranging from Orthodox Catholics to the Disciplines (U.S.A.) and the Salvation Army. The Oxford Conference was divided into five sections. Eliot's section dealt with the economic order. On the evening of July 16, Eliot addressed a plenary session in the Town Hall, titled "The Church as an Ecumenical Society." He opened by saying,

> The question of War and Peace, of absolute and or relative Pacifism, is the most conspicuous. Not one communion, I venture to say—and my own is not one of the least divided—has an unanimous opinion about the relation of the temporal and the spiritual power. I only mention this, to remind you of the obvious fact that before the various communions can agree completely, each must agree with itself. Each must decide for itself what is obligatory for its members, and what may be left to private judgment.

See T. S. Eliot, "The Church as an Ecumenical Society," *London Times*, July 17, 1937, and *The Church Times*, July 23, 1937, in the Houghton Library, Harvard University. In an appendix to *The Idea of a Christian Society*, originally a broadcast talk delivered in February 1937, he commented, "It must be said bluntly that between the church and the world there is no permanent modus-vivendi possible" (Appendix, *The Idea of a Christian Society* (New York: Harcourt, Brace, 1940), 72.

2. In March 1939, Eliot gave the Boutwood Foundation Lectures at Corpus Christi College, Cambridge (published later as *The Idea of a Christian Society*) bemoaning the erosion of Christian tradition. In response to what he called a "negative culture," he lamented:

> I do not think that it can remain negative, because a negative culture has ceased to be efficient in a world where economic as well as spiritual forces are proving the efficiency of cultures which, even when pagan, are positive; and I believe that the choice before us is between the formation of a new Christian culture, and the acceptance of a pagan one.

3. Contrary to the image of Eliot's hard-hearted response to Vivienne's condition presented in Michael Hastings's play *Tom and Viv* (he also co-wrote the screenplay for the film of the same title), his second wife, Valerie

Eliot, maintains that Tom didn't visit Vivienne because he was following his doctor's advice. She maintains that Northum Berland House, where Vivienne resided, was a glorified nursing home rather than a mental hospital. Furthermore, she adds, they had been separated for five years, and at the time of Vivienne's commitment, necessitated by her unstable mental state, Eliot was away in the country. In a letter to Eliot (dated August 14, 1938), Vivienne's brother, Maurice Haigh-Wood, makes it clear that Eliot did not take part in his first wife's institutionalization. Both doctors felt strongly that she should be put into a home (from a letter cited in Blake Morrison, "The Two Mrs. Eliots," *The Independent on Sunday*, April 24, 1994, 5). Robert Sencourt (*T. S. Eliot: A Memoir* [New York: Delta, 1973], 173), Eliot's friend, reports that

> If he could have forgotten Vivienne, she could not forget him. She would return to his office in Russell Square and try to waylay him on the stairs, but when it was suggested that he might see her he answered, and rightly, that it would be madness to do so. There are stories of her coming to his lectures wearing on her back a placard bearing the words "I am the wife he abandoned" and she was to be a regular attendee of his plays.

4. Returning to his Wishwood home after an absence of eight years, his wife having died in the absence, Harry finds his manor house essentially unchanged. In disgust he declares:

> I am the old house
> With the noxious smell and the sorrow before morning,
> In which all past is present, all degradation
> Is unredeemable. As for what happens—
> Of the past you can only see what is past
> Not what is always present. That is what matters. (CPP 234)

What matters most to Harry is the "one end" within the flux of time. He discovers that instead of seeking, he has always been fleeing, and that searching for the "one end" involves suffering the frustrating consequences of reversing one's way in the world. Harry's spiritual quest goes beyond the first world of the *Burnt Norton* rose garden and leads toward the darker world of *East Coker*, for Harry's journey involves confronting death. Commenting on Harry's condition, Agatha, Lady Monchensey's younger sister in the play, indicates that he has already been led across the frontier of death. "For him death is now only on this side," she remarks. "For him danger and safety have another meaning." Harry needs to learn what is revealed in *East Coker*, namely that the seeker must confront the way of renunciation and pass through a dark night of spiritual death in order to endure the light of spiritual rebirth. Eliot refused to allow John Gielgud to take the part of Harry because he "wasn't religious enough finally to understand the motivation of the character." Peter Ackroyd notes that the play is a "static drama of explication in which symbols of guilt and fear are the most significant elements" (*T. S. Eliot: A Life* [New York: Simon & Schuster, 1984], 246, 247).

5. T. S. Eliot, "Last Words," *Criterion* 18, no. 71 (January 1939): 274.

6. It was to East Coker that Eliot traced his earliest ancestors (to July 1563, Katherine Eliot). The church register dates back to 1560, at which time there were four "Eliots" living in East Coker. When Andrew Eliot set out from West County village, East Coker, in pursuit of religious freedom, he settled in Salem, Massachusetts. Subsequently Eliot's grandfather, the Rev. William Greenleaf Eliot, left Salem for St. Louis, Eliot's birthplace. The cemetery of St. Michael's Church contains tombstones so worn that they "cannot be deciphered." To the right of the church door was (and still is) an oval memorial plaque upon which are inscribed the first and last lines of *East Coker*—"In my beginning is my end. . . . In my end is my beginning." It was in St. Michael's Church on January 4, 1965, that Eliot's ashes were buried.

7. T. S. Eliot talks about himself and the "Drive to Create," interview by John Lehmann, *New York Times Book Review* (November 29, 1953), 5, reprinted in *T. S. Eliot: Four Quartets, A Casebook:* ed. Bernard Bergonzi (New York: Macmillan, 1969), 23.

8. Bonamy Dobrée, "T. S. Eliot: A Personal Reminiscence," in *T. S. Eliot: The Man and His Work*, ed. Allen Tate (New York: Delta, 1966), 83.

9. Paul Murray, *T. S. Eliot and Mysticism: The Secret History of Four Quartets* (London: Macmillan, 1991), 62. Murray's book is a valuable resource for studying *Four Quartets* from a mystical viewpoint. Rowan Williams writes: "What Paul Murray's book does is to look patiently at the *Quartets* in the light of what we know Eliot was reading and thinking, and to spell out how the poems realize the different levels or stages of faith through which Eliot himself was passing" ("T. S. Eliot and Mysticism: A Discussion," *Doctrine and Life* [September 1993]: 396).

10. T. S. Eliot, Letter to William Force Stead, August 9, 1930, Beinecke Rare Book and Manuscript Library, Yale University. A. David Moody calls Eliot's three wartime quartets "patriotic poems." He bases his observation on a remark (subsequently canceled) that Eliot had made in the first draft of his "The Three Voices of Poetry": "The last three of my quartets are primarily patriotic poems." For Moody, even though Eliot canceled the remark, "it comes as near as a single sentence could to providing the key to

them" (*Thomas Stearns Eliot: Poet*, 2nd ed. [Cambridge: Cambridge University Press, 1994], 203).

11. Thomas Merton, *New Seeds of Contemplation* (New York: New Directions, 1961), 59.

12. Eliot once noted that Ecclesiastes is "as near to pure literature or pure poetry as anything in the Bible." He made this remark in an "Unpublished Address" to the Women's Alliance at Kings Chapel, Boston, on December 1, 1932. A copy of the manuscript exists at the Houghton Library of Harvard University.

13. Edward Lobb, "Limitation and Transcendence in 'East Coker,'" *Words in Time: New Essays on Eliot's Four Quartets*, ed. Edward Lobb (Ann Arbor: University of Michigan Press, 1993), 28.

14. See Sir Thomas Elyot, *The Boke of the Governour* [1531], ed. H. H. S. Croft (1883), vol. 1, book 1, chapter 21, 233–38. Eliot's comment on this passage is referenced in Helen Gardner, *The Composition of Four Quartets* (London: Faber & Faber, 1978), 99. For a fuller account of the relationship between this passage and Elyot's *The Boke of the Governour*, see James Sweeney's "'East Coker': A Reading," in *T. S. Eliot: A Selected Critique*, ed. Leonard Unger (New York: Rinehart, 1948). The archaic spelling links the reader to a time of more traditional moral and doctrinal teachings, which, as Ronald Bush suggests, in *T. S. Eliot: A Study in Character and Style* (New York: Oxford University Press, 1984), "has the line of harmony but is anchored in darkness" (213).

15. See Sir James George Frazer, *The Golden Bough: A Study in Magic and Religion*, vol. 9: *Spirits of the Corn and of the Wild*, 3rd ed. (New York: Macmillan, 1935), 233. In volume 12 of *The Golden Bough*, *Balder the Beautiful: The Fire-Festivals of Europe and the Doctrine of the External Soul*, Frazer notes: "Young people and children dance and sing round the bonfires, and leap over the embers to secure good crops or a happy marriage within the year, or as a means of guarding themselves against colic" (107). In 1923, in London, Havelock Ellis published *The Dance of Life*, which doubtlessly reached Eliot's attention as well. In his foreword, Ellis writes that while sometimes "gay and trivial," sometimes "highly respectable," the dance is "a symbol of life in that it appeals to a general rhythm which marks not only human but also cosmic life. As such, dancing is the primitive expression of religion and love. Among pre-historic peoples, for example, dance was both worship and prayer, whether among the Swahili of Africa, the Sahmans of Northern Siberia, or the Greco-Roman Dionysian rituals." According to Ellis, not only did the chief or Shaman dance, but the gods danced as well. Ellis remarks that, in early Catholic ritual, "at the Eucharist the faithful gesticulated with their

hands, danced with their feet, flung their bodies around (40)." See Havelock Ellis, *The Dance of Life* (New York: Modern Library, 1929), 39.

16. Quoted in Gardner, *Composition*, 99.

17. Martin Buber, *The Origin and Meaning of Hasidism*, trans. Maurice Friedman (New York: Harper Torchbook, 1960), 170. In the larger Buberian context, "sacramental existence" includes holy insecurity (what is to happen cannot be known in advance), holy intent (hallowing the everyday), and awareness that creation/revelation/redemption occur in every moment. Sacramental existence, for the Hasidic tradition and for Buber, points to the meaning-giving covenant (binding or joining) between humans and the eternal partner in concrete situations. Sacramental consecration, therefore, depends on and manifests God's grace.

18. Martin Buber, *The Way of Man: According to the Teachings of Hasidism* (New York: Citadel, 1950), 38. In *The Way of Man* Buber provides six commentaries on Hasidic stories that point to the unified path of becoming uniquely human. The act of "heart-searching" initiates each person's "particular way," or unique task, which activates and is activated by a determined "resolution" to "begin with oneself" *and*, at the same time, "not to be preoccupied with oneself." The fulfillment and significance of "heart-searching," along with this entire course of action, culminates "here where one stands." In this interdynamic process, the human task is to enter into holy conversations with the world, thus liberating the divine spark (the mysterious spiritual substance) living in everyone and everything. By hallowing the everyday, in ever new ways, a person comes to find the great treasure, the fulfillment of human existence—the Divine Presence—and is transformed again and again in the process.

19. Consider for instance, Buber's understanding of love. Where does love occur—inside a person or between persons? Buber writes that while feelings accompany love, they do not constitute love. While feelings dwell *in* a person the way a person dwells *in* the world, a person in love dwells *in* the mutual presence of love. Real love is deep bonding between partners, and a loving relationship proceeds from the voluntarily assumed responsibility of one person for the other. See Martin Buber, *I and Thou*, trans. Ronald Gregor Smith, 2nd ed. (New York: Scribner, 1958), 15.

20. Dante Alighieri, *The Divine Comedy: The Carlyle-Wicksteed Translation* (New York: Modern Library, 1932), 11.

21. Eliot, *The Idea of a Christian Society*, 63–64, quoted in Moody, *Thomas Stearns Eliot: Poet*, 203–4.

22. Edward Lobb, "Limitations and Transcendence," 26. See also Jefferey M. Perl, *Skepticism and Modern Enmity: Before and After Eliot* (Baltimore: Johns Hopkins University Press, 1989). Perl recalls Eliot's lecture

notes from the Philosophy 24a lectures of Masaharu Anesaki at Harvard. Anesaki, it should be recalled, introduced Eliot to the Madhyamika philosophy of Nagarjuna. Perl writes:

> the Middle Way is not perspectivistic in the European sense: its core project is not to extend validity to countless points of view. Nagarjuna articulates two categories of perspective from which the world is viewed. There is the standpoint nirvana, or the absolute (this is the perspective of the enlightened). There are the standpoints of *samsara*, or the conventional (the perspectives of the pre- and unenlightened).
>
> From the standpoint of the absolute, no distinction exists between the absolute and the conventional. The absolute is a set of relations (the term used is "dependent coordination," pratityas-amutpada). From the standpoints of the conventional, however, there exists a radical distinction between conventionality and ultimacy. For the unenlightened nirvana is a goal—not here, not this, not now—to be *achieved.* (57)

For Nargarjuna, the operative opposites are the Absolute (*Nirvana*) and the relative (*Samsara*). For Eliot the corresponding pair are the timeless and time. From the viewpoint of the timeless, there is no distinction between itself and time-bound reality. However, from the standpoint of time, the distinction holds.

23. *The Rule of St. Benedict*, trans. Anthony Mersel and M. L. del Mastro (Garden City, NY: Image Books, 1975), 57. In the seventh chapter of Benedict's *Rule*, he describes twelve degrees of humility:

1. Constantly watching against sin;
2. Not loving one's own will;
3. Submitting to superiors in obedience;
4. Holding fast to patience amid rough times;
5. Confessing one's sins;
6. Confessing one's unworthiness;
7. Admitting that one is less than others;
8. Maintaining the common rule of the monastery;
9. Keeping silent until questioned;
10. Not being over-ready to laugh;
11. Speaking reasonable words with a moderate voice;
12. Keeping a moderate bearing. (57–61)

24. T. S. Eliot, Letter to Paul Elmer More, January 11, 1937, Princeton University Library.

25. Ronald Schuchard, *Eliot's Dark Angel: Intersections of Life and Art* (New York: Oxford University Press, 1999), 15.

26. St. John of the Cross, *The Collected Works of St. John of the Cross*, trans. Kieran Kavanaugh and Otilio Rodrigues (Washington, DC: ICS Publications, 1979), 74–75. In 1927, Eliot compared the mysticisms of St. John of the Cross and Dante: "An equally genuine mysticism is expressed in the verses of St. John of the Cross; this is not a statement, but a riddling expression; it belongs to great mysticism, but not to great poetry" ("The Sulurist," *Dial* 83, no. 3 [September 1927]: 260).

27. W. B. Yeats, *The Collected Poems of W. B. Yeats* (New York: Macmillan, 1956), 203.

28. Martin Heidegger, *Discourse on Thinking*, trans. John N. Anderson and E. Hans Freund (New York: Harper Torchbooks, 1966), 55.

29. Jay, *Eliot and the Poetics of Literary History*, 218.

30. St. John of the Cross, *The Ascent of Mount Carmel*, in *The Complete Works of St. John of the Cross*, trans. and ed. E. Allison Peers, 3rd ed. (Westminster, MD: Newman, 1953), book 1, chapter 8, 59. This volume (first published in 1935) was in Eliot's library. As Abraham H. Maslow writes about what he calls peak-experience: "To say this in a different way, perception in the peak-experience can be relatively ego-transcending, self-forgetful, egoless, unselfish. It can come closer to being unmotivated, impersonal, desireless, detached, not needing or wishing. Which is to say, that it becomes more object-centered than ego-centered" (*Religions, Values, and Peak Experiences* [New York: Penguin, 1977], 62). Of course, St. John's path of negation includes the negation of the soul's object-orientation as well.

31. Paul Murray, *T. S. Eliot and Mysticism*, 91. According to Eliot, "one must always keep strictly to the path of detachment, only in the end to arrive at the point where one already is rather than some place outside of time." To say, as Murray does, that St. John "makes no comment whatever on the subject of ecstasy" is to read both St. John and Eliot too literally. That Eliot read parts of St. John in the original Spanish (as Murray himself indicates) suggests, to me, that "ecstasy," in Eliot's mind, more clearly than "pleasure," translated St. John's intention into the nearest English equivalent. To be detached from pleasure would have been, for Eliot, the more noble spiritual accomplishment.

32. Nagarjuna, *Fundamentals of the Middle Way*, in Frederick J. Streng's *Emptiness: A Study in Religious Meaning* (Nashville: Abingdon, 1967), 212, 204. In this treatise, Nagarjuna, through a series of dialectical maneuvers, demonstrates that philosophical concepts (such as causation, time, and action) do withstand rigorous analysis and are in fact empty of identity. Even

the concept of nirvana cannot stand up to his scrutiny and must be negated as a concept (though not as a realization).

Eliot's paradoxes recall Nagarjuna's teaching of the annihilation of self and what the Rinzai Zen tradition calls "no-mind," or dying while alive, or what the Japanese philosopher Nishida once called "absolutely contradictory self identity." While I do not want to insinuate that Eliot was a Buddhist in disguise, or that Eliot's poetry must be interpreted through a Buddhist-oriented hermeneutic, I would suggest that part of the reason Eliot chose the language of St. John of the Cross was because it resonated so profoundly with Buddhist insights into nothingness, the implications of which helped shape his spiritual journey.

Kitaro Nishida, in *Intelligibility and the Philosophy of Nothingness* (trans. Robert Schinzinger [Tokyo: Maruzen, 1959], 163), speaks of the "absolute contradictory," which Richard DeMartino translates as "absolutely contradictory self-identity." Shinichi Hisamatsu, a student of Nishida, presented this matter in his own way: "seeing into one's True Nature not being anything, is every-thing, and being everything, is not anything." For Hisamatsu, "absolute negation" is "absolute affirmation," and "absolute affirmation is in itself absolute negation." See Hisamatsu, "The Characteristics of Oriental Nothingness," *Philosophical Studies of Japan* 2, 1957, 93. In Hisamatsu's understanding, the "Nothingness state of myself" is no other than "Myself being Nothingness" (76).

33. *Collected Works of St. John of the Cross*, 67. At the time Eliot was writing *East Coker*, the following passage from St. John (*The Ascent of Mt. Carmel*, book 2, chapter 7) was central to his spiritual consciousness:

> To follow Christ is to deny self; this is not that other course which is nothing but to seek oneself in God, which the very opposite of love. For to seek self in God is to seek for comfort and refreshment from God. But to seek God in Himself is not only to be willing to be deprived of this thing and of that for God, but to incline ourselves to will and choose for Christ's sake whatever is most disagreeable, whether proceeding from God or from this world; this is to love God.

34. T. S. Eliot, Letter to Anne Rider, March 10, 1941: "I am glad, by the way, that you like Part IV [of *East Coker*], which is in a way the heart of the matter" (quoted in Gardner, *Composition*, 109).

35. Quoted in Gardner, *Composition*, 109 (italics mine).

36. T. S. Eliot, "A Dialogue on Dramatic Poetry," in *Selected Essays*, new

ed. (New York: Harcourt, Brace, 1950), 36. In this regard, I recall a conversation with Eliot's close friend George Every, at Oscott College in 1989, in which Every said, "Eliot's anthropological approach to religion is older than his Hindu interest in religion," referring to Eliot's 1913 paper in Royce's seminar. Every continued: "Eliot argued there that the only historical fact about primitive religion is its ritual; the rest is an interpretation of interpretations. What we can be sure of [in the Christian tradition] is that there was a rite with bread and wine, and it is the same rite which has elaborated and developed its meaning."

37. Eliot's guiding purpose in *East Coker* IV, according to A. D. Moody, is "not simply to stimulate feeling" but "to intensify the apprehension of the metaphysical truth which should have been its object" (Moody, *Thomas Stearns Eliot: Poet*, 219). Even more than intensifying our apprehension of a metaphysical truth, Eliot's purpose in this section involves the two sides of participation—namely, of choosing and of being chosen.

38. "The supreme archetype of the downward or negative way is the Passion, Death and Burial of Christ. Eliot's fourth movement, by an extended image of the 'wounded surgeon' at work upon the soul, shows how life's fitful fever finds its cure through the piercing love of the Redeemer" (Grover Smith, *T. S. Eliot's Poetry and Plays* [Chicago: University of Chicago Press, 1950], 269).

39. In 1928, the year that he announced his conversion to the Anglo-Catholic church, Eliot published an internal dialogue on the relation between art and religion. Called "A Dialogue on Dramatic Poetry," a central concern of the imagined dialogue was the relation between drama and liturgy. In the dialogue, two dramatis personae (characters designated "E" and "B") express Eliot's pre- and postconversion attitudes toward the Anglo-Catholic Mass. E's preference for liturgy has a wide adaptability; for B, the question is not about whether the Mass is dramatic but rather about the relation of drama to the Mass.

Back and forth, the two imagined personae exchange their different views. The earlier Eliot (i.e., E) argues that Mass substituted "the consummation of the drama for religion," and that "the only dramatic satisfaction that I find now is in a High Mass well performed." In response, the older, postconversion Eliot (i.e., B) remarks that he once knew a man who held this view (the younger Eliot) who was solely interested in the Mass being aesthetically pleasing. "His attention," notes B, "was not on the meaning of the Mass, for he was not a believer but a Bergsonian, who focused on the art of Mass." B then continues that "religion is no more a substitute for drama than drama is a substitute for religion." What finally differentiates the twenty-two-year-old American graduate student studying in Paris with

Bergson from the devout, thirty-nine-year-old British poet, critic, and businessman is "participation" at Mass: "In participating we are supremely conscious of certain realities, and unconscious of others. But we are human beings, and crave representations of which we are conscious, and critical, of these other realities. We cannot be aware solely of divine realities. We must be aware also of human realities" ("Dialogue on Dramatic Poetry," in *Selected Essays*, 35–36).

40. In a June 1940 memorial lecture on William Butler Yeats, Eliot remarked: "Towards middle age a man has three choices: to stop writing altogether, to repeat himself with perhaps an increasing skill of virtuosity, or by taking thought to adapt himself to middle age and find a different way of working" ("Yeats," in *On Poetry and Poets* [New York: Noonday, 1961], 297). For Eliot, balancing and reconciling opposites—through acts of inclusion and transmutation—became an element of that "different way of working," as well as a key element of his religious sensibility.

41. Eliot's affinity for the middle way, in religion and politics, in philosophy and poetry, opened up a means by which to overcome, in language, the false imperative of extremity in every day life. Always skeptical of reductive, overly simplistic perspectives, Eliot drew upon multiple understandings of the "middle way." The sheer joy (and madness) of the reader's task is to apprehend (and even be apprehended by) various combinations of these nuances. As we will see in the *Quartets*, Eliot's reference to the middle path in no way represents either a pruning or a selection of one understanding over another; rather, it is his way of mediation, of including and transmuting, of always forming wider wholes. In terms of the poet's entering into the presence of immediate relationship with the natural world, the "middle way" evokes the spirit of spontaneous mutuality, of common fruitfulness, enveloping and connecting the poet to the rose garden or to the dancers. For this reason Eliot observed in a 1927 essay on John Bramhall that extreme thinking may too easily transform into the opposite of itself. Middle-way thinking, Eliot continued, "requires discipline and self-control, it requires both imagination and a hold on reality" ("John Bramhall," *Selected Essays*, new ed., 316).

Of the Anglican church, Eliot wrote: "The *via media* which is the spirit of Anglicanism was the spirit of Elizabeth in all things. . . . In its persistence in finding a mean between Papacy and Presbytery the English Church under Elizabeth became something representative of the finest spirit of England of the time" ("Lancelot Andrewes," in *Selected Essays*, 302–3).

To the extent that the poet is caught in the limitation of chronological time, "middle" suggests any place between extremes. To the extent that he participates in the freedom of timeless moments, however, "middle" suggests an awareness or realization transcending the extremes of action and inaction. The phrase "the middle of the way" also echoes the Buddha's middle-way path, reconciling opposites that arise not from knowledge but from direct experience. Analogously, in the preceding movement, the Eucharist became meaningful when situated in middle-way immediacy: the importance of the Eucharist is not only that the communicant reconciles the physical and physiological differences between himself or herself and Jesus by eating the body but, as Augustine suggested in the *Confessions* (7:10), also that Christ literally becomes the communicant. Thus, when Eliot notes that he is "in the middle way," he registers both the temporal fact that he is growing older and the contemplative act of seeking, and struggling to speak from, a middle-way awareness.

42. Moody, *Thomas Stearns Eliot: Poet*, 220.

43. Gardner indicates that Eliot deleted a line from the conclusion that would have made these lines read: "For a further union, a deeper communion, Aranyaka, the forest or the sea." She writes: "he wisely dropped the reference to 'Aranyaka, the forest.' The Aranyakas are sacred books whose name can be interpreted as meaning either that they were written in the forests by forest hermits, or that they were written for those who, after a life of action, have retired to the forests" (*Composition*, 113).

44. William Spanos, "Hermeneutics and Memory: Destroying T. S. Eliot's *Four Quartets*," *Genre* 11, no. 4 (Winter 1978): 552.

45. The "vast waters" (which become in *The Dry Salvages* the sea all around us) contain the "petrel and the porpoise." The petrel is a small bird that flies so close to the water that it appears to be walking on water. Hence, the name "Petrel," the little Peter, directs the reader's attention to the church. The porpoise, according to sailors, often appears in the waters just before a storm at sea and is thus associated with Christ as the one who calms the storm.

3. *The Dry Salvages*: Rediscovering the New World

1. T. S. Eliot, Letter to William Force Stead, June 20, 1930, Beinecke Rare Book and Manuscript Library, Yale University. Biographer Lyndall Gordon comments on the significance of Eliot's evolving use of "the American imagination" at this stage in his life, especially as it manifested "the dream of self-transformation" presumably particular to the American way of life: "In his last years Eliot returned more often to his native country, and in the last important interview, the *Paris Review* interview of 1959, stressed the American origins of his poetry: '. . . in its sources, in its emotional springs, it comes from America'" ("The American Eliot and 'The Dry Salvages,'" in

Words in Time: New Essays on Eliot's Four Quartets, ed. Edward Lobb [Ann Arbor: University of Michigan Press, 1993], 38).

2. Gregory Jay, *T. S. Eliot and the Poetics of Literary History* (Baton Rouge: Louisiana State University Press, 1983), 230.

3. Rear-Admiral Samuel Eliot Morison, quoted in Helen Gardner, *The Composition of Four Quartets* (London: Faber & Faber, 1978), 128.

4. See A. David Moody, *Thomas Stearns Eliot: Poet*, 2nd ed. (Cambridge: Cambridge University Press, 1994), 222–34. In *Tracing T. S. Eliot's Spirit: Essays on His Poetry and Thought* (Cambridge: Cambridge University Press, 1996), Moody writes: "Eliot was an American, and a poet. But was he an American poet?" (3). Answering his own question, he writes: "Eliot, clearly, is not an American poet in the sense that Whitman and Williams and Olson are. His poetry is as much English and European as it is American. It aspires to a vision and a wisdom not of any one nation or culture. But Eliot's is an English and European poetry that only an American could have written, and it is the American component that makes the difference" (16). Applying this view to *The Dry Salvages*, Moody writes: " 'The Dry Salvages' might be called Eliot's New World Quartet, not only because it returns to his American sources, but because it discovers a new meaning in them, a meaning which goes back to the religious origins of New England. It goes back with a difference, because it seeks a world that is new in every moment" (14).

5. T. S. Eliot, "Wordsworth and Coleridge," in *The Use of Poetry and the Use of Criticism* (London: Faber & Faber, 1933), 78–79. Gordon comments: "Eliot's career circled back so that the sources of his own life, the Mississippi River and Cape Ann, came to stand for the source of all life. Despite his adaptation to England, his adoption of English religion, manners, and clothes, and despite marriages to English women, his poetry led him back to 'the source of the longest river,' and to the silence the child heard between two waves of the sea" ("The American Eliot," 50).

6. T. S. Eliot, "The Influence of Landscape on the Poet," *Daedalus* 89, no. 2 (Spring 1960), 422. Eliot also notes:

> Well. I came East too, at the age of seventeen, to a school not remote from Brookline; and as far back as I can remember and before, my family had spent every summer on the New England coast. So my personal landscape is a composite. In St. Louis, my grandmother—as was very natural—wanted to live on in the house that my grandfather had built; my father, from filial piety, did not wish to leave the house that he had built only a few steps away; and so it came to be that we lived on in a neighbourhood

which had become shabby to a degree approaching slumminess, after all our friends and acquaintances had moved further west. And in my childhood, before the days of motor cars, people who lived in town stayed in town. So it was, that for nine months of the year my scenery was almost exclusively urban, and a good deal of it seedily, drably urban at that. (422)

In light of these remarks, Eloise Knapp Hay ("Conversion and Expatriation: T. S. Eliot's Dual Allegiance," in *The Fire and the Rose: New Essays on T. S. Eliot*, ed. Vinod Sena and Rajiva Verma [New York: Oxford University Press, 1992], 2) poses the question of Eliot's American identity, and then suggests an answer:

> How could Eliot, as an expatriate, make these statements, and how did he legitimize his appearance in the anthologies of both British and American literature, despite his alienation from America through most of his writing life? Reviewing his life, we see that Eliot's sense of patriotism was determined from the start by what he considered to be a poet's primary loyalty: his dedication to his language. Throughout his life he held that, despite extreme differences in the cultural ideologies of England and the United States, the two nations had between them one language.

7. In a letter to Frank Morley, Eliot's close friend John Hayward writes: "Tom was worried that the title might appear too remote and, particularly, that it might not occur to his readers (as it didn't [*sic*] to me) that it was a proper name" (Letter [xxviii] to Frank Morley, January 1941, Collection of King's College, Cambridge).

Acknowledging the prodigious achievement of *Four Quartets*, Donald Davie has expressed surprise at how *The Dry Salvages* "sticks out among the rest [of the *Quartets*] like a sore thumb." He then proceeds to make a case against *The Dry Salvages*. Since Davie's writings, over the years, have instigated discussions both for and against his views, I repeat his central argument here:

> At first sight it is not only incongruous with the others, strikingly different in conception and procedure, but different unaccountably and disastrously. One could take it by itself and prove convincingly that it is quite simply *rather a bad poem*.
>
> It is hardly too much to say that the whole of this third quartet is spoken by a nameless persona; certainly it is spoken through a mask, *spoken in character,* spoken in character as the American.

See "T. S. Eliot: The End of an Era," in *T. S. Eliot: A Collection of Critical Essays*, ed. Hugh Kenner (Englewood Cliffs, NJ: Prentice-Hall, 1962), 192, 200 (italics in original).

Derek Traversi notes, in *T. S. Eliot: The Longer Poems* (New York: Harcourt, Brace, Jovanovich, 1976), that there has been a tendency among commentators to find *The Dry Salvages* the least satisfactory poem in the series.

> Some have found that there is too much *prose* in this part of
> the sequence, too much repetition of what they find to be tired
> and dispirited motives. Others—more deeply dissatisfied—have
> considered that the underlying thought is lacking in precision
> or fails to contribute [to expand the argument.] Others again . . .
> have argued that the descent, as they feel it to be, from poetry to
> prose is a structural necessity, a stage of false, or at least prema-
> ture resolution, through which the poetry has to pass before it
> can recover. (152)

8. Quoted in Gardner, *Composition*, 51–52.

9. Samuel Eliot Morison, "The Dry Salvages and the Thocher Shipwreck," *American Neptune* 25, no. 4 (1965): 233–47, cited by Gardner, *Composition*, 31–53. About these rocks, in *T. S. Eliot: A Study in Character and Style* (New York: Oxford University Press, 1984) Ronald Bush notes:

> Along with their primary symbolism, the rocks also represent
> the seat of some of Eliot's childhood memories. Mantra-like, they
> seem to have helped him release a complex vision of his early
> life. Writing the poem, Eliot addressed a long-standing part of
> his private mythology (an ancestor of his, he suspected, had been
> shipwrecked there), and he and a friend were once storm-bound
> on a neighboring island. (215)

And Gardner (*Composition*) writes:

> The Atlantic off the great promontory of Cape Ann is studded
> with rocks and reefs. It is a dangerous and difficult coast, as
> well as a supremely beautiful one. Eliot and his older brother,
> Henry, were taught to sail on its waters by an ancient mariner
> of Gloucester and became expert at navigating its hazards. Later
> they sailed in Henry's boat, the Elsa; and in his Harvard days
> Eliot sailed in vacations with a college friend, Harold Peters. In
> the same year as he wrote the preface to Mowrer's *This American
> World*, 1928, he wrote an unsigned publishers' preface to James B.

Connolly's tales of Gloucester fishermen, Fishermen of the Banks,
writing with authority as one who know the seamen and their
hard life. (50)

10. Quoted by M. W. Childs, "From a Distinguished Former St. Louisan,"
St. Louis Post-Dispatch, October 15, 1930.

11. Interestingly, when we look at Eliot's first notes for the poem (as
reproduced in Gardner, *Composition*, 118.), "River" does not appear in his
rough schema:

1. Sea picture—general
2.   —particular
            problem of permanence
            of past pain
3. Past error can only be reconciled
   in eternity. Arjuna & Krishna.
4. Invocation to the B.V.M.
                meaning of "mother" & "father."
5. Generalisation: Liberation from
            the past is liberation from the
            future. To get beyond time &
            at the same time deeper into
            time. the Spirit & the Earth.

Commentators have been critical about Eliot's opening to the poem, "I
do not know much about gods." A. David Moody writes: "There is a discon-
certing flatness about the start of The Dry Salvages." He questions whether
it is a lapse "or does Eliot know that this is a cliché and bathos, and is he
doing a straight-faced parody?" (*Thomas Stearns Eliot: Poet*, 222). Donald
Davie points out that Eliot's tone here is an embarrassment—"who could
conceivably start a conversation like that without condemning himself from
the start as an uncomfortable poseur?" ("T. S. Eliot: The End of an Era," in
T. S. Eliot, Four Quartets: A Casebook, ed. Bernard Bergonzi [London: Macmillan, 1969], 154). To Davie's ear, the opening lines are a type of "strident
uncertainty in the poet," and seem like a "journalistic cliché." According to
Davie's assessment *The Dry Salvages* is a "bad poem" characterized by "strident uncertainty in the poet and a correspondingly acute embarrassment
in the hearer"; language that is "re-symbolist and old fashioned," grotesque,
a "dismal jocularity," and "lame gabble"; and rhythms that are "trundling"
and suffer from "woolliness rather than clarity." Following the lead of Hugh
Kenner, Davie explains these stylistic faults by postulating that *The Dry Salvages* is really, in effect, a parody of the other *Quartets* and "is spoken in

character as the American." While not without some merit, these criticisms fail to do justice to two facts. First, the *Quartets* are a four-fold reality; no single component of the pattern can be decontextualized without reference to all of the parts. By calling *The Dry Salvages* a parody of *Burnt Norton* and *East Coker*, Davie implies that there is no development from the earlier two to the last, which leaves unanswered the questions of why Eliot would want to spend five movements merely parodying himself. Moreover, Davie neglects the fact that Eliot develops a consistent persona throughout the *Quartets*. He calls the persona of *The Dry Salvages* the American, as if he somehow differed from the Englishman of the other poems, or as if he were someone totally new. Neglecting the unfolding voice is puzzling, for statements made in *The Dry Salvages* depend upon statements made elsewhere in the poems, and the philosopher-poet's discoveries are only understandable in light of discoveries made in the previous *Quartets*.

On the positive side, Traversi writes that the opening movement is "one of Eliot's most sustained and evocative pieces of writing" (*T. S. Eliot: The Longer Poems*, 153). And Helen Gardner writes: "The first movement of 'The Dry Salvages' is particularly beautiful and bold in its diction, its variations of phrasing, and its rhythms" (*The Art of T. S. Eliot* [London: Faber & Faber, 1949], 10).

12. In his introduction to the Cresset Library edition of *Huckleberry Finn* (New York: Cresset, 1950), Eliot suggested one possible line of commentary on his use of the river in the first movement of the poem:

> Mark Twain makes you see the River, as it is and was and always will be. . . . As with Conrad, we are continually reminded of the power and terror of Nature, and the isolation and feebleness of Man. . . . It is as a native that he accepts the River God, and it is the subjection of Man that gives to Man his dignity. For without some kind of God, Man is not even very interesting. But Mark Twain is a native, and the River God is his God. (xii–xiii, xv)

13. Nancy K. Gish, *Time in the Poetry of T. S. Eliot: A Study in Structure and Theme* (Totowa, NJ: Barnes & Noble, 1981), 108.

14. Moody, *Thomas Stearns Eliot: Poet*, 206. Paul Murray suggests that Eliot "has come at last, it would seem, to realize that any theory of mysticism which regards the sphere of time past as 'a mere sequence', and which would therefore direct all a man's energies towards the simple attainment of a state of ecstasy, or a state of 'holy' indifference, is in large part mistaken (*T. S. Eliot and Mysticism: The Secret History of Four Quartets* [London: Macmillan, 1991], 105). I would argue that the *Quartets* do not express any theory of mysticism. But I would agree with Murray that the focus of Eliot's

wartime quartets is "the grace and the strength to apprehend the point of intersection of the Timeless with Time" (106), provided that we mean by this a dialogic intelligence and not a mystical disembodiment.

15. Martin Buber, *The Knowledge of Man: A Philosophy of the Interhuman*, trans. Maurice Friedman and Ronald Gregor Smith (New York: Harper & Row, 1965) 105, 107. While Heraclitus did not say "We," he would not have denied, Buber asserted, "that one cannot follow the logos more adequately than by saying 'We'. . . ." Buber continued:

> The genuine We is to be recognized in its objective existence, through the fact that in whatever of its parts it is regarded, an essential relation between person and person, between I and Thou, is always evident as actually or potentially existing. For the word always arises only between an I and a Thou, and the element from which the We receives its life is speech, the communal speaking that begins in the midst of speaking to one another (106).

According to Buber, this appreciation of a "We" which over-spans opposites "has attained its highest expression" through the poet Friedrich Hölderlin (1770–1843) when he wrote, "since we [are] a dialogue and have been able to hear from one another" (109). When we *are* the dialogue, when dialogue becomes a choral antiphony, for Hölderlin (and for Buber) we then stand before the divine countenance.

16. Martin Buber, *The Knowledge of Man*, 106. This is possible, as Buber wrote, because

> speech in its ontological sense was at all times present wherever men regarded one another in the mutuality of I and Thou; wherever one showed the other somehting in the world in such a way that from then on he began really to perceive it; wherever one gave another a sign in such a way that he could recognize the designated situation as he had not been able to before; wherever one communicated to the other his own experience in such a way that it penetrated the other's circle of experience and supplemented it as from within, so that from now on his perceptions were set within a world as they had not been before.

17. Accompanied by music and dancing, *The Rock: A Pageant Play* was commissioned by forty-five churches in the diocese of London and tells of the coming of Christianity.

18. See Martin Buber, *I and Thou*, trans. Ronald Gregor Smith (New York: Scribner, 1958), 128. In Buber's 1923 classic, a genuine meeting (in which redeeming reciprocity occurs) between a person and what comes to meet that person (nature, another person, or spirit becoming forms) is said to involve

choosing and being chosen and, simultaneously, acting and surrendering into a reciprocal relationship. According to Buber, similar criteria hold for a genuine encounter with the spirit of a text as it becomes language. To enter into a meaningful dialogue with a text, Buber proposes making the words immediately present, as if hearing the voice of the speaker; turning with one's whole being toward the speaker; adopting an attitude of personal engagement toward the text; and receiving the indivisible wholeness of something spoken.

19. In a 1948 broadcast talk on "The Unity of European Culture," Eliot spoke of his interest in Indian languages and philosophy, noting: "Long ago I studied the ancient Indian languages and while I was chiefly interested at that time in Philosophy, I read a little poetry too; and I know that my own poetry shows the influence of Indian thought and sensibility."

Though first attracted to Sanskrit, Eliot also studied Pali (a dialect of Sanskrit), the language of the Buddha and of the Theravadan scriptures. The Pali canon opened new philosophical possibilities for Eliot.

Agreeing that India's influence on Eliot was lifelong, Eliot's long-time friend George Every has remarked: "I think that what he learned from India is better centralized in the *Gita* than in any other Buddhist text. If he thought of being a Buddhist, and I'm not sure that he did, it was because he was looking for some way of universalizing himself" (recorded conversation with the author at Oscott College, Sutton Coldfield, Birmingham, England, May 27, 1989).

20. T. S. Eliot, *After Strange Gods* (New York: Harcourt, Brace, 1934), 43. Eliot's statement about the influence of Indian thought on his poetry is well known. However, he has also observed that "a good half of the effort of understanding what the Indian philosophers were after—and their subtleties make most of the great European philosophers look like school-boys—lay in trying to erase from my mind all the categories and kinds of distinction common to European philosophy from the times of the Greeks" (40).

21. Ibid., 41.

22. T. S. Eliot, "Dante," in *Selected Essays 1917–1932* (New York: Harcourt, Brace, 1932), 219. Years later, toward the end of his publishing career, Eliot wrote an extended essay on George Herbert in which he remarked: "The present writer is very thankful for having had the opportunity to study the *Bhagavad Gita* and the religious and philosophical beliefs, so different from his own, with which the *Bhagavad Gita* is informed" (*George Herbert* [London: British Council, 1962], 24).

23. Many critics have expressed reservations about the aesthetic quality of this section. Helen Gardner notes that "to introduce Krishna at this point is an error and destroys the poem's imaginative harmony." Elsewhere she writes: "I imagine that the reason for the introduction of the *Gita* here

is that the poem contains so much of Mr. Eliot's past that inevitably his explorations of Hindu metaphysics find a place in it" ("Four Quartets: A Commentary," in *T. S. Eliot: A Study of His Writings by Several Hands*, ed. Balachandra Rajan [London: Dennis Dobson, 1947], 69). She continues that "in their view of history and the time-process Christianity and Hinduism are most irreconcilably opposed; the incarnations of Vishnu give no significance to history, as does the unique Incarnation of Christian belief"(70). In my view, it was precisely this seeming irreconcilability that so attracted Eliot; it is his middle way sensibility that opened a deeper complementarity between Hindu and Christian views of time and history. More recently, however, Gardner would seem to have changed her mind since her initial hesitation. In *The Composition of* Four Quartets, she notes that while Eliot quotes Krishna's teaching on detached action and reincarnation, he "translates the idea into his own [Christian] terms" (57). Agreeing with Gardner, Balachandra Rajan writes: "Mr. Eliot is never happy in the maze of oriental-metaphysics and his wanderings this time are uncomfortably sinuous" ("The Unity of the Quartets," in *T. S. Eliot: A Study of His Writings by Several Hands*, 87).

24. Ramesh Chandra Shah, *Yeats and Eliot: Perspectives on India* (Atlantic Highlands, NJ: Humanities, 1983), 111. Speaking of Eliot's use of the "one Annunciation," Shah notes that "other cultures have expressed the same mystery in different ways. Eliot approaches the problem of reality both from a Christian point of view and from that of a rationalist monist philosophy" (114). I would suggest rather that Eliot expresses his experience of reality through an ongoing interreligious dialogue that includes more than just Christianity and monist philosophy. According to Narsingh Srivastava, by suggesting a strong parallelism between Eastern and Occidental ideas, between Krishna and Christ, "Eliot seems to have evolved a new method of inclusion and synthesis" which "widens the perspective of his metaphysical problem and its solution" ("The Ideas of the Bhagavad Gita in Four Quartets," *Comparative Literature* 29, no. 2 [Spring 1977]: 99). Srivastava continues that "Eliot is interested in the emotional validity and the essential unity of seemingly unrelated ideas rather than epistemological identity, and he uses these ideas in a pattern of intuitive realization rather than of analysis."

25. Raimundo Panikkar, *The Intrareligious Dialogue* (New York: Paulist, 1978), 31–32.

26. It becomes important here, according to Buber, to raise the question, especially in light of the dialogical character of language about whether one can enter into a genuine dialogue with one's self. In a 1957 dialogue between Martin Buber and Carl Rogers at the University of Michigan, at one point Rogers shifted the topic of discussion from dialogue between

two persons (e.g., therapist and client) to another type of meeting—the person's relationship to himself. Rogers remarked that in his practice he noticed that some clients reported extremely vivd encounters with aspects of the self.

Buber, however, was skeptical. A significant difference exists, for Buber, between interpersonal dialogue with a unique other and intrapersonal dialogue with an aspect of one's self. Missing in the latter is the possibility of a moment of surprise. Being surprised by an aspect of one's self remains phenomenologically and existentially different from being surprised by the uniqueness of the other. In the former case, the possibility of surprise is conditioned and limited to one's own understanding and awareness; in the latter, surprise is not restricted to my experience and embodies what can be known in no other way. But Rogers persisted. He expressed a desire to play recordings of interviews for Buber in which "surprise" does, in fact, occur for some of his clients. This segment of their dialogue ended with each agreeing that meeting "otherness" within oneself deserved a different designation. "You call something dialogue which I cannot call so," Buber remarked; "I would want another term between dialogue and monologue for this." See the appendix to Buber's *The Knowledge of Man*, 177–79. The significance of this discussion will be revisited in the second movement of *Little Gidding* in the next chapter.

27. By appealing to Indic teaching, Eliot simultaneously echoes the Hindu teaching of a permanent, unchanging, unborn, undying *atman* (true self at the center of all personal life) and the Buddhist notion of *anatta*, which is translated into English as "no-self." In the Buddhist doctrine, the self is a continuous, ever-changing aggregate of impulses arising from form, sensation, perception, volition, and consciousness.

Harold McCarthy suggests that the philosophical orientation of Theravada Buddhism and of Eliot's *Quartets* are parallel. In each, there is a profound awareness of the ambiance "of impermanence and suffering," a realization that human life is in universal bondage to suffering; in each, there is the realization that, while impermanence and suffering can be transcended, this transcendence can only come within the time-process itself, in the midst of birth and death; in each, the mode of transcendence is detachment and compassion "which comes with knowledge, reconciliation, and inner control; an awareness of the difficulty of this mode (what we have referred to as the meditative posture) and that this path is extremely dependent on each individual's resources" ("T. S. Eliot and Buddhism," *Philosophy East and West* 2 [April 1952]: 54). It has already been suggested that many critics, in their attempt to demonstrate the Christian motifs in the *Quartets*, underemphasize the Indic themes. McCarthy's convincing article corrects this misunderstanding, though, at points, it unnecessarily squeezes Eliot's ideas into the Buddhist pattern of the four noble truths.

28. T. S. Eliot, "Goethe as the Sage," in *On Poetry and Poets* (New York: Farrar, Straus and Cudahy, 1957), 264.

29. To address oneself to complementary and contradictory points of view, Panikkar suggests the need for a "dialogical dialogue." Differing from a dialectical dialogue, in which each voice is locked within preestablished points of view, and from eclectic syncretistic dialogue, which uncritically assimilates distinct religious elements, a dialogical dialogue involves both self-other and self-self. Its only assumption, though not like a rule postulated before dialogue can take place, is that as I proceed toward a deeper, clearer understanding of the other, I proceed as well toward a deeper, clearer understanding of myself. To this extent it "is religious encounter in faith, hope, and love" in which "the very vitality of religion manifests itself" (*The Intrareligious Dialogue*, 35).

30. The *Gita* speaks clearly about Krishna's self-understanding:

> For whenever the law of righteousness [*dharma*]
> Withers away and lawlessness [*adarma*]
> Raises its head,
> Then do I regenerate myself on earth. (IV:7)

> For the protection of the good,
> For the destruction of evil doers,
> For the setting up of righteousness,
> I come into being, age after age. (IV:8)

> He who knows my divine birth
> And mode of operation [*karma*]
> Having left his body, is never born again [*moksha*]:
> He comes to Me. (IV:9)

While the term "avatar" refers to the descent of any deity on earth, it is applied most frequently to appearances of Vishnu, the Preserver. The term appeared relatively late in classical Hindu thought; it does not occur in the classical *Upanishads*. There are various lists of avatars, which include animals (e.g., the horse-head, the swan, the fish, the tortoise, and the boar), a dwarf, and great humans like Krishna, Rama, and even the Buddha (added later possibly to attract Buddhist believers). The origins of Krishna are uncertain. The *Mahabharata* provides no details of his birth and few of his youth. He does have a human body in the *Gita*. Geoffrey Parrinder summarizes the principal implications of the avatar under twelve rubrics: (1) the avatar is real; (2) the human avatars take worldly birth; (3) the lives of avatars mingle divine and human; (4) the avatars finally dies; (5) there may be historicity in some avatars; (6) avatars are repeated; (7) the example and character of the avatars is important; (8) the avatar comes with work to do; (9) the avatars show some reality in the world; (10) the avatar is a guarantee of revelation; (11) avatars reveal a personal God; and (12) avatars reveal a God of grace (*Avatar and Incarnation* [New York: Oxford University Press, 1982], 120–26).

31. Several commentators have pointed out that the poet in the poem assumes the role of a modern-day Arjuna. The poet remarks "that the future is a faded song," which imagistically paraphrases some of the reasons Krishna used to urge Arjuna to fight. Since the true Self [*atman*] is unborn and undying, there never was and never will be a time when it does not exist; just as one passes from youth to old age, so the dweller in this body passes, at death, into another form, another kind of body. Even if the *atman* does not exist eternally and is subject to rebirth, still Arjuna should fight because as death is certain for him who is born, so rebirth is certain for him who dies. It is the caste duty of a warrior to take up arms and fight, and most important, Arjuna should realize that it is not winning and losing that are important but how he fights. This last argument, also known as *karma yoga*, if understood and assimilated, liberates one from the wheel of death and rebirth. In essence, *karma yoga* states that one should perform every act without thinking about the fruits of that action but rather to realize the "inaction in action, and action in inaction" (*Bhagavad Gita* IV:18).

32. Whereas the third movement of *East Coker* speaks of abstention from movement, of waiting meditatively without hope or love, and of St. John's way of negation, here the *via negativa* is cross-pollinated by Krishna's dialogue with Arjuna. Action and the way of nonaction, in the field on *dharma*, are one:

> Abandon attachments to the fruits of action, and act without acting.
> Your business is with action alone; not by any means with fruit.
> Let not the fruit of action be your motive (to action).
> Let not your attachment be fixed on inaction.
>
> Having recourse to devotion, O Dhanangaya!
> Perform actions, casting off (all) attachment, and being equable
>   in success
> or ill-success;
> [Such] equability is called devotion.

The Bhagavad Gita II:47-48, trans. Kashinath Trimbk Telang, in *The Sacred Books of the East*, ed. Max Müller (Delhi: Motilal Barnarsi, 1881), 7:48–49.

33. The second chapter of the *Bhagavad Gita* stresses two paths to enlightenment—the contemplative path consisting of knowledge (*jnana yoga*) and the active path consisting of devotion (*bhakti yoga*) and selfless action (*karma yoga*). A hint of these two ways has already been presented in *Burnt Norton*, where the poet evokes St. John's "Dark Night of Sense" (the active way) and the "Dark Night of the Soul" (the passive, contemplative way). To consider the past and future with an "equal mind" is not, however, to choose between the contemplation associated with memory or the action associated with moving forward. It is, rather, to progress by the way of actionless activity, which is neither active nor inactive as we ordinarily conceive of these terms. To "fare forward" means reaching neither into the past nor toward a future, but remaining fully present through nonattached activity. As Derek Traversi observes: "[This awareness] means increasingly detachment from any notion which regards the present self as a final reality, points to the exploration of what East Coker called 'another intensity,' another and more inclusive order of consciousness" (*T. S. Eliot: The Longer Poems*, 174).

34. Rajnath, "Whitman, Eliot, and the Bhagavad Gita," *Comparative Literature Studies* 20 (Spring 1983): 100.

35. Both Hindu true-self realization and the Heraclitian flux ("you cannot step twice into the same river") are implied in the poet's emphasis on the necessity of moment-to-moment dying into life (Philip Wheelwright, "Eliot's Philosophical Themes," in *T. S. Eliot: A Study of His Writing by Several Hands*, 105). See also Wheelwright's *The Burning Fountain: A Study in the Language of Symbolism* (Bloomington: Indiana University Press, 1968), 266–68.

36. Nancy Duvall Hargrove, *Landscape as Symbol in the Poetry of T. S. Eliot* (Mississippi: University Press of Mississippi, 1978), 165. Raymond Preston notes the severe contrast between this lyric and what preceded it, and he attributes it to the development in the poem of an attitude "of resignation, humility, and faith" in the face of the agony of existence (*Four Quartets Rehearsed* [London: Sheed & Ward, 1946], 47).

37. Elisabeth Däumer, "Charlotte Eliot and 'Ash Wednesday's' Lady of Silences" (an abstract), *T. S. Eliot Society Newsletter* 28 (Spring 1996): 2. Däumer notes that in *Ash-Wednesday* Eliot "symbolized the mother as the 'author' of the poet's transformation and resurrection into new self," and that Eliot's "mother-centered narrative of conversion" moves from "salutation" to the "matriarchal trinity." His concluding prayer is an "alternative narrative, in which the mother herself, endowed with divine authority, guides the poet's individuation and conversion." Noting that biographers have portrayed Eliot's mother, Charlotte, as a "frustrated artist" with a "sti-

fling concern" for her son, Däumer concludes that: "Charlotte Eliot's literary and social ambitions (which found support in specifically Victorian notions of maternal authority) nurtured in her son the conviction that women held an authoritative and influential position with regard to language and culture." In the second movement of *Ash-Wednesday*, written shortly after his mother's death, the lady becomes a "lady of silences" (lady Beatrice, lady Mary).

38. Dante writes: "Virgin Mother, daughter of thy son; / Humble beyond all creatures a more exalted; / Predestined turning point of God's intention; / Thy merit so ennobled human nature / That its divine Creator did not scorn / To make himself of the creature of His creature" (Canto XXXIII, *The Paradiso: A Verse Rendering for the Modern Reader*, trans. John Ciardi [New York: Mentor, 1961], 360). Moody reminds us that this quotation, the first line from the final canto of the *Paradiso*, "is presumably an allusion to all that is said there. The prayer is the culmination of Dante's love poetry; and it is spoken by a Doctor of the Church [St. Bernard], as a member of the Church of Heaven." While the voice of the poet appears to be "alone in the promontory" at the end of *East Coker*, he "is now joined in prayer with his fellow Christians, with all who are involved in the one action of Incarnation" (*Thomas Stearns Eliot: Poet*, 233).

39. Another fascinating interreligious perspective is offered by Zen Buddhist Gishin Tokiwa. He compares Mary to Maya, the mother of Gautama Buddha. Tokiwa indicates that Maya has been called, in certain Buddhist traditions, *tathagata-garbha* (or "womb of the Buddha"). *Tathagata-garbha* represents, for Tokiwa, the emptying of individual self and the realization of a formless, or original, self. The womb thus represents the original way of being of all humankind. He then compares the *tathagata-garbha* to the Christian concept of the "Mother of God" (*Theotokos*): "in St. Mary I see what Buddhists call the Buddha's womb (*tathagata-garbha*)." "Mary stands for all human being, all humanity," and therefore, like Maya, represents the original way of being for all humanity—suffering and peace at the same time (Gishin Tokiwa, "Chan [Zen] View of Suffering," *Buddhist-Christian Studies* 5 [1985]: 108).

40. While referring to Eliot's own earlier poem, this movement of *The Dry Salvages* also recalls the delight-provoking power of Dante's exalted passage elevating Mary:

> I am angelic Love, that circles round
> The Joy Sublime that issues from the womb
> Which is the resting place of our desire:
> I shall encircle thee, O Heavenly Lady

Till thou wilt join thy Son, to make this sphere
Yet more divine, because thou art within it . . .
To follow that bright flame incoronate
Which rose on high, after her glorious seed . . .
Stretch upward with its flame, so that their love
For Mary was made manifest to me
They afterward remained there in my sight
Singing *Regina Coeli* with such joy
That its delight has never parted from me. (*Paradiso*, Canto
XXIII)

For a provocative study of Mary in three traditions (Judaism, Christianity, and Islam) see Mishael Caspi and Sascha Cohen, *Still Waters Run Deep: Five Women of the Bible Speak* (Lanham, MD: University Press of America, 1999), especially chapter 5, "Mary."

41. The lady of *Ash-Wednesday*, however, is more a compound image who includes not only Mary but also an Isis-like goddess figure.

42. Ronald Schuchard, *Eliot's Dark Angel: Intersections of Life and Art* (New York: Oxford University Press, 1999), 156.

43. Gardner, *The Art of T. S. Eliot*, 171–72.

44. Hints of liturgical language throughout the *Quartets* reinforce Eliot's sacramental sensibilities and remind readers that they are being brought into the presence of a mystery beyond, yet incarnate within, language. The name of the prayer is taken from the first word of the three verses—*Angelus Domini nuntiavit Mariae* (The angel of the Lord declares unto Mary). The "Hail Mary" prayer is divided into three groups of fifty and is called *rosarium* after Mary's title *Rosa Mystica*. Originally, as early as the fourteenth century, the *Angelus* was said in the evening at the tolling of the bell. The morning and midday prayers were added later, the latter being the most recent addition, although there is some disagreement among Catholic Church historians about how closely, initially, the *Angelus* was associated with the ringing of the bell (the bell may, instead, have announced Compline, which was said at sundown). Today, bells with the *Ave Maria* inscription are numerous throughout England.

45. Cleo McNelly Kearns, *T. S. Eliot and Indic Traditions* (New York: Cambridge University Press, 1987), 251, 257, appeals to the distinction that Eliot made between revealed religions ("where one is right and the other wrong") and the "wisdom of poetry," where such differences are not obligatory. Kearns aptly states: "The appeal to this wisdom of poetry, allowing as it does a transcendence, for a time, of ordinary discursive logic, makes sense of the appeal to Mary, the fulfillment of the figure or type of wisdom

in the passage Eliot cited from Ecclesiastes, who "glor[ies] in the midst of her people, and governs the poem's close."

46. Pondering possible interactions between Krishna and Mary produces insightful alterations, reconfigurations, and clarifications of each figure. Signified differences as well as mutual implications resonate simultaneously. Neither is reduced; each is transfigured. Rather than settling simply for univocal or equivocal relationships, the poet's cross-cultural juxtapositions evoke a double reverberation: similarities-in-differences *and* differences-in-similarities. As a result, the poetry facilitates a more accurately nuanced account of spiritual experience, which both modifies (deconstructs) previously held understandings and reforms initial viewpoints. Contradictory wisdoms correspond, not by some logical order, or linear direction, but by the simultaneity of a cross-dimensional synchronicity.

47. In keeping with W. B. Yeats's criticism of Eliot's poetry—that he "writes out of his own mind"—Maurice Friedman specifically points to the dualism that exists between "the saint" and "the rest of us." "Only the saint is able to find authentic existence; he alone is able to find the point at which the timeless intersects the line of time that otherwise moves meaninglessly around the surface of the sphere. Most of us are not saints and cannot dedicate and devote our lives as they do" (*To Deny Our Nothingness: Contemporary Images of Man* [New York: Delacorte, 1967], 97). On the other hand, for Denis Donoghue the poetry is saved by the way it mixes in (to quote William James) "some austerity and wintry negativity, some roughness, danger, stringency, and effort" (*Words Alone: The Poet T. S. Eliot* [New Haven: Yale University Press, 2000], 294).

48. Leonard Unger, *T. S. Eliot: Moments and Patterns* (Minneapolis: University of Minnesota Press, 1956), 159; italics mine.

49. As Eliot wrote in an article published shortly after he finished writing *Four Quartets*, poetry is capable of bringing figures of the Divine into contemplative play, and poetry primarily is "a kind of humble shadow of the Incarnation whereby the human is taken up into the divine" ("The Aims of Poetic Drama," *Adam* 17 [November 1949]: 12). In *T. S. Eliot's Poetry and Plays* (Chicago: University of Chicago Press, 1950) Grover Smith observes:

> In "The Dry Salvages," Eliot's imagery of the line between hither and farther shore supplements that of the railway journey symbolizing the timeless, fluctuating "now." Both symbols modernize the Buddha's own reference to the two "shores," desire and nirvana. (Nirvana is sometimes figured also as the ocean into which the river of life empties.) The Buddha said in the Dhammapada: ". . . for who there is neither this nor that shore, nor both, him,

the fearless and unshackled, I call indeed a Brahmana." Eliot's fusion of ideas from Hinduism and Buddhism, with a nod to the fortuitous parallels in Heraclitus, has an almost ironic use in the poem. (282)

50. For example, while Krishna and Christ are the two holy incarnations most visibly suggested in *The Dry Salvages*, the figure of Buddha is in the background. That is, just as Christ is the reconciliation of God and humans, so the Buddha incarnates the ultimate *dharma* (truth-of-life). One of the Buddhist's terms for incarnation, *tathagata* (one-who-has-thus-attained), for instance, means "thus he comes" and "thus he goes." The Buddha comes and goes with no external designs upon life, with nothing excluded from his presence. In this sense, Buddha incarnates love, truth, and wisdom and, in so doing, reconciles the illusory distinction between past and future. Yet there remains one significant difference—one does not enter into a personal relationship with God through Buddha as one can through Christ or Krishna.

In a personal conversation on May 27, 1989, at Oscott College, north of Birmingham, England, Eliot's friend George Every told me:

> When Buddhists, especially Mahayanans, talk about Buddha-nature, this is something rock bottom, absolutely rock bottom to everyone. There is something common to each human being, and I think Eliot came to see that it was *this* that was taken up by Christ. Being risen with Christ is really being in that universal man which has been taken up by God.

51. See *A Catalogue of an Exhibition of Manuscripts and First Edition of T. S. Eliot* (Austin: University of Texas Humanities Research Center, 1961), 24. See also Gardner, *Composition*, 146. Gardner indicates that in response to Geoffrey Faber's query "Does Incarnation mean 'The Incarnation' (of Christ) or the incarnation of every human spirit?" Eliot had no response (145). Commenting on the reason for Eliot's silence in response to this query, Paul Murray is persuaded not "that Eliot considered the inquiry somehow irrelevant or meaningless, but rather that the only possible reply he felt he could make to such a fundamental question had, in fact, already been made within and by the poem itself" (*T. S. Eliot and Mysticism*, 77). Murray further indicates that Eliot's view of incarnation cannot be reduced to "a mere abstract formula, or to an intellectual statement of belief," nor does he "require us to accede to even one part of his own belief" (84–85).

If Eliot wanted to restrict his meaning to its Christian connotation, then he might have written "The Incarnation," and would not have removed the following line contained in an early version of the manuscript: "And Atone-ment makes action possible." Kearns suggests that Eliot's use of the term "Incarnation" in *The Dry Salvages* is "less a signifier for a predetermined doctrinal content than a 'half-object,' a truth half-glimpsed in the inter-stices between an Indic and a Christian point of view" (*T. S. Eliot and Indic Traditions*, 252). Kearns's remarks are influenced by her reading of Bradley and his use of the term "half-object," which results when points of view encounter each other, resulting in the "transformation of each [point of view], not into the other, but into a 'third center of feeling.'" Kearns seems to equate the "third center of feeling" with a third term or point of view between, say, Christ and Krishna. Eliot's language, I feel, does not warrant this interpretation.

I cannot agree with critics like P. S. Sri, who remarks that "the basic concern that animates Eliot's 'raid on the inarticulate' (EC)—the aware-ness of the fact of human bondage in time and the possibility of human freedom in eternity—is absolutely universal and may well be called the *philosophia perennis* that surfaces variously time and again in the religious and philosophical traditions of the East and West" (*T. S. Eliot, Vedanta and Buddhism* [Vancouver: University of British Columbia, 1985], 120). Eliot was far too attuned to cultural and linguistic peculiarities to unify every-thing into one vision. Recall that one reason for his not becoming Buddhist was that he could never really understand its nuances, not being raised in a Buddhist culture. Eliot's is not the grand religious narrative as we find in Aldous Huxley's perennial philosophy. Rather, Eliot practiced intrareli-gious dialogue.

I can, however, agree with Sri that Eliot's attraction to the Indic tradi-tion (especially the teachings of Krishna and Buddha), while retaining his strong identity with Christianity, is not viewed as a contradiction from the Hindu point of view, which sees Christ as an avatar through whom one can seek liberation just as one can through Krishna. As Sarvepalli Radhakrish-nan notes, in Hinduism "intellect is subordinated to intuition, dogma to experience, outer expression to inward realization," and "religion is not correct belief but righteous living" (*The Hindu View of Life* [New York: Mac-millan, 1968], 13, 37).

52. Through "middle way" dynamics between Krishna and Mary, Krishna and Christ, and between Christ and Buddha, Eliot evokes the redemptive power of incarnation. It would be inaccurate and shortsighted to limit the "one end" to its Christian associations only. "Incarnation," in the poem, takes broader associations, not just Christian, not even just religious. More deeply, incarnation becomes the "impossible union" of multilevel anti-theses, including "the point of intersection of the timeless / With time." Not

interested in unifying, fusing, or reconciling Indic and Christian thought, Eliot allows each its own voice and subtle intonations, maintaining uniqueness in tension, without surrendering his own Christianity.

Smith (*T. S. Eliot's Poetry and Plays,*) writes:

> Though a Buddhist might read the closing lines of *The Dry Salvages* without feeling that they were strange to his beliefs, and though he might understand by "temporal reversion" something consistent with his habitual idea of personal karma, this fact need not make *The Dry Salvages* heterodox for Christians. It is, after all, a poem; it does not affect to pronounce dogma. But most real theology, in contradistinction to commentary, was once also poetry. Eliot in *Burnt Norton* and *The Dry Salvages* reached in poetry a level which, without extravagance, one might call creative theology. (286)

53. T. S. Eliot, Letter to William Force Stead, April 10, 1928, Beinecke Rare Book and Manuscript Library, Yale University.

54. Evelyn Underhill, *Mysticism: A Study in the Nature and Development of Man's Spiritual Consciousness* (New York: Dutton, 1911), 120.

55. Commenting on the language of the second half of part V of *The Dry Salvages*, Moody writes that "each sentence has its own distinct meaning and form; yet the whole passage is a seamless statement through which the thinking flows lucidly and powerfully" (*Thomas Stearns Eliot: Poet,* 236). Moody comments that the phrasing is exactly right, "so the whole is organically articulate."

4. *Little Gidding*: Choosing Between Two Worlds

1. See Helen Gardner, *The Composition of Four Quartets* (London: Faber & Faber, 1978), 153–57. Eliot had misgivings with the form of *Little Gidding*—which to some represents "the phoenix cry of modernist poetry" and to others "announces the extremes of post-modernist verse" (Ronald Bush, *T. S. Eliot; A Study in Character and Style* [New York: Oxford University Press, 1983], 227).

Eliot feared that he would become trapped by the established structure of the former *Quartets* and that *Little Gidding* would be an elegant parody of what he had already produced. He sent the first draft to his long-time friend and trusted critic John Hayward on July 14, 1941. Later, on August 5, Eliot wrote to Hayward: "The defect of the whole poem [*Little Gidding*], I feel, is the lack of some acute personal reminiscence (never to be explicated, of course, but to give power from well below the surface)." See the Eliot-Hayward correspondence in King's College Library, Cambridge; quoted by Gardner, *Composition*, 22, 24. In a 1941 letter to Bonamy Dobrée, Eliot wrote: "I am afraid that I have been overproducing, and at last trying to make poetry out of unseasoned material" ("T. S. Eliot: A Personal Reminiscence," in *T. S. Eliot: The Man and His Work*, ed. Allen Tate (New York: Dell, 1966), 86. Eliot was referring to the fact that each of the first three *Quartets* had a personal, experiential significance: the rose garden illumination of Burnt Norton, his ancestral village of East Coker, and the Dry Salvages rocks by which he often sailed as a young man. As a result of Eliot's misgivings, the poem was shelved, and it was not until the end of 1942 that *Little Gidding* was published. Ironically, the resulting poem contains some of Eliot's most masterful lines. "It should be clear that the whole work has a fully developed and complex organization, and that the later Quartets do not simply repeat the structure of Burnt Norton three times over," for "what happens is that the first Quartet is expanded and developed into the larger work" (A. David Moody, *Thomas Stearns Eliot: Poet*, 2nd ed. [Cambridge: Cambridge University Press, 1994], 242.

2. Ronald Schuchard, "If I Think, Again, of This Place: Eliot, Herbert and the Way to Little Gidding," in *Words in Time: New Essays on Eliot's Four Quartets*, ed. Edward Lobb (Ann Arbor: University of Michigan Press, 1993), 52. When the Ferrars bought the medieval church in 1625, it was largely in ruins. After they restored its nave it was mostly destroyed in a 1646 Puritan raid, then rebuilt in 1714 by Ferrar's nephew John. The medieval tower, an example of English classical architecture, was originally built in 1634 in honor of the poet-preacher George Herbert, who had joined the community. When Herbert took charge of the original restoration, he tried to preserve its medieval exterior while accommodating its interior layout to facilitate seventeenth-century worship patterns. Wanting to symbolize the equal influence of prayer and preaching, he had two identical pulpits placed (one to the right and one to the left) in the central nave. Narrow bench pews lined the two walls so that congregants faced one another across the aisle. The communion table, then, was carried to the middle of the chancel so that worshipers could stand around it.

3. Quoted in Schuchard, "If I Think, Again," 64. Eliot's remarks about Herbert, shortly after he finished writing *Little Gidding*, indicate the devotional and metaphysical spirit of the poem. Eliot wrote: "What has at first the appearance of a succession of beautiful but separate lyrics, comes to reveal itself as a continued religious meditation with an intellectual framework; and the book as a whole discloses to us the Anglican devotional spirit of the first half of the seventeenth century" ("What Is Minor Poetry?" in *On Poetry and Poets* [London: Faber & Faber, 1957], 45).

4. See Gardner, *Composition*, 62. Based on her access to the first draft of George Every's play, she suggests that "it was Mr. Every's play ["Stalemate or the Head of a King" set at Little Gidding on May 4, 1646] that linked fire with Little Gidding in Eliot's mind, and that his memory of it colored the discussion of victory and defeat in Part III" (63). Gardner quotes from a letter Eliot wrote on February 26, 1936 to Every, in which Eliot said, "I am ashamed not to have got round to studying your play sufficiently to report to you."

5. Little Gidding today is a tiny hamlet in the county of Huntingdonshire north of London on the M 1 motorway, about eighteen miles northwest of Cambridge on the A 604, which becomes the A 1. Southwest of Peterborough, one takes the B 660 to Great Gidding and then travels east, a mile and a half, to Little Gidding. Arriving at a junction with the road linking Hamerton with Sawtry, the entrance to the Community of Christ the Sower at Little Gidding is through a farmyard and across a field.

In 1947, under the leadership of Robert Van de Weyer, a second Little Gidding community (the community of Christ the Sower) came into existence (formally in the autumn of 1981) comprised of members from various parts of the Christian spectrum (Catholic, Anglicans, Free Church, and Quakers). The rules are simple and evolve from a model of leadership in which the whole community appoints pastors who act as guides or advisors. See Van de Weyer's *Little Gidding: Story & Guide* (London: Lamp, 1989). An ecumenical form of worship, inspired by Ferrar and Herbert's identification with the high-church tradition, led to the composition of *The Little Gidding Prayer Book* (London: SPCK, 1986). Located in a clearing surrounded by tall shade trees, the chapel (approximately sixty feet long by seventeen feet wide) is plain and unimposing. The façade at the west end is composed of dull gray stone. The sides and the rear of the church are composed of red brick. In front of the door is the raised, rectangular, gray tombstone of Ferrar (1592–1637). The interior walls of the chapel are paneled; narrow benches line both sides of the aisle. At one end of the chapel is a brass eagle lectern and on the east wall, behind it, are brass tablets (on which are engraved the Lord's Prayer, the Ten Commandments, and the Apostle's Creed), above which is a window that depicts the crucifixion. The door is usually unlocked, and the chapel empty—a perfect place "to put off / Sense and notion."

6. Gardner, *Composition*, 157. Gardner writes that the outline shows "that he had come to see the seasons and the four elements as an organizational element in the sequence of the four poems."

7. Martin Buber, *Good and Evil: Two Interpretations*, trans. Ronald

Gregor Smith and Michael Bullock (New York: Scribner, 1952), 58. Speaking of the way Eliot uses "everyday things to mirror the sublime," M. C. Bradbrook writes: "This landscape, at once the country round Little Gidding, and that landscape of the heart where the flames reappear after the long march across . . . broken stones recalls, with the matter-of-fact conclusion about 'the early afternoon,' that the poet is talking of a physical journey, though the spring he sees—the hedgerow blanched with snow as with blossom—is 'not in time's covenant'" (*T. S. Eliot* [London: Longmans, Green, 1950], 33).

8. Quoted by William Levy and Victor Scherle, *Affectionately, T. S Eliot* (London: J. M. Dent and Sons, 1968), 41–42.

9. Stephen Spender, "Remembering Eliot," in *T. S. Eliot: The Man and His Work*, 59.

10. Martin Buber, *Eclipse of God* (New York: Harper Torchbook, 1952), 126. Buber is quick to indicate that the requisite concentration of the one who prays is assailed by the human tendency toward "subjectivized reflection." Buber identifies the assailant as consciousness, "the over-consciousness of this [person] here that he is praying, that he is *praying*, that *he* is praying." Buber then suggests that "the subjective knowledge of the one turning-towards about his turning-towards, the holding back of an I which does not enter into the action with the rest of the person, an I to which the action is an object—all this depossesses the moment, takes away its spontaneity" (126).

In response to this assailant, for Buber, acts of "turning" stream through all of the spheres of existence and renew the world. In fact, "turning" is a double movement: first, in dialogue we turn *away from* everything that would prevent us from entering into genuine relationship with the other, and second, we turn *toward* whoever or whatever presents itself to us. In other words, the double movement requires turning away from self-preoccupation, and toward entering-into-relationship. In our lives there is always, writes Buber, a "special something" that takes center stage. Whether that "special something" is an object of enjoyment, or principle of belief, it can frustrate the essential movement of turning. Turning, in the end, requires practice and mental awareness. See Martin Buber, *I and Thou*, trans. Ronald Gregor Smith, 2nd ed. (New York: Scribner, 1958). 100–101, 105, 120.

11. Quoted in Levy and Scherle, *Affectionately*, 128–29.

12. A. L. Maycock, *Nicholas Ferrar of Little Gidding* (New York: Macmillan, 1938), 194. In a similar fashion, one could suggest that the way of "prayer beyond words" was grasped by Thomas Merton when he wrote: "Since contemplation is the union of our mind and will with God in a

supreme act of pure love that is at the same time the highest knowledge of Him as He is in Himself, the way to contemplation is to develop and perfect our mind and will and our whole soul" (*New Seeds of Contemplation* [New York: New Directions, 1961], 133). In fragment 34 Heraclitus writes: "Fire lives in the death of earth, air in the death of fire, water in the death of air, and earth in the death of water" (cited in Philip Wheelwright, *Heraclitus* [New York: Atheneum, 1968], 37). It is uncertain whether Eliot read the *Tibetan Book of the Dead*, but the Tibetans speak of death as well in terms of the four elements. Just as life depends on the interaction of four basic elements—earth, water, fire, and air—the process of dying begins with the dissolution of these elements. The earth element of the body's functions is first absorbed by the water element in the body, which is then dissolved and absorbed by the fire element. When at last, whether the process takes years or weeks, the fire element dissolves into air, heat escapes from the body. During this time, if one can meditatively be aware that nothing exists independently of mind, then one will become enlightened to Buddha nature. An "elemental" reading of *Four Quartets* from this point of view could shed light on some interspiritual possibilities not detailed here.

13. T. S. Eliot, *Selected Essays*, new ed. (New York: Harcourt, Brace, 1950), 308–9.

14. For a further discussion of interactions among these three faces of death, see Kenneth Paul Kramer, *The Sacred Art of Dying: How World Religions Understand Death* (New York: Paulist, 1988), especially chapter 1.

15. Moody, *Thomas Stearns Eliot: Poet*, 246.

16. See Gardner, *Composition*, 168.

17. T. S. Eliot, "What Dante Means to Me," in *To Criticize the Critic* (Lincoln: University of Nebraska Press, 1965), 128; italics mine. About this section Gardner (*Composition*) writes:

> This passage gave Eliot more trouble than any other section of the poem. He was here attempting to sustain a style consistently over a long span, whereas his natural genius was towards the paragraph. He also committed himself to a strict and difficult verse-form, an approximation to the terza rima of Dante, a meter in which few English poets have been successful. Here, again, he was writing against his natural bent which was towards a rhythmically flexible verse. Many lines, phrases, and words were revised again and again, and argued over. (171)

When I come to this section, I often think of the literary critic Hugh Kenner. As well as lecturing on Eliot at San José State University (for the 1988 Eliot Centenary), Kenner attended a seminar on Eliot's poetry and critical writings. Toward the end of the class, after he had spoken almost exclusively about *The Waste Land*, I asked him to speak about *Four Quartets*. With more passion than Eliot reading Eliot, he responded simply and eloquently, with no introduction, by reciting from memory the entire Dantesque encounter with the "compound ghost" imaged here.

18. See Kristian Smidt, "T. S. Eliot and W. B. Yeats," *Review des languages vivantes* (Brussels), reprinted in *The Importance of Recognition: Six Chapters on T. S. Eliot* (Tromsø: Norbye, 1973). Smidt quotes a letter he received from Eliot, which specified that he "was thinking primarily of William Yeats." Given Eliot's own remarks about Yeats, and the fact that an early version of *Little Gidding* IV was drafted on the verses of pages containing Eliot's notes for his June 1940 memorial lecture on Yeats (delivered in Dublin), several critics have noted that Eliot had Yeats's "A Dialogue of Self and Soul" in mind during the writing of this section. Leonard Unger writes that "no other single poem of Yeats corresponds so extensively" (*Eliot's Compound Ghost: Influence and Confluence* [University Park: Pennsylvania State University Press, 1981], 113).

19. Unger, *Eliot's Compound Ghost*, 112–13. Unger instructively titles the conclusion to his *Eliot's Compound Ghost* with three words, each of which captures an element of Eliot's intention—"Echo, Mirror, Ghost," 103.

20. Bush, *T. S. Eliot*, 230, 231.

21. Gardner, *Composition*, 67. Gardner writes: "It is impossible to hazard a guess as to what 'dead masters' or 'master' Eliot had originally in mind; but the obvious debt to the *Inferno* (Canto XV) suggests he had in mind masters to whom he owed reverence and gratitude but from whom he felt himself severed. Eliot thought of Hell and Purgatory as eternal states known to men here in time, and in this scene of 'meeting nowhere, no before and after' the distinction between the dead and the living is blurred. The ghost is 'compound' but so is the poet" (185).

22. Grover Smith, "Tourneur and Little Gidding; Corbiére and East Coker," *Modern Language Notes* 65 (June 1950): 420–21.

23. Maurice Johnson, "The Ghost of Swift in 'Four Quartets,'" *Modern Language Notes* 64 (April 1949): 273.

24. Cleanth Brooks in a graduate course in English literature at Yale University (Spring semester, 1967).

25. Cleo McNelly Kearns, *T. S. Eliot and Indic Traditions* (New York: Cambridge University Press, 1987), 259.

26. A. Walton Litz, "The Allusive Poet," *Yale Review* 78, no. 2 (Winter 1989): 262.

27. Derek Traversi, *T. S. Eliot: The Longer Poems* (New York: Harcourt Brace Jovanovich, 1976), 190. These remarks would seem to be in keeping

with Eliot's own comments about why he altered an earlier identification of the "compound ghost"—"Are you here, Sr Brunetto?"—to "What! are *you* here?" Responding to Hayward's disapproval, Eliot wrote that there were two reasons for the change: "The first is that the visionary figure has now become somewhat more definite and will no doubt be identified by some readers with Yeats though I do not mean anything so precise as that. However, I do not wish to take the responsibility of putting Yeats or anybody else into Hell and I do not want to impute to him the particular vice which took Brunetto there. Secondly, although the reference to that Canto is intended to be explicit, I wished the effect of the whole to be Purgatorial which is much more appropriate" (quoted in Gardner, *Composition*, 176).

28. Gardner, *Composition*, 179. Gardner writes: "In this No Man's Land, between two worlds, Eliot may well have had in mind, mingling with the dead, others, still living, from whom he was divided by 'thought and theory' but from whom he had learned to cherish 'essential moments' or 'epiphanies.' Both in the first and the second version, the ghost speaks with Eliot's own voice. It is, in a profound sense, a meeting with himself when he encounters 'a familiar compound ghost' who is 'Both intimate and unidentifiable' " (185). Gregory Jay suggests that the "insertion of the universalizing 'we' depersonalizes the encounter, reminding us as readers that the scene is also an allegory of our own meeting with this text, that we are also the 'I' and Eliot is also 'some dead master' " (*T. S. Eliot and the Poetics of Literary History* [Baton Rouge: Louisiana State University Press, 1983], 239).

D. W. Harding has suggested that this meeting between the poet and the ghost is "the logical starting point of the whole poem" ("Little Gidding: A Disagreement in Scrutiny," in *T.S. Eliot: Four Quartets*, ed. Bernard Bergonzi [London: Macmillan, 1969], 64).

29. In *T. S. Eliot and Dante* (New York: Macmillan, 1989), Dominic Manganiello explores the parallel relationships between Dante and his master Brunetto, and between Eliot and his admiration for Yeats as the major poet of his age. Yeats glorified the poetic imagination and believed, as Brunetto did, that by his artistry "man makes himself eternal" (*Inferno* XV:85). In order to escape from becoming enslaved by prosaic, tradition-bound systems, Yeats attempted to create his own system, "an almost infallible church of poetic tradition" (*The Autobiography of William Butler Yeats* [New York: Collier, 1969], 77). Also like Brunetto, Yeats believed that a person is "self-sufficing and eternal" (*Letters of W. B. Yeats*, ed. Allan Wade [London: Rupert Hart-Davis, 1954], 805). Both as a classicist and as a Christian, Eliot (like Dante before him) rejected or altered this romantic assertion that one can redeem the created order (and in the process be re-

deemed) by the power of poetic creativity. The difference between them, Manganiello remarks, "lies between 'self-renewal' and being 'renewed'" (*T. S. Eliot and Dante*, 150). Manganiello notes that Eliot once remarked that Yeats subscribed, as Eliot could not, "to the Arnoldian tenet, poetry can replace religion" (T. S. Eliot, *After Strange Gods* [New York: Harcourt, Brace, 1934], 48). When the dead master quotes Mallarmé's pronouncement—"To purify the dialect of the tribe" (*"Donner un sens plus pur aux mots de la tribe"*)—he captures both the crucial similarity and the crucial difference between them. While the philosopher-poet recognizes the need to purify speech, the method by which this is accomplished, rather than glorifying the medium of one's own words, "requires a purged or redeemed speech, a willingness on the part of the poet, as in 'Marina,' to resign his speech for that unspoken."

30. In an early draft of this section, Eliot wrote:

> Remember rather the essential moments
>> That were the times of birth and death and change
>> The agony and the solitary vigil.
>
> Remember also fear, loathing, and hate,
>> The wild strawberries eaten in the garden,
>> The walls of Poitiers, and the Anjou wine,
>
> The fresh new season's rope, the smell of varnish
>> On the clean oar, the drying of the sails,
>> Such things as seem of least and most importance.
>
> So, as you circumscribe this dreary round,
>> Shall your life pass from you, with all you hated
>> And all you loved, the future and the past.
>
> United to another past another future,
>> (After many seas and after many lands)
>> The dead and the unborn, who shall be nearer
>
> Than the voices and the faces that were most near.
>> This is the final gift of earth accorded—
>> One soil, one past, one future, in one place.

This passage remarkably and comprehensively focuses the central current of the *Little Gidding* passage and points to implications of timeless immediacies in the present moment. See Gardner, *Composition*, 183.

31. Buber, *The Knowledge of Man*, 104–5. However, Buber reminded us that this working together can in no way "be conceived of as a team hitched to the great wagon; it is a strenuous tug-of-war for a wager, it is battle and strife." Yet this tension between speakers, Buber continued, "insofar as it

lets itself be determined by the logos it is a common battle and produces the common out of the extremist tension, when it takes place in the service of the logos, arises ever anew the harmony of the lyre" (105).

32. Traversi, *T. S. Eliot: The Longer Poems*, 195. Traversi writes:

> It is clear that the passage we have been considering represents in more senses than one, a decisive stage in the ordering of the *Quartets*. The poet is, we have suggested . . . confronting himself, seeming to arrive at some estimate of what his life-time of creative endeavor has achieved, what it can mean to him and what its significance can be in relation to the human undertaking—the "tradition" in which he is incorporated with the writers of the past—to which he has sought to make his contribution.

Parenthetically, it can be mentioned here that the ghost's dialogue depends on listening to the silence from which language arises. Beyond judgments, beyond associations (more typical ways of responding to what one hears/reads), his discernment-listening delves into the possibility of what is and is not heard (that is, what is normally excluded from consideration, especially alien points of view, are now considered). In conversations between religious points of view, one comes to recognize the significance of listening to the other, and the possibility that the conversation thus becomes.

33. Buber, *The Knowledge of Man*, 86. Genuine meeting, for Buber, is immediate, personal, and reciprocal. The other of this meeting is not restricted to a person, but includes animals, aesthetic objects, nature, inspirited forms, and God. Through entering into a genuine dialogic relationship with the other in any form, I am no longer subject to causality and fate, no longer determined by space and time. Indeed, genuine meeting does not take place primarily in space and time; rather, space and time take place within genuine meeting. When grace and will combine, my sense of selfhood no longer depends primarily on the objectified realm of daily interactions. At least four elements describe this interhuman dynamic: *turning* (truthfully, fully, without reserve) toward who or what encounters me; *making* (the other) *present* by coexperiencing, as much as possible, what the other is thinking, feeling, and sensing, and including this awareness in my response; *receiving* the other as a partner through genuine listening, both to what is said and what is unsaid; and *confirming* my partner by accepting and affirming him or her both now and into the future without necessarily agreeing with everything said (see Martin Buber, *The Knowledge of Man: A Philosophy of the Interhuman*, trans. Maurice Friedman and Ronald Gregor Smith [New York: Harper & Row, 1965], 85). When these elements are mutually encountered, dialogue is fulfilled.

34. The image of God as "absolute Person" in the last pages of the "Postscript" to *I and Thou* is one of Buber's most significant contributions to theological thought. Buber's shift in emphasis from the image of the "eternal *Thou*" to the "absolute Person" brings attention to, and characterizes, the immanence-presence dimension of the "eternal *Thou*." In no way, however, does Buber limit God to any particular image, let alone to the image of God as "Person." Buber does not mean, by "absolute person," that God is a person but rather that "unlimited Being becomes as absolute person, my partner" by creating me "in order to love me and be loved by me" because "in our human mode of existence the only reciprocal relation with us that exists is a personal one" (*Eclipse of God*, 97).

35. Buber, *I and Thou*, 136–37. According to Buber, God's speaking penetrates through every genuine interhuman relationship, especially when the words of others stand out as "instruction, message, demand." When turning to God with unreserved spontaneity, I bring all other relationships before God, to be transformed in God's presence. Our conversations with God and God's conversation with us not only happens alongside of the everyday but also penetrates into our lived reality. In event-upon-event, happening-upon-happening, the personal address of God, through others, enables us to take a stand, to make decisions, and to continue in a direction of movement.

36. See Eloise Knapp Hay, *T. S. Eliot's Negative Way* (Cambridge: Harvard University Press, 1982), 186.

37. The three conditions of human nature are attachment (*rajas*), detachment (*sattva*), and indifference (*tamas*).

38. Eliot quoted in Gardner, *Composition*, 197. Detachment has always been a monastic art to be cultivated. As Thomas Merton writes: "The secret of interior peace is detachment. . . . You will never be able to have perfect interior peace and recollection unless you are detached even from the desire of peace and recollection" (*New Seeds of Contemplation*, 128, 129).

39. Louis Martz frames the conclusion of his essay "Origins of Form in *Four Quartets*" ("Origins of Form in Four Quartets," in *Words in Time*) by highlighting the significance of the last three lines quoted above.

> in the last two quartets the truly meditative voice, concentrated in its quest, grows more and more confident, until, in the middle of "Little Gidding," the voice can say: "See, now they vanish, / The faces and places, with the self which, as it could, / loved them, / To become renewed, transfigured, in another pattern." This is the "pattern / Of timeless moments" that the meditative voice has sought to discover, and now discovers

in this place of the "secluded chapel," "A symbol perfected in death." (203)

40. In her "Thirteenth Revelation" Julian writes: "Sin is necessary [behovely] but all will be well, and all will be well, and every kind of thing will be well" (*Showings*, trans. Edmund Colledge and James Walsh [New York: Paulist, 1978], 224). In response to a question by Hayward about his use of the term "behovely," Eliot wrote:

> This line and the two which follow and which occur twice later constitute a quotation from Juliana of Norwich. The beautiful line, the presence of which puzzles you toward the end of page II, comes out of *The Cloud of Unknowing*. My purpose was this: there is so much 17th century in the poem that I was afraid of a certain romantic effect and I wanted to check this and at the same time give greater historical depth to the poem by allusions to the other great period, i.e. the 14th century. Juliana and *The Cloud of Unknowing* represent pretty well the two mystical extremes or, one might say, the male and female of this literature.

It should be noted that in an earlier draft Eliot wrote: "No one is wholly alive No man is free from sin and sordid or petty weakness" (cited in Gardner, *Composition*, 70, 206).

41. See Paul Murray, *T. S. Eliot and Mysticism* (London: Macmillan, 1991), 152.

42. Julian of Norwich, *Showings*, XIV, chapter 41, 249.

43. Ibid., XIV, chapter 41, 248. In keeping with the Christocentric nature of "beseeching," Eliot had originally intended to conclude Part III of *Little Gidding* with an adaptation of the first four lines of the prayer *Anima Christi*, ascribed to St. Ignatius Loyola, which Eliot probably knew from an Anglo-Catholic devotional manual: "Soul of Christ, sanctify them, Body of Christ, let their bodies be good earth, Water from the side of Christ, wash them, Fire from the heart of Christ, incinerate them" (see Gardner, *Composition*, 206).

44. Moody, *Thomas Stearns Eliot: Poet*, 257.

45. The image of fire here, from which one needs to be redeemed, also echoes the Buddha's "Fire Sermon" (to which Eliot referred in his notes to *The Waste Land*), which begins: "All things, O priests, are on fire." In response to the rhetorical question—"And what, O priests, are all these things which are on fire?"—the Buddha distinguishes between the sensory organs (the eye, the ear, the nose, the tongue, and the body) and the mind, which includes ideas, consciousness, impressions, and sensations. All these are on fire:

With the fire of passion, say I, with the fire of hatred, with
the fire of infatuation; with birth, old age, death, sorrow,
lamentations, misery, grief, and despair are they on fire.

See Henry Clarke Warren, *Buddhism in Translations* (New York: Atheneum, 1969), 352. Eliot refers, in *The Waste Land* (footnote to line 308) to
Buddha's "Fire Sermon" as "corresponding in importance to the Sermon on
the Mount," and to Henry Clarke Warren as "one of the great pioneers of
Buddhist studies in the Orient." Perceiving that sensory organs and minds
are ablaze, the Buddha concluded that one should "conceive an aversion"
for all forms—the sensory organs and the sensations of mind—and thereby
become "divested of passion," free from the cycle of death and rebirth.

46. Bede Griffiths, *The Marriage of East and West* (Springfield, IL:
Templegate, 1982), 36. Griffiths, an English Benedictine monk, at fifty went
to India to find "the other half of my soul," as he put it. In 1968, he came to
the Shantivanam Ashram, in Tamil Nadu (founded in 1950 by Jules Monchanin and Henri Le Saux). This Christian community, adapting itself to
Hindu ways of life and thought, is dedicated to the mutual transformation
of both Vedanta Hinduism and Benedictine Christianity through experiential dialogues. In the process, the interfaith dialogian is called to journey
beyond all religions, scriptures, and creeds to pass beyond this world of
signs, each of which will also pass away "when the Reality, the thing signified, is revealed." Finally, Griffiths writes, "God himself, in so far as he can
be named, whether Yahweh or Allah or simply God, is a sign, a name for
the ultimate Truth, which cannot be named" (42).

47. T. S. Eliot, Preface in *The Testament of Immortality*, ed. N. Gangalee (London: Faber & Faber, 1940), 136. In his Preface, Eliot writes that
"the perceptive reader will be struck not least by the fusion of Eastern and
Western Culture in the anthologist's mind and heart" (10). See also Murray,
Eliot and Mysticism, 208, where he discusses this passage.

48. *The Cloud of Unknowing*, ed. James Walsh (New York: Paulist, 1981),
chapter 2 117.

49. Ibid., 173.

50. Raimundo Panikkar, "Some Words Instead of a Response," *Cross
Currents* 29, no. 2 (Summer 1979): 194. Paraphrasing Eliot's words "to know
the place for the last time," Panikkar speaks of the need for a new innocence: "The new innocence is not a repetition of the old, which cannot be
thematically searched and yet which is the kind of light that illumines all
our enterprises." There is always more to achieve, a higher realization, a new
beginning-end to be reached. The goal is not the end itself but the search, or,
to put it slightly differently, not the exploration itself but detachment from

exploration. The one end and one way of all our exploring is to arrive at "complete simplicity" (the "wisdom of humility" in *East Coker* II), to know it "for the first time" (the "impossible union" of *The Dry Salvages* V), and in the process, to hear "the stillness / Between two waves of the sea." This "stillness" opens the here and now condition of complete simplicity, the motive purified in the ground of beseeching. Reminiscent of *The Dry Salvages*— "(And the time of death is every moment)"—in a middle-way perspective, the place is known not only for the first time but for the last time as well.

51. William Spanos, "Hermeneutics and Memory: Destroying T. S. Eliot's Four Quartets," *Genre* 11, no. 4 (Winter 1978): 564.

52. Dante, *The Paradiso: A Verse Rendering for the Modern Reader*, trans. John Ciardi (New York: Mentor, 1961), 363. Speaking about Dante in 1950, Eliot remarked that he regarded Dante's poetry "as the most persistent and deepest influence upon my own verse" ("What Dante Means to Me," 125). Apocalyptic "tongues of flame," "in-folded / Into the crowned knot of fire," sweep through Dante's *Divine Comedy* as well, finally gathering together in the "multifoliate rose," on which countless angels alight like bees, "their faces full of living flame," that illuminates the *Paradiso*. Dante's vision of God in the final Canto of *Paradiso* is a vision of "One," the "Point," "First Power," "Creator," "Eternal Light," "Infinite Worth," and "Love." Dante writes: "I saw the universal form / That binds these things." Tongues of flame—both human desire and purgatorial purification—are necessarily in-folded (relationally bonded) in what, extrapolating from Dante, we can call "love's knot" (XXXIII:91), which binds without entangling.

53. Gardner, *Composition*, 233, 224. As Cleo McNelly Kearns indicates, the word "one" invoked, for Eliot, "a long tradition of metaphysical, psychological and religious debate, a debate in which Indic and Christian points of reference play a particularly important, though not the only role." Just as the supernatural Pentecostal fire and the natural rose are one, the natural, or Heraclitian, fire and the mystic rose confirm each other (Kearns, *T. S. Eliot and Indic Traditions*, 266). Kearns mentions the Brihadararyaka Upanishad (4.4.1-1) and the words of Christ "I and the Father are one" (John 10:30) as possible frames of reference.

54. I agree with William Spanos that Eliot does not attempt to "resolve the immediate tensions of the be-ing of language (to fill the gaps) and thus transform its differences into identity" (Spanos, "Hermeneutics and Memory," 566). Like other fundamental distinctions spread throughout the *Quartets* (e.g. end and way, "lotos" and rose, stillness and movement, unbeing and being, beginning and end, darkness and light, strength and submission, the way up and the way down, the way forward and the way back, attachment and detachment), Eliot holds their tension together. He

is not, however, content to remain caught between poles (to have "had the experience but missed the meaning"). Rather, he brings opposites together "in a way that makes less of their oppositions and disjunctions than of their capacity to indicate or suggest by their very differences a third point of view" (Kearns, *T. S. Eliot and Indic Traditions*, 230). This third point of view—what Dante called the ethical meaning—refers to what Aristotle, in the *Nicomachean Ethics* called the "mean" between two extremes (II:7). In this mode of understanding, one no longer must choose between contradiction but, instead, must navigate a passage that contains elements of each. But this does not complete the interpretative act for Dante or for Eliot. For example, the primal moment in the *Burnt Norton* rose garden, which in a way generates the entire poem, occurs when "the pool was filled with water out of sunlight" and in that timeless moment, "the lotos rose, quietly, quietly." Here conflicting Indic and Christian allusions are juxtaposed. Literally, they are opposed. Ethically, they present the opportunity for mediation. Mystically, however, these opposites are empty of dualistic identity, for "then a cloud passed and the pool was empty." Literally, of course, the pool was dry. Mystically, the lotus and rose are empty, void of inherently binary identity. The poet here affirms the immediacy of a "here and now" presence in which a literal, an ethical, and a mystical meaning are enfolded and must be apprehended as "the future / And the past with an equal mind" (DS III). To know the place for the first time is to realize the "impossible union" of contrary points of view.

55. When asked in a 1949 interview about his favorite period in Italian literature, Eliot replied: "Dante, and then Dante, and then Dante" (Giorgio Zampa, 'Eliot e Danté', *La Stampa*, January 6, 1965, 11 as cited in Manganiello, *T. S. Eliot and Dante*, 1). In light of this affection, to understand the final lines of *Little Gidding* as fully as possible it will be helpful to refer to Dante's discussion of the "polysemous" meaning of *The Divine Comedy*, in which he distinguished between a literal meaning (what the letter conveys) and an allegorical meaning (what the letter signifies). See *Dantis Alagherii Epistlae: The Letters of Dante*, trans. Paget Toynbee (Oxford: Clarendon, 1966), 199. Of the *Divine Comedy*, Dante remarks that its literal subject is "The state of souls after death," and its allegorical subject is whether a person, according to one's merits or demerits, "is deserving of reward or punishment by justice" (200). Elucidating this distinction, Dante expands signified or allegorical meaning to include the ethical and the mystical. While the true subject of a literary work must be considered, first, from the literal or historical point of view, a text's whole meaning must be analyzed, as well, from an allegorical (from the Latin meaning "strange" or

"different") perspective. If we apply these distinctions to the finale of *Little Gidding,* especially in the context of the middle way, Eliot's presentation of opposites, not limited to fire and rose, find a clarifying structure. Literally, in the realm of time, space, and history, they remain separate, not one. Suggestive of his fear of being misrepresented or misunderstood, Eliot once responded to a question about the meaning of his lines in the first movement of *Little Gidding*—"And what the dead had no speech for, when living, / They can tell you, being dead"—by remarking, "Once he is dead, the acts of his life fall into proper perspective and we can see what he was tending toward."

Conclusion: Interspiritual Practices

1. T. S. Eliot, Letter to William Force Stead, August 9, 1930, Beinecke Rare Book and Manuscript Library, Yale University.

2. John Cooper, *T. S. Eliot and the Ideology of Four Quartets* (Cambridge: Cambridge University Press, 1995), 136. Cooper takes the phrase "a new life of the spirit" from Denis Donoghue, *The Ordinary Universe: Soundings in Modern Literature* (New York: Macmillan, 1968), 260.

3. See Martin Buber, *A Believing Humanism,* trans. Maurice Friedman (New York: Simon & Schuster, 1967), 52, 147, 174. Buber speaks of creatively responding to another person—through ideas, through art, and through pure action—by virtue of "spirit." In its human manifestation, spirit animates the quality of our responses to others. Analogous to grace (indeed the very expression of grace), spirit exists primarily between persons, and then within persons. Indeed, according to Buber, spirit generates the energy of pure relationships. Buber writes: "he who knows the breath of the Spirit trespasses if he desires to get power over the Spirit or to ascertain its nature and qualities. But he is also disloyal when he ascribes the gift to himself" (*I and Thou,* trans. Ronald Gregor Smith, 2nd ed. [New York: Scribner, 1958], 129–30).

4. Buber, *I and Thou,* 39. Spirit always remained a central part of Buber's lifework. In *I and Thou,* spirit (*Geist*) is named as an essential element of person-with-person meetings. In the beginning of Part II, for instance, Buber suggests that the "component" of interpersonal relationship that often remains hidden, or goes unnoticed, is spirit, and that "spirit in its human manifestation is a response of man to his *Thou*" (39). Reading consecutively through the Buber endnotes in this book (see note 37 of the introduction), one can notice the meaningful significance of Buber's dialogic philosophy for key transformational moments in Eliot's *Quartets.* One of my cardinal appropriations of Buber's thought is his view that the presence of "spirit" and

the manifestation of transcendence in the world occur simultaneously. Spirit enters the world interactively as the oscillating sphere of "the between," as the immediate embracing of dialogical partners by redeeming reciprocity. Neither subjective experience nor objective phenomenon, "the between" is the interactive presence of spirit-filled mutuality and, as such, animates an ever-renewing, ever-unique, ever-dialogical relationship to the Eternal One. Through the dawning of spirit, the poet, in places in *Four Quartets*, enters a direct, immediate, timeless relationship to the world. When viewed against Buber's Hasidic-influenced thought, existence is made sacramental; the identity-in-difference relationship between the root center of the human soul and "holy sparks" contained within things and persons manifests.

5. Raymond Preston, "T. S. Eliot as a Contemplative Poet," in *T. S. Eliot: A Symposium for His Seventieth Birthday*, ed. Neville Braybrook (New York: Ferrar, Strauss & Cudahy, 1958), 161–62.

6. T. S. Eliot, Preface in *Thoughts for Meditation: A Way to Recovery from Within*, ed. Nagendranath Gangulee (London: Faber & Faber, 1951), 13. In this context I vividly recall discussing my interest in the poem with Eliot's long-time friend George Every at Oscott College in Birmingham, England, May 27, 1989. Surrounded by the monastic simplicity of his room, Every sat back in a wooden chair behind a table-desk and said: "I have often thought that I would not want to write a book *about* Eliot, but to bring Eliot into something else, and *this* may be the right thing to do." In response, I suggested that by weaving interreligious imagery throughout *Four Quartets*, Eliot had been ahead of his time. Every nodded vigorously. "Yes," he said. "Yes! I agree. The aspect of Eliot that has not been properly recognized is the intercultural, ecumenical aspect. I suppose it is true that it reaches its most mature form in the *Quartets*."

7. Eliot, Preface in *Thoughts for Meditation*, 13. In a preface written for Simone Weil's *The Need for Roots*, Eliot commented on Weil's interest in various religious traditions:

> Her attitude may appear to be dangerously close to that of those universalists who maintain that the ultimate and esoteric truth is one, that all religions show some traces of it, and that it is a matter of indifference to which one of the great traditions we adhere. Yet she is saved from this error—and this is a matter for admiration and thankfulness—by her devotion to the person of Our Lord. (*The Need for Roots: Prelude to a Declaration of Duties Toward Mankind* [New York: Putnam, 1952], ix)

8. Indicative of his comparative interest in contemplative religious traditions is Eliot's attraction to Frithjof Schuon's *The Transcendent Unity of*

Religions (published in English by Faber & Faber, 1907). Eliot was drawn to Schuon's expression of the sameness, or what he called "transcendental unity," of these traditions, which Schuon held was rooted in the mystery of God's nonduality with the world. Schuon's main contention was that we should not distinguish primarily among religions but between *esoteric* and *exoteric* believers within religious traditions. Esoteric believers are mystical, while exoteric believers (constituting the majority of religious cultures) tend to externalize God; while esoteric believers realize the nonduality between the absolute and the finite, exoteric believers dwell in the comfort of creeds, doctrines, dogmas, and ritual practices. Eliot wrote, "I have met with no more impressive work in the comparative study of Oriental and Occidental religions" (quoted in Huston Smith's Introduction to Frithjof Schuon's *The Transcendent Unity of Religions* [New York: Harper & Row, 1979], ix).

9. T. S. Eliot, *Knowledge and Experience in the Philosophy of F. H. Bradley* (New York: Farrar, Strauss, 1964), 147–48.

10. The descending spiritual direction especially, though not exclusively, evoked in the first two quartets, combined with the ascending spiritual direction especially, though not exclusively evoked in the second two quartets, coordinates grace and effort in ways that reinforce the intersection of Eliot's artistic and spiritual life. While the first two practices primarily represent the way down and only secondarily the way up, the second two practices are primarily rooted in the way up (nonattached action and purification) and only secondarily reflect a downward way (detachment and deprivation). By bringing together the spiritual practices of St. John and Julian, and those of Krishna and Patanjali, Eliot exemplifies a necessary reciprocity (primary/secondary to secondary/primary and vice versa) between the negative way of renunciation (the way down) and the positive way of incarnation (the way up).

11. St. John of the Cross, *Collected Works, Dark Night of the Soul*, II, chapter 6, 339.

12. Ronald Schuchard, "Eliot, Herbert and the Way to 'Little Gidding,'" in *Words in Time: New Essays on Eliot's Four Quartets*, ed. Edward Lobb (Ann Arbor: University of Michigan Press, 1993), 69.

13. Buber, *A Believing Humanism*, 144. By "psychologizing the world" Buber means "the transference of the world into the soul," in which the fundamental and essential relationship between "I" and the world ceases to exist. Perhaps we can come to understand the meaning of Eliot's words better here by placing them against a backdrop of their opposite—the irrational, unreal, internalized "I." Buber speaks of the fundamentally difficult problem of humankind's insistence on seeing the world through a

psychological filter of judgments and assessments: "That the world faces me and that between us the real happens, this essential basic relation from which our life receives its meaning is injured if the world is so far removed within the soul that its non-psychic reality is obliterated, that this fundamental relation of I to world ceases to be able to be a relation of I to Thou" (144). According to Buber, an individual who primarily observes things as objects—arranges them, orders them, separates them, and connects them without necessarily feeling the weight of their importance—is not able to enter into genuinely interhuman relationships with others.

14. Martin Buber, *The Origin and Meaning of Hasidism*, trans. Maurice Friedman (New York: Harper Torchbooks, 1960), 105. Buber continues, in language that remarkably echoes and enriches the meaning of Eliot's timeless moments, by indicating that the redemptive moment "does not mean that the moment becomes a mystical timeless now, rather that it is filled with time: in the wavering fraction of time, the fullness of time announces itself—not as a happening in the soul, but as a bodily happening in the world, out of the concrete meeting between God and man" (106–7). I can hear Eliot agreeing with Buber when Buber writes: "Here then, the world is neither transfigured into something wholly spiritual, nor overcome by the spirit. The spirit does not embrace a holy world, rejoicing in its holiness, nor does it float above an unholy world, clutching all holiness to itself: it produces holiness, and the world is made holy" (*Israel and the World: Essays in a Time of Crisis* [New York: Schocken Books, 1948], 180–81).

Works Cited

Ackroyd, Peter. *T. S. Eliot: A Life*. New York: Simon & Schuster, 1984.

Avnon, Dan. *Martin Buber: The Hidden Dialogue*. Twentieth-Century Political Thinkers. Lanham, MD: Rowman & Littlefield, 1998.

Bakhtin, Mikhail. *Speech Genres and Other Late Essays*. Trans. Vern McGee. Austin: University of Texas Press, 1986.

Bergonzi, Bernard. *T. S. Eliot*. New York: Collier Books, 1972.

———, ed. *T. S. Eliot: Four Quartets: A Casebook*. London: Macmillan, 1969.

Blamires, Harry. *Word Unheard: A Guide through Eliot's Four Quartets*. London: Methuen, 1969.

Bradbrook, M. C. *T. S. Eliot*. London: Longmans, Green, 1950.

Bradley, F. H. *Appearance and Reality*. Ed. Richard Wollheim. Oxford: Oxford University Press, 1969.

Braybrooke, Nelville, ed. *T. S. Eliot: A Symposium for His Seventieth Birthday*. New York: Farrar, Straus, and Cudahy, 1958.

Brett, Raymond Lawrence. *Reason and Imagination: A Study of Form and Meaning in Four Poems*. London: Oxford University Press for the University of Hull, 1960.

Buber, Martin. *A Believing Humanism*. Trans. Maurice Friedman. New York: Simon & Schuster, 1967.

———. *Between Man and Man*. Trans. Ronald Gregor Smith. New York: Macmillan, 1948.

———. *Eclipse of God*. New York: Harper Torch, 1952.

———. *Good and Evil: Two Interpretations*. Trans. Ronald Gregor Smith and Michael Bullock. New York: Scribner, 1952.

———. *I and Thou*. Trans. Ronald Gregor Smith. 2nd ed. New York: Scribner, 1958.

———. *Israel and the World: Essays in a Time of Crisis*. New York: Schocken Books, 1948.

———. *On Judaism*. Ed. Nahum N. Glatzer. New York: Schocken Books, 1967.

———. *The Knowledge of Man: A Philosophy of the Interhuman*. Trans. Maurice Friedman and Ronald Gregor Smith. New York: Harper & Row, 1965.

———. *The Origin and Meaning of Hasidism*. Trans. Maurice Friedman. New York: Harper Torchbook, 1960.

———. *The Way of Man: According to the Teachings of Hasidism*. New York: Citadel, 1966.

Buber, Martin, and Franz Rosenzweig. *Scripture and Translation*. Trans. Lawrence Rosenwald. Bloomington: Indiana University Press, 1994.

Bucke, R. M. D. *Cosmic Consciousness: A Study in the Evolution of the Human Mind*. Library of the Mystic Arts. New Hyde Park, NY: University Books, 1961.

Bush, Ronald. *T. S. Eliot: A Study in Character and Style*. New York: Oxford University Press, 1983.

Caspi, Mishael, and Sascha Cohen. *Still Waters Run Deep: Five Women of the Bible Speak*. Lanham, MD: University Press of America, 1999.

A Catalogue of an Exhibition of Manuscripts and First Edition of T. S. Eliot. Austin: University of Texas Humanities Research Center, 1961.

Childs, Donald. *T. S. Eliot: Mystic, Son and Lover*. London: Athlone, 1997.

Clubb, Merrell D. "The Heraclitean Element in Eliot's *Four Quartets*." *Philosophical Quarterly* 40, no. 1 (January 1961): 19–33.

Cooper, John. *T. S. Eliot and the Ideology of Four Quartets*. Cambridge: Cambridge University Press, 1995.

Dante Alighieri. *The Divine Comedy: The Carlyle-Wicksteed Translation*. New York: Modern Library, 1932.

———. *The Paradiso: A Verse Rendering for the Modern Reader*. Trans. John Ciardi. New York: Mentor, 1961.

Däumer, Elisabeth. "Charlotte Eliot and 'Ash Wednesday's' Lady of Silences." *T. S. Eliot Society Newsletter* 28 (Spring 1996): 2.

Donoghue, Denis. *The Ordinary Universe: Soundings in Modern Literature*. New York: Macmillan, 1968.

———. *Words Alone: The Poet T. S. Eliot*. New Haven: Yale University Press, 2000.

Drew, Elizabeth. *T. S. Eliot: The Design of His Poetry*. New York: Scribner, 1949.

Eliot, T. S. *After Strange Gods*. New York: Harcourt, Brace, 1934.

———. *Christianity and Culture*. New York: Harcourt, Brace, 1940.

———. *Complete Poems and Plays 1909-1950*. New York: Harcourt Brace Jovanovich, 1952, 1969.

———. "The Church as an Ecumenical Society." *London Times*. July 17, 1937.

———. "I," in Gustav Aulén et al., *Revelation*. Ed. John Baillie and Hugh Martin. London: Faber & Faber, 1937.

———. *The Idea of a Christian Society*. London: Faber & Faber, 1939.

———. "The Influence of Landscape on the Poet." *Daedalus* 89, no. 2 (Spring 1960).

———. Introduction in Blaise Pascal's *Pensées*. Trans. W. F. Trotter. New York: Dutton, 1958.

———. Introduction in Dyuna Barnes's *Nightwood*. New York: Harcourt, Brace, 1937.

———. Introduction in G. Wilson Knight's *The Wheel of Fire: Interpretations of Shakespearean Tragedy*. New York: Meridian, 1930.

———. Introduction in Mark Twain's *Huckleberry Finn*. New York: Cresset, 1950.

———. *Inventions of the March Hare: Poems 1909–1917*. Ed. Christopher Ricks. London: Faber & Faber, 1996.

———. *Knowledge and Experience in the Philosophy of F. H. Bradley*. New York: Farrar, Straus, 1964.

———. "Last Words." *Criterion* 18, no. 71 (January 1939).

———. *Notes Towards the Definition of Culture*. London: Faber & Faber, 1948.

———. *On Poetry and Poets*. London: Faber & Faber, 1957.

———. *Poems Written in Early Youth*. London: Faber & Faber, 1967.

———. "The Preacher as Artist." *Athenaeum*. November 28, 1919.

———. Preface in Simone Weil's *The Need for Roots: Prelude to a Declaration of Duties Toward Mankind*. New York: Putnam, 1952.

———. Preface in *The Testament of Immortality*. Ed. Nagendranath Gangulee. London: Faber & Faber, 1940.

———. Preface in *Thoughts for Meditation: A Way to Recovery from Within*, ed. Nagendranath Gangulee. London: Faber & Faber, 1951.

———. *The Sacred Wood*. New York: Harper & Row, 1920.

———. *Selected Essays*. New ed. New York: Harcourt, Brace, 1950.

———. *Selected Essays, 1917–1932*. New York: Harcourt, Brace, 1932.

———. "The Sulurist." *Dial* 83, no. 3 (September 1927): 260.

———. *To Criticize the Critic*. Lincoln: University of Nebraska Press, 1965.

———. Unpublished Address to the Women's Alliance at King's Chapel, Boston. December 1, 1932.

———. *The Use of Poetry and the Use of Criticism*. London: Faber & Faber, 1933.

———. *The Varieties of Metaphysical Poetry*, ed. Ronald Schuchard. London: Faber & Faber, 1993.

Eliot, Valerie, ed. *The Letters of T. S. Eliot*. Vol. 1. London: Faber & Faber, 1988.

Ellis, Havelock. *The Dance of Life*. New York: Modern Library, 1929.

Ellis, Steve. *The English Eliot: Design, Language, and Landscape in Four Quartets*. New York: Routledge, 1991.

Elyot, Sir Thomas. *The Boke of the Governour* [1531], book 1, chapter 21, ed. H. H. S. Croft (1883), vol. 1.

Fowlie, Wallace. *Journal of Rehearsals: A Memoir.* Durham, NC: Duke University Press, 1977.

Frazer, Sir James George. *The Golden Bough.* Vol. 2. New York: Macmillan, 1935.

Friedman, Maurice. *The Affirming Flame: A Poetics of Meaning.* New York: Prometheus, 1999.

———. *To Deny Our Nothingness: Contemporary Images of Man.* New York: Delacorte, 1967.

———. *Encounter on the Narrow Ridge: A Life of Martin Buber.* New York: Paragon House, 1991.

Frye, Northrop. *T. S. Eliot: An Introduction.* New York: Barnes & Noble, 1963.

———. "T. S. Eliot and Ezra Pound: Collaborators in Letters." *Atlantic Monthly* 225 (January 1970).

Gardner, Helen. *The Art of T. S Eliot.* London: Faber & Faber, 1949.

———. *The Composition of* Four Quartets. London: Faber & Faber, 1978.

Gish, Nancy K. *Time in the Poetry of T. S. Eliot: A Study in Structure and Theme.* Totowa, NJ: Barnes & Noble, 1981.

Gordon, Lyndall. *Eliot's Early Years.* Oxford: Oxford University Press, 1977.

———. *Eliot's New Life.* New York: Farrar, Straus and Giroux, 1988.

———. *T. S. Eliot: An Imperfect Life.* New York: Norton, 1998.

Griffiths, Bede. *The Marriage of East and West.* Springfield, IL: Templegate, 1982.

Hargrove, Nancy Duvall. *Landscape as Symbol in the Poetry of T. S. Eliot.* Jackson: University Press of Mississippi, 1978.

Hay, Eloise Knapp. *T. S. Eliot's Negative Way.* Cambridge: Harvard University Press, 1982.

Heidegger, Martin. *Discourse on Thinking.* Trans. John N. Anderson and E. Hans Freund. New York: Harper Torchbooks, 1966.

Hindu Scriptures. Trans. R. C. Zaehner. London: Dutton, 1966.

Howarth, Herbert. *Notes on Some Figures behind T .S. Eliot.* New York: Houghton Mifflin, 1964.

Jay, Gregory. *T. S. Eliot and the Poetics of Literary History.* Baton Rouge: Louisiana State University Press, 1983.

Johnson, Maurice. "The Ghost of Swift in 'Four Quartets.'" *Modern Language Notes* 64 (April 1949): 273.

Julian of Norwich. *Showings.* Trans. Edmund Colledge and James Walsh. New York: Paulist, 1978.

Kavanaugh, Kieran and Otilio Rodrigues. *The Collected Works of St. John of the Cross*, Washington DC: ICS Publications, 1979.

Kearns, Cleo McNelly. *T. S. Eliot and Indic Traditions*. Cambridge: Cambridge University Press, 1987.

Kenner, Hugh. *The Invisible Poet*. New York: Harcourt, Brace, 1959.

——, ed. *T. S. Eliot: A Collection of Critical Essays*. Englewood Cliffs, NJ: Prentice-Hall, 1962.

Kepnes, Steven. *The Text as Thou: Martin Buber's Dialogical Hermeneutics and Narrative Theology*. Indianapolis: Indiana University Press, 1992.

Kierkegaard, Søren. *Repetition: An Essay in Experimental Psychology*. Trans. Walter Lowrie. New York: Harper Torch, 1964.

Kramer, Kenneth Paul. *Martin Buber's I and Thou: Practicing Living Dialogue*. New York: Paulist, 2003.

——. "A New Kind of Intellectual: Eliot's Contemplative Withdrawal." *Religion and Literature* 31, no. 3 (Autumn 1999): 43–75.

——. *The Sacred Art of Dying: How World Religions Understand Death*. New York: Paulist, 1988.

Levy, William and Victor Scherle. *Affectionately, T. S. Eliot*. New York: Lippincott, 1969.

Lehmann, John. Interview with T. S. Eliot. *New York Times Book Review*. November 29, 1953, 5. Reprinted in *T. S. Eliot: Four Quartets: A Casebook*. Ed. Bernard Bergonzi. New York: Macmillan, 1969.

Litz, A. Walton. "The Allusive Poet." *The Yale Review* 78, no. 2 (Winter 1989): 262.

Lobb, Edward, ed. *Words In Time: New Essays on Eliot's Four Quartets*. Ann Arbor: University of Michigan Press, 1993.

Lynen, John. *The Design of the Present: Essays on Time and Form in American Literature*. New Haven: Yale University Press, 1969.

MacCallum, H. Reid. "Time Lost and Regained." In *Imitation and Design and Other Essays*, ed. William Blisset. Toronto: University of Toronto Press, 1963.

Manganiello, Dominic. *T. S. Eliot and Dante*. New York: Macmillan, 1989.

Martz, Louis. *The Meditative Poem: An Anthology of Seventeenth-Century Verse*. New York: New York University Press, 1963.

——. *The Poem of the Mind: Essays on Poetry English and American*. New York: Oxford University Press, 1966.

——. *The Poetry of Meditation*. New Haven: Yale University Press, 1954.

Maslow, Abraham H. *Religions, Values, and Peak Experiences*. New York: Penguin, 1977.

Matthews, T. S. *Great Tom: Notes towards the Definition of T. S. Eliot*. New York: Harper & Row, 1974.

Matthiessen, F. O. *The Achievement of T. S. Eliot*. New York: Oxford University Press, 1959.

Maycock, A. L. *Nicholas Ferrar of Little Gidding*. New York: Macmillan, 1938.

Merton, Thomas. *Contemplation in a World of Action*. New York: Doubleday, 1971.

———. *New Seeds of Contemplation*. New York: New Directions, 1961.

Moody, A. David. "*Four Quartets*: Music, Word, Meaning and Value." In *The Cambridge Companion to T. S. Eliot*. Cambridge: Cambridge University Press, 1994.

———. *Thomas Stearns Eliot: Poet*. 2nd ed. Cambridge: Cambridge University Press, 1994.

———. *Tracing T. S. Eliot's Spirit: Essays on His Poetry and Thought*. Cambridge: Cambridge University Press, 1996.

Moore, Ronald. *Metaphysical Symbolism in T. S. Eliot's Four Quartets*. Stanford Honors Essays in Humanities 9. Stanford, CA: Stanford University, 1965.

Morison, Samuel Eliot. "The Dry Salvages and the Thacher Shipwreck." *The American Neptune* 25, no. 4 (1965): 233–47.

Morrison, Blake. "The Two Mrs. Eliots." *The Independent on Sunday*. April 24, 1994.

Müller, Max, ed. *The Sacred Books of the East*. Delhi: Motilal Barnarsi, 1881.

Murray, Paul. *T. S. Eliot and Mysticism: The Secret History of Four Quartets*. London: Macmillan, 1991.

Nagarjuna. *Fundamentals of the Middle Way*. In Frederick J. Streng's *Emptiness: A Study in Religious Meaning*. Nashville: Abingdon, 1967.

Nishida, Kitaro. *Intelligibility and the Philosophy of Nothingness*. Trans. Robert Schinzinger. Tokyo: Maruzen, 1959.

Panikkar, Raimundo. *Blessed Simplicity: The Monk as Universal Archetype*. New York: Seabury, 1982.

———. *The Intrareligious Dialogue*. New York: Paulist, 1978.

———. "Some Words Instead of a Response." *Cross Currents* 29, no. 2 (Summer 1979): 194.

Parrinder, Geoffrey. *Avatar and Incarnation*. New York: Oxford University Press, 1982.

Perl, Jefferey M. *Skepticism and Modern Enmity: Before and After Eliot*. Baltimore: Johns Hopkins University Press, 1989.

Preston, Raymond. *Four Quartets Rehearsed*. London: Sheed & Ward, 1946.

Radhakashnan, Sarvepalli. *The Hindu View of Life*. New York: Macmillan, 1968.

Rajan, Balachandra, ed. *T. S. Eliot: A Study of His Writings by Several Hands.* London: Dennis Dobson, 1947.

Reinan, Peter. *Recurring Patterns in T. S. Eliot's Prose and Poetry: A Stylistic Analysis.* Bern: A. Francke, 1978.

The Rule of St. Benedict. Trans. Anthony Mersel and M. L. del Mastro. New York: Image Books, 1975.

St. John of the Cross. *The Ascent of Mount Carmel.* In *The Complete Works of St. John of the Cross.* Ed. and trans. E. Allison Peers. 3rd ed. Westminster, MD: Newman, 1953.

Schuchard, Ronald, ed. *T. S. Eliot: The Varieties of Metaphysical Poetry.* London: Faber & Faber, 1993.

———. *Eliot's Dark Angel: Intersections of Life and Art.* New York: Oxford University Press, 1999.

Schuon, Frithjof. *The Transcendent Unity of Religions.* New York: Harper & Row, 1979.

Scofield, Martin. *T. S. Eliot: The Poems.* New York: Oxford University Press, 1999.

Sena, Vinod. "The Lotos and the Rose: The *Bhagavad Gita* and T.S. Eliot's *Four Quartets.*" In *The Fire and the Rose: New Essays on T. S. Eliot.* Edited by Vinod Sena and Verma Rajiva. Delhi: Oxford University Press, 1992.

Sena, Vinod, and Rajiva Verma. "Conversion and Expatriation: T. S. Eliot's Dual Allegiance." In *The Fire and the Rose: New Essays on T. S. Eliot.* Edited by Vinod Sena and Verma Rajiva. Delhi: Oxford University Press, 1992.

Sencourt, Robert. *T. S. Eliot: A Memoir.* New York: Delta, 1973.

Seymour-Jones, Carole. *Painted Shadow: A Life of Vivien Eliot, First Wife of T. S. Eliot, and the Long-Suppressed Truth about Her Influence on His Genius.* London: Constable, 2001.

Shah, Ramesh Chandra, *Yeats and Eliot: Perspectives on India.* Atlantic Highlands, NJ: Humanities, 1983.

Smidt, Kristian. *The Importance of Recognition: Six Chapters on T. S. Eliot.* Tromsø: Norbye, 1973.

Smith, Grover. *T. S. Eliot's Poetry and Plays.* Chicago: University of Chicago Press, 1950.

Spanos, William. "Hermeneutics and Memory: Destroying T. S. Eliot's *Four Quartets.*" *Genre* 11, no. 4 (Winter 1978): 523–73.

———. *Repetitions: The Postmodern Occasion in Literature and Culture.* Baton Rouge: Louisiana State University Press, 1987.

Spender, Stephen. "Remembering Eliot." In *T. S. Eliot: The Man and His*

Work: A Critical Evaluation by Twenty-Six Distinguished Writers. Ed. Allen Tate. New York: Delacorte, 1966.

Sri, P. S. *T. S. Eliot: Vedanta and Buddhism.* Vancouver: University of British Columbia Press, 1985.

Stead, William Force. "Mr. Stead Presents an Old Friend." *Alumnae Journal of Trinity College* 38, no. 2 (Winter 1965).

Steiner, George. *Language and Silence: Essays of Language, Literature, and the Inhuman.* New York: Atheneum, 1967.

Sullivan, J. W. N. *Beethoven: His Spiritual Development.* New York: Vintage, 1927.

Tate, Allen, ed. *T. S. Eliot: The Man and His Work: A Critical Evaluation by Twenty-Six Distinguished Writers.* New York: Delacorte, 1966.

Taylor, Charles. *Sources of the Self: The Making of the Modern Identity.* Cambridge: Harvard University Press, 1989.

Teasdale, Wayne. "The Interspiritual Age: Practical Mysticism for the Third Millennium." *Journal of Ecumenical Studies*, 34, no. 1 (Winter 1997): 74–91.

Thompson, Eric. *T. S. Eliot: The Metaphysical Perspective.* Crosscurrents: Modern Critiques. Carbondale: Southern Illinois University Press, 1963.

Timmerman, John H. *T. S. Eliot's Ariel Poems: The Poetics of Recovery.* Lewisburg, PA: Bucknell University Press, 1994.

Toynbee, Paget, trans. *Dantis Alagherii Epistlae: The Letters of Dante.* Oxford: Clarendon, 1966.

Traversi, Derek. *T. S. Eliot: The Longer Poems.* New York: Harcourt Brace Jovanovich, 1976.

Underhill, Evelyn. *Mysticism: A Study in the Nature and Development of Man's Spiritual Consciousness.* New York: Dutton, 1911.

Unger, Leonard. *Eliot's Compound Ghost: Influence and Confluence.* University Park: Pennsylvania State University Press, 1981.

———. *T. S. Eliot: Moments and Patterns.* Minneapolis: University of Minnesota Press, 1956.

———, ed. *T. S. Eliot: A Selected Critique.* New York: Rinehart, 1948.

Van de Weyer, *Little Gidding: Story and Guide.* London: Lamp, 1989.

Wade, Allan, ed. *Letters of W. B. Yeats.* London: Rupert Hart-Davis, 1954.

Walsh, James. *The Cloud of Unknowing.* New York: Paulist, 1981.

Warren, Henry Clarke. *Buddhism in Translations.* Cambridge: Harvard University Press, 1900.

Weinblatt, Alan. *T. S. Eliot and the Myth of Adequation.* Ann Arbor: UMI Research, 1984.

Weitz, Morris. "T. S. Eliot: Time as a Mode of Salvation." *The Sewanee Review* 60 (1952): 48–64.

Wheelwright, Phillip. *The Burning Fountain: A Study in the Language of Symbolism.* Bloomington: Indiana University Press, 1968.

———. *Heraclitus.* New York: Atheneum, 1968 [1959].

Yeats, W. B. *The Autobiography of William Butler Yeats.* New York: Collier, 1969.

———. *The Collected Poems of W. B. Yeats.* New York: Macmillan, 1956.

Index

Note: page numbers in italics refer to photographs.

CPSIA information can be obtained
at www.ICGtesting.com
Printed in the USA
FSHW020501180619
59167FS